# CHILDHOOD DEPRESSION

# CHILDHOOD DEPRESSION
# A Place for Psychotherapy

Edited by
*Judith Trowell*

with
*Gillian Miles*

Foreword by
*Michael Rustin*

Routledge
Taylor & Francis Group
LONDON AND NEW YORK

First published 2011 by Karnac Books Ltd.

Published 2019 by Routledge
2 Park Square, Milton Park, Abingdon, Oxon OX14 4RN
52 Vanderbilt Avenue, New York, NY 10017, USA

*Routledge is an imprint of the Taylor & Francis Group, an informa business*



**British Library Cataloguing in Publication Data**

A C.I.P. for this book is available from the British Library

ISBN 9781780490045 (pbk)

Edited, designed, and produced by Communication Crafts

*In memory of*
*Professor Israel Kolvin, David Campbell,*
*and Hartwin Sadowski*

# *CONTENTS*

## IV Research



## V Conclusions

# *SERIES EDITOR'S PREFACE*

*Margot Waddell*

Since it was founded in 1920, the Tavistock Clinic has developed a wide range of developmental approaches to mental health which have been strongly influenced by the ideas of psychoanalysis. It has also adopted systemic family therapy as a theoretical model and a clinical approach to family problems. The Clinic is now the largest training institution in Britain for mental health, providing postgraduate and qualifying courses in social work, psychology, psychiatry, and child, adolescent, and adult psychotherapy, as well as in nursing and primary care. It trains about 1,700 students each year in over 60 courses.

The Clinic's philosophy aims at promoting therapeutic methods in mental health. Its work is based on the clinical expertise that is also the basis of its consultancy and research activities. The aim of this Series is to make available to the reading public the clinical, theoretical, and research work that is most influential at the Tavistock Clinic. The Series sets out new approaches in the understanding and treatment of psychological disturbance in children, adolescents, and adults, both as individuals and in families.

The research study described in *Childhood Depression: A Place for Psychotherapy* was, as Michael Rustin says in his Foreword, "a pioneering response to the challenge that the demand for 'evidence-based' practice was posing for child and adolescent mental health services".

The authors of this book, and Judith Trowell in particular, are to be congratulated for demonstrating that a sound research base can be established for the provision of psychotherapy for the treatment of children and adolescents.

# ACKNOWLEDGEMENTS

We are very grateful and thankful to Professor Issy Kolvin, who initiated this Project but did not live to see its completion. Special thanks also to Dr Hartwin Sadowski, who worked alongside Professor Kolvin.

We would also like to thank Professor John Tsiantis and the Greek team, as well as Professor Fredrik Almqvist and the Finnish team. All contributed enormously to the Biomed/ERC multicentre study, of which the London arm was one of three sites.

The Childhood Depression Project was a special opportunity for everyone involved. We are very grateful to the young people and their families, who were generous in their commitment and in their support of the research. The therapists and supervisors were dedicated and impressive. The research team worked to do justice to all the hard work and to demonstrate that these troubled young people and their families were able to benefit from, and make use of, the help offered.

Taking part in an international research study provided a special opportunity for learning and professional development through creative exchanges across the three sites: Athens, Helsinki, and London. The multi-professional research meetings in the three countries during the Project were times for rich exchanges of ideas and shared experience of the work, contributing to the development of our thinking within the overall Project about the nature of childhood depression and the effectiveness of our therapeutic interventions.

We would like to acknowledge the vision of Professor Israel Kolvin and Dr Hartwin Sadowski in the work they did in setting up the Project, and we are grateful to our colleagues in Athens and Helsinki for their commitment and dedication and to Professor Dick Harrington for his support after the death of Professor Kolvin.

Our thanks also go to Gillian Miles for the work involved in editing and bringing together the papers, with the skilful help of Dr Pamela Davenport.

## *Confidentiality*

Throughout the accounts in this book of the work with the children, young people, and their families, we have been conscious of the need to protect the identities of the individuals. To this end, some details have been changed and every effort made to protect the confidentiality of the individual families.

## *Declaration of interest*

This study was funded in part by the European Community: Concerted action contract No. BMH4-CT98-3231 DG12-SSMI. Central coordination of the Project took place at the Tavistock Clinic, London. While developing the Project, Professor Kolvin was funded by the Leverhulme Foundation.

## *Copyright acknowledgements*

We are grateful to the editors of the *Journal of Psychoanalytic Psychotherapy* for permission to publish chapter 6, first printed in that Journal in September 2010, Vol. 24, No. 3; to the editors of *European Child and Adolescent Psychiatry* for permission to publish chapter 12, first printed in that Journal in April 2007, Vol. 16, No. 3; and to the editors of the *Journal of Family Therapy* for permission to publish chapter 14, which is an edited version of the paper that is to appear in a forthcoming issue of that Journal.

# *ABOUT THE EDITORS AND CONTRIBUTORS*

## *London*

**Sara Barratt** is a consultant systemic psychotherapist at the Tavistock Clinic, where she is Team Leader of the Fostering, Adoption and Kinship Care Team. She is a tutor and consultant to supervisors on the Master's course in systemic psychotherapy and a tutor on the Systemic Supervision Training. She teaches on other systemic psychotherapy trainings in the UK and Malta. In addition, she is a consultant and trainer to local authority child care staff and a psychotherapist in general practice.

**Vicky Bianco** was, at the time of the Childhood Depression Project, Head of Family and Systemic Psychotherapy for City and Hackney Child & Adolescent Mental Health Service. Prior to that she was a systemic psychotherapist in the Department of Child & Family Psychiatry at Queen Elizabeth Hospital for Children, Hackney, which together with Great Ormond Street Hospital was part of the Special Hospitals Trust.

**David Campbell** [1943–2009] was a consultant clinical psychologist in the Child and Family Department of the Tavistock Clinic, where he worked as a systemic/family therapist and a course organizer, supervisor, and teacher for various family therapy courses. In addition, he worked as a consultant to teams and small organizations in the public services. He was the author of several books on the subject and was co-editor of Karnac's Systemic Thinking and Practice Series.

**Jane Cassidy** is a child & adolescent psychotherapist who trained at the Tavistock Clinic and now works mainly in private practice, with children, adolescents, and parents. She is Chair of the Child and Adolescent Division of the Tavistock Society of Psychotherapists and Allied Professionals. She has a particular interest in transgenerational issues in families and is currently working on a doctoral thesis using her clinical work from this research project on childhood depression.

**Emilia Dowling** is a Chartered Consultant Clinical Psychologist & Family Psychotherapist (UKCP registered) who worked at the Tavistock Clinic for many years, where she was Head of Child Psychology. Currently she works in private practice and is a member of the Institute of Family Therapy. Her interests include systemic consultation with families, schools, and General Practice, and working with families during and after separation and divorce. In all areas of her work she is particularly interested in the child's perspective. She has published widely and co-edited with the late Elsie Osborne, *The Family and the School: A Joint Systems Approach with Problems with Children* (1985/1994). She is co-author with Gill Gorell-Barnes of *Working with Children and Parents through Separation and Divorce* (2000), and co-editor with Arlene Vetere of *Narrative Therapy with Children and Their Families* (2005).

**Henia Goldberg** qualified in family therapy at the Tavistock Clinic. At the time of the Project, she was employed by NELMHT Barking & Dagenham, working for The Acorns Early Intervention Service, a local authority-run service, aiming to prevent children of 4 to 7 years from school exclusion and promoting their mental health by providing a one-year intensive joint school–home therapeutic intervention for them and their families.

**Agathe Gretton** is a child & adolescent psychotherapist. Born in Paris, she graduated in European Literature. She trained at the Tavistock Clinic and has a particular interest in adolescents. She worked for some years at the Brent Centre for Young People and currently works in the NHS and in private practice.

**Jackie Hall** works as a child & adolescent psychotherapist in a Looked After Children's Service in Bromley CAMHS and in the Child and Family Directorate at the Tavistock Clinic. She is a visiting lecturer at the Tavistock and is particularly interested in the development of multi-agency work with children and families in the community.

**Ilan Joffe** is a consultant child & adolescent psychiatrist in the Child & Adolescent Mental Health Service at the Hertfordshire Partnership NHS Foundation Trust. His research interests include treatment of depression in children and adolescents, eating disorders in adolescents, and ethnicity factors in relation to childhood mental health.

**Sue McNab** is a family psychotherapist working in adult services for the Oxfordshire & Buckinghamshire Mental Health Partnership NHS Trust. She is also a clinical supervisor on the Master's in Systemic Psychotherapy at the Tavistock Centre.

**Gillian Miles** is an adult psychotherapist, and member of the British Association of Psychotherapists. As a member of the Depression Study research team, she was a Senior Clinical Lecturer in Social Work in the Child and Family Department of the Tavistock Clinic, where her work included assessment, clinical work with families, and work with parents in a multidisciplinary setting.

**David Pentecost** is consultant systemic psychotherapist and Head of Systemic Psychotherapy in the Islington Child Mental Health Service. He is a visiting lecturer and tutor at the Institute of Family Therapy, London. He has authored several papers on systemic psychotherapy within child mental health and has a specialist interest in the application of systemic practice to neuro-developmental disorders such as ADHD. He is author of *Parenting the ADHD Child* (2000) and Honorary Teaching Fellow at Birkbeck College, University of London.

**Maria Rhode** is Emeritus Professor of Child Psychotherapy at the Tavistock Clinic/University of East London, Honorary Consultant Child Psychotherapist at the Tavistock Clinic, and Associate of the British Psychoanalytical Society. She has co-edited three books—*Psychotic States in Children; The Many Faces of Asbergers' Syndrome*; and *Invisible Boundaries: Psychosis and Autism in Children and Adolescents*—and has published many papers and book chapters. She lectures widely in the UK and abroad and was the supervisor for half of the individual cases described in this book.

**Judith Trowell** is Honorary Consultant Child Psychiatrist and former Chair of the Child and Family Department, Tavistock Clinic, and is Professor of Child Mental Health at the University of Worcester (formerly West Midlands NIMHE). She is a psychoanalyst, Past Chair Person and Co-Founder of Young Minds, and Chair of Voice. Her research includes psychotherapy outcome studies, adult mental health and child protection, and comparative outcome studies. Her training interests are court work and psychodynamic psychotherapy.

### *Helsinki*

**Fredrik Almqvist,** Professor of Child Psychiatry, The Hospital for Children and Adolescents, Department of Psychiatry, Faculty of Medicine, University of Helsinki.

**Finn Ferdinand Garoff,** University of Helsinki, Institute of Behavioural Sciences and Department of Child Psychiatry, Hospital for Children and Adolescents.

**Kati Heinonen,** University of Helsinki, Institute of Behavioural Sciences.

**Anu-Katriina Pesonen,** University of Helsinki, Institute of Behavioural Sciences.

*Athens*

**Stelios Christogiorgos**, Department of Child Psychiatry, Athens University Medical School.

**Gerasimos Kolaitis,** Department of Child Psychiatry, Athens University Medical School, Aghia Sophia Childrens Hospital, Athens.

**Effie Layiou-Lignos**, Department of Child Psychiatry, Athens University Medical School, Aghia Sophia Childrens Hospital, Athens.

**Olga Maratos,** Department of Child Psychiatry, Athens University Medical School, Aghia Sophia Childrens Hospital, Athens.

**Valeria Pomini,** Department of Child Psychiatry, Athens University Medical School, Aghia Sophia Childrens Hospital, Athens.

**Eleni Stavrou**, child psychiatrist, child & adolescent psychotherapist, Athens.

**Vlasis Tomaras,** Department of Child Psychiatry, Athens University Medical School, Aghia Sophia Childrens Hospital, Athens.

**John Tsiantis,** Professor of Child Psychiatry, Department of Child Psychiatry, Athens University Medical School, Aghia Sophia Childrens Hospital, Athens. President of the European Union of Medical Specialists (UEMS), Section of Child and Adolescent Psychiatry.

**Marie-Ange Widdershoven-Zervaki**, clinical psychologist, child & adolescent psychotherapist, Athens.

# *FOREWORD*

*Michael Rustin*

The demand in contemporary health services for a proven scientific base for all permitted treatments has provoked severe difficulties in the field of mental health provision. Mental illnesses are by their nature more subject to variable definition and interpretation than are many, although not all, kinds of physical illness. Particular difficulties of measurement arise in relation to the various kind of psychotherapeutic—in contrast to pharmacological—treatments, since their inputs are more difficult to deliver in a standardized way than are drugs. All forms of mental health treatment pose problems in regard to the measurement of improvement, and this is perhaps especially the case for psychotherapeutic interventions, where even feasible and desired outcomes may evolve in the context of the treatment process itself, as possibilities for development are revealed that might previously have been hidden. In recent years—for example, in Lord Layard's Improving Access to Psychological Therapies project—it has often been held that cognitive behavioural therapy (CBT) has a more scientifically proven "evidence-base" than do psychoanalytic or family therapies, though in reality the evidence base for CBT in the treatment of many mental health conditions, especially where these are severe and long-lasting, is far from strong. The preference accorded to CBT is probably as much a consequence of the targeted focus of its treatments on specific symptoms or behavioural problems, which makes the measurement of intended outcomes more feasible, as it is of its larger proven efficacy.

In the field of child and family mental health, particular problems arise in the adoption of predominantly pharmacological solutions to illnesses. The alleviation through drug treatments of symptoms of psychotic illness or depression in chronically or acutely ill adult patients is now the form of treatment most commonly provided. This has achieved significant benefits—for example, in permitting the treatment of many patients "in the community" (although with varying levels of care) where formerly they would have been incarcerated for long periods in mental hospitals. But to many people it does not seem desirable to extend this model of quasi-medical drug treatment to mental illnesses among children, when this can be avoided. Children are nearly always being cared for in families (though not necessarily their families of birth), so the earlier need to reduce a large population of mentally ill patients in hospital is not a reason—economic or otherwise—for the long-term administration of drugs to them. In any case, a problem is now being reported from the United States of the large-scale addiction of adults to prescription drugs. Furthermore, it seems in principle undesirable to establish a dependence in children on pharmacological treatments when this can be avoided, especially where such treatments address the symptoms—such as behavioural problems—rather than the underlying causes of difficulty or disturbance. Practitioners of psychoanalytic and systemic family therapy have always believed that their interventions could bring permanent and lasting improvements in the mental health of many of their patients, often putting them back on course towards a fairly normal course of development. It is an advantage for the practitioners of child and adolescent mental health that their patients are still young, with most of their lives before them, and that they can still mostly depend on the dedicated commitment of their families. Thus it seems particularly worthwhile to test the hypothesis that such treatments can be effective in the treatment of serious mental illness in young people.

The research study described in this book was a pioneering response to the challenge that the demand for "evidence-based" practice was posing for child and adolescent mental health services. Its aim was to examine whether or not properly structured and managed psychotherapeutic treatments, in the modalities of both individual psychoanalytic psychotherapy and systemic family therapy, could bring improvements in young adolescent patients (from age 9 to 15 years) who had been diagnosed prior to their treatment as suffering from severe depression. The achievement of this aim required that modifications were made to everyday practices of diagnosis, treatment, and the measurement of outcomes, to meet scientific requirements. Thus the sample of patients was selected through specific diagnostic tests in order to ensure comparability between patients, and the sample was randomly assigned to either individual psychoanalytic psychotherapy (with parallel support work with parents) or systemic family therapy. The administering of the therapies was standardized as far as was feasible, given the relatively open-ended nature of the treatment methods themselves. With both these forms of psychotherapy, a great deal of initiative in regard to what is brought into the treatment situation rests with the patient, the therapists' responsibilities being to respond to what emerges in treatment sessions in ways that enable patients to learn from their understanding. This conception of therapy limits the extent of standardization of the delivery of treatment which is possible without compromising the essence of both of these treatment methods. "Standardization" thus took the form of ensuring that treatments were delivered by therapists with comparable training, within standard settings, and within a fixed number of sessions known to both therapists and the young people and their families from the outset. All of the therapies were supervised on a regular basis, by experienced and well-qualified clinical supervisors, to ensure that a good and as far as possible equivalent quality of treatment was provided to all patients in the samples. The same psychological tests were administered to all patients at the same specified intervals—prior to treatment, at the conclusion of treatment, and at six-month follow-up. To facilitate analysis of the clinical data after the completion of the treatments, recordings were made of all the treatment sessions. For the individual psychotherapy, audio-recordings were made and subsequently transcribed;

for the systemic family therapy treatments, video-recordings were made, consistent with common practice in this form of therapy. Therapists were also required to make detailed clinical notes of their work, which would be available for analysis in relation to the electronically recorded data and their transcripts.

These methods permitted quantitative methods to be used to evaluate the outcome of these treatments, as later chapters in the book describe. The outcomes of treatment were found to be extremely positive for both modes of psychotherapy, and in all three of the treatment centres—London, Helsinki, and Athens. The study provided a convincing confirmation of the hypothesis that these treatment methods were effective with patients of this age group and with this severity of depression. The fact that randomly selected patients benefited from whichever of the therapeutic modalities they were assigned to was a fortunate occurrence for the Childhood Depression Project, since it encouraged a spirit of cooperation rather than rivalry to develop between the different teams. There was also a significant and interesting difference between the pattern of treatment outcomes for the two therapeutic methods. In the sample of systemic family therapy patients, there was a more immediate reduction in the symptoms of depression than with the individual psychotherapy patients. But the improvement in the latter group continued longer—evidence, perhaps, of what has been termed a "sleeper effect" of psychoanalytic treatment methods.

The collection of "qualitative" data on the treatment process, through recordings, transcripts, and detailed clinical notes, has made possible the detailed analysis of what happened during the treatments themselves, and several examples of these analyses, in their various dimensions (including work with parents and the supervision process) are presented in the various chapters in the book. The clinical case study has long been the principal method by which knowledge of theory and technique has been advanced in both psychoanalytic and systemic family therapy, and it is valuable that this Project enables such cases to be studied in conjunction with quantitative measures of outcome. Several of the questions specifically raised by the framing of this research study have been explored through the data. One of these is how to explain the differences between the two treatment modalities employed, a question provoked by the somewhat different pattern of the outcomes in both cases. A second is the implication of providing sessions once-weekly for individual psychotherapy versus every two weeks for systemic family therapy, especially given professional concerns about whether "work in depth" can in reality be provided in treatments of this limited frequency. A third question concerns the consequences of providing treatment within a rigidly fixed timeframe of sessions, rather than as treatments without a predetermined duration and end-point that might otherwise be offered to patients suffering from depression of this degree of severity. Could evidence be found of the consequence of such a fixed duration, and what adaptation did therapists need to make to ensure that a known date of ending did not undermine the treatment process? (The interests of those patients who needed further clinical support after the completion of the Project could be safeguarded without compromise to the scientific integrity of the study.) On both of these counts, the study provided evidence that such constraints of frequency and duration need not be harmful to the outcomes of psychotherapeutic treatment for these conditions. Not only, therefore, did this study demonstrate that these treatments were each effective, but also that effectiveness could be achieved by means of a limited allocation of therapeutic resources.

This study has already had beneficial outcomes in demonstrating the efficacy of these forms of psychotherapy and of the feasibility of scientific research into treatment outcomes using both quantitative and qualitative methods. Further studies—a study at the Tavistock and Portman NHS Foundation Trust of psychoanalytic psychotherapy for adult patients suffering from severe depression, and a larger (IMPACT) study into severe adolescent depression involving the University of Cambridge, the University of Liverpool, and University College London and many NHS Trusts including the Tavistock and Portman—are currently taking place. These further studies have in part been made possible by the example set by the Childhood Depression Project.

# PART I

# INTRODUCTION

CHAPTER ONE

# The Childhood Depression Project

*Judith Trowell & Emilia Dowling*

The incidence of depression in children has increased markedly over the last few years. Children do not just get better of their own accord. They go on to lead limited lives, underachieving at school, at risk of consuming drugs and alcohol, and finding themselves increasingly in social isolation, suffering repeated depressive episodes. If, in addition, these children have symptoms of anxiety, their prognosis is all the more worrying.

According to research carried out by Harrington and Dubicka (2002), of the children who suffer one episode of major depressive disorder or of dysthymia, 26% had experienced another episode in the first year. By the second year this figure had risen to 40%, and by the fifth year there was a 72% risk of a further episode.

As clinicians in the field of child and family mental health, we are committed to address "unhappiness" in children through relationship therapies, rather than with medication. When the opportunity arose to set up an international research study with the support of BioMed, we decided to embark on a project to explore what works to alleviate childhood depression.

## *Why write this book?*

Why did we undertake the Project with depressed young people that we want to tell you about? Through the work of the Project we came to understand a great deal about depression in children and young people, and about ways of helping them and their families. We know now that depression in children is often masked by stroppy and difficult behaviour, by lack of interest in school work and activities, and withdrawal from the peer group, sometimes leading to school refusal. We hope that reading this book will help you to recognize childhood depression, even when masked by these behaviours, and to develop some ideas about working with them. We are now more aware of how many depressed children and adolescents there are. Many professionals and parents recognize such states of mind in children but are unsure how to help. In part, this book is for teachers, social workers, primary mental health workers, nurses, and health visitors, alongside child and adolescent mental health workers. We hope that what emerges will enable the recognition of depression in children and adolescents, as well as the development of useful interventions for the young people and their worried and troubled families. We are also including some of the research papers that came out of the Project, which may be of more relevance to researchers in the field.

## *What is childhood depression?*

Everyone becomes sad at times. Life has bad experiences and difficulties, so it is appropriate to be sad. It becomes *depression* when the sadness persists and cannot be lifted. One must think of depression when a child talks about feeling low, sad, or empty and of how this feeling is there most days. However, many depressed young people will not tell you they feel sad or low but, instead, will be irritable, scratchy, snappy, and generally fed up with those around them. They may also lose interest in activities they previously enjoyed and find no pleasure in anything much. They may not be aware of this themselves, but others around them notice. There can also be a definite falling off of the capacity to concentrate and learn, and they may say that they find it difficult to think. This can lead to feeling useless, worthless, and a burden. They can feel guilty and think that things that go wrong, or went wrong in the past, are their fault. Not surprisingly, when such depressive thoughts set in, some begin to wonder whether life is worth living, whether those around them would be better off without them. Such thinking can result in suicidal feelings, but these can also arise from their irritable and angry state of mind. If a young person has a plan to end it all, or has made attempts to do so, this must be taken very seriously.

Other symptoms of depression might be physical, a loss of appetite and weight, or sometimes increased appetite and weight gain. There may be sleep problems, either an inability to sleep or sleeping for hours on end, and this often becomes a long-term pattern. At the same time, the young person may complain about always feeling tired and lacking in energy, unable to get on with anything.

When these problems emerge quite quickly and are severe, reference is made to major depressive disorder. Once established, this state can last for some time, but the child usually recovers in about six months. Further episodes may follow, and other family members may have similar experiences of depression. However, sometimes such a state of mind grows slowly, is less severe, and is not so obviously worrying, just more chronic. Then, if it has lasted for at least a year, it is called dysthymia. Dysthymia is quite common and often goes unrecognized. However, it severely limits the young person's capacity to engage in school and home activities, or to make something of his or her life. It is possible to suffer from both depression and dysthymia, the one superimposed on the other, and then it is called double depression.

## *Our Project*

The Tavistock Clinic in North London has a large Child and Family Department, which is part of the NHS and undertakes clinical work with troubled children, young people, and their families. In addition, the Department provides training for a range of mental health professionals—psychologists, psychiatrists, social workers, child psychotherapists, family therapists, teachers, and nurses—to help them in their work and their understanding of families, children, and young people.

The two main interventions practised and taught in the Department are systemic family therapy, and psychoanalytic psychotherapy for children and adolescents. In a climate of evidence-based practice, it seemed important to explore whether we could demonstrate the effectiveness of the skills we were using and teaching. Another of our aims was to compare these two forms of psychological therapy, to see if either was better able to address different aspects of depression in young people and their families.

In order to set up such a study, we needed additional research funding, alongside the available NHS resources in the Clinic. Funding bodies were approached. The European Research Council (ERC) expressed interest and offered support, provided that we expanded our Project to include thinking about the response to treatment of depressed young people in different parts of the European Union. We had strong links with a number of European colleagues, and the teams that most wanted to join such a study were the Greek team in Athens and the Finnish team in Helsinki. Having secured their cooperation, we were able to secure funding for the research from Brussels (BioMed/ERC) and proceeded to set up the Project.

The Project has been an impressive and brave undertaking, the first such research project to take place within the Clinic, and it has demonstrated the possibility of bringing together different cultures in an attempt to validate the effectiveness of the two clinical approaches and to understand more about childhood depression.

## *This Project*

The London Research Team, together with colleagues from the Maudsley Hospital in South London, had already completed a psychotherapy outcome study looking at the effectiveness of short-term therapeutic interventions with sexually abused girls (Trowell, Kolvin, et al., 2002). Within this study, baseline psychopathology showed that 57% of these girls suffered from major depressive disorder. With that in mind, it was decided to plan a further outcome study looking at the response of depressed young people (between 9 and 15 years old) either to individual psychotherapy with parent work alongside or to family therapy. There were several implied benefits from our collaboration with the research teams in Athens and Helsinki: to increase the research numbers (the sample size), to promote psychological therapies in Greece and Finland, and to think about their effectiveness in the light of cultural differences.

Extensive planning and training meetings were involved in setting up and carrying out the research across the three countries. For the research team, a battery of research instruments had to be agreed, the timing of assessments clarified, and the therapy settings and procedures agreed. As a condition of the research, Brussels required written manuals for the therapists and the recording of all sessions, with audiotapes for the individual therapy and videotapes for the family therapy. Whereas family therapists were used to videotaping sessions in their everyday practice, individual child therapists were not accustomed to such procedures, and we needed to reach an agreement for such recording to take place. A further research requirement was that of monitoring the therapeutic process at intervals across the time span of the therapies. To this end, the young people and their parents were asked throughout the therapy to complete monthly questionnaires with the research psychologist. Supervision needed to be arranged for all the therapists. Bearing in mind the differences in approach, the research team worked out and agreed the frequency of sessions for the family therapy and the individual child and parent work (Kovacs, 1986). There were 30 sessions of individual therapy for the child, with 15 sessions of parent work alongside, and there were 14 sessions of family therapy. Since family therapy sessions were less frequent, the work for both arms of the Project spanned approximately the same period of time.

In all three centres there were fewer referrals than had been hoped. In London, referrals to the Clinic were monitored, and the Childhood Depression Inventory (CDI; see Glossary: Research Measures) was sent out by post to all those children and young people where depression seemed a possible factor in the referral. Where the score was high, and within the limits set by the

Project, the child and parents were offered an appointment with the research team.

In the course of the study, which took place over four years, 72 children and young people were recruited across the three countries. These children were then randomly allocated across the two treatment modalities: 35 to individual therapy, with parent work alongside, and 37 to family therapy. In all there had been 110 referrals, of which 26 had declined to take part (mainly in Athens). Twelve were excluded, either because they were not sufficiently depressed or because they needed hospital admission, which automatically excluded them from the study.

An extensive battery of research instruments was used for the assessments at the beginning and end of treatment and at the six-month follow-up. In the research chapters in this book, reference will be made to the following (see also the Glossary: Research Measures):

- Kiddie-SADS
- Children's Global Assessment Scale
- Childhood Depression Inventory
- Moods and Feelings Questionnaire
- Birmaher Anxiety Scale
- Beavers Interactional Scales
- demographic questionnaires: Cambridge (I. Goodyer), Newcastle (I. Kolvin)
- process notes for individual child psychotherapy
- audiotapes for individual child psychotherapy
- videotapes for family therapy

We have learnt much that seemed important to share about childhood depression. The clinical lessons have implications for professionals and their practice, for those who commission treatment, and for young people and their families. We have also spent time considering the meaning of the diagnosis of childhood depression. Genetic issues and neuro-endocrine factors are being explored elsewhere. The essence of this book concerns family factors, emotional and psychological factors, how these young people and their families functioned, and what needed to be done to help them.

### *How the research context affected our clinical practice*

A number of research issues arose that changed the way clinical teams usually worked—for example, the audiotaping and video-recording mentioned above.

Clinical practice was also changed with the need to hold research interviews at the beginning and end of treatment, and at the follow-up research interview six months later. The family therapists found it particularly hard to adjust to this and to the fact that the young person already had a label of "depression" attached to him or her before they started their work with the family. Again, many referring clinicians found the idea of random allocation between the two treatment modalities problematic, wanting to offer what they individually believed would be helpful. This had a considerable effect on referrals. As we have said, referrals into the Project were slow, and consequently the final research numbers were below those needed for really conclusive data analysis. In spite of this, we did recruit 72 families across the three countries and were able to offer evidence of the effectiveness of treatment within this group of families, both at the point after the end of therapy and at follow-up six months later.

Throughout, it was challenging for the clinicians to find themselves part of a research project and feeling that their work was under scrutiny. Additionally, they were not used to working within the fixed schedule required by the research, with a clearly marked timetable of the number of possible treatment sessions. Initially, as they became involved with the families, many found this restriction painful and encountered what they felt to be a conflict between the research and the clinical work.

It is important to acknowledge that we were aware that other interventions, such as cognitive behavioural therapy, could have been included. However, at the time a big study in this area of work was under way in Manchester, and another had been undertaken in the United States (for further discussion, see chapter 12). We spent time considering the inclusion of drug treatment with the newer antidepressants, only one of which is licensed for young people; we decided against the inclusion of such a group. Where children were already on medication at the time of referral, they needed to stop their medication to enter the study. Again, if anyone was felt to need antidepressants for clinical reasons while in treatment on the Project, they had to leave the study.

## *The families*

In the main, the chapters in this book describe the work with the families seen in the London arm of the study, though we include one clinical study from Greece. The research papers (chapters 12 to 14) concern all the families in the wider Project, across the three countries. As will be seen, there were interesting aspects to these particular families included in the Project, and interesting differences emerged between families across the three countries. Many of the London families had a mixed ethnic background, which was not found in either Greece or Finland. Again, many London families had lone parents, while neither Athens nor Helsinki had any lone parents within the study. At the point of referral, the London young people were either completely out of school, or in school but not learning, some spending all day at home, often in bed. In Athens, because of the stigma attached to mental health problems, most of the children were referred for learning difficulties, and there was a danger that naming depression could lead to the family leaving the Project. In contrast to London, there were few community services to support the families in Athens; there was no Educational Psychology service, no Educational Social Workers, and the main support for families became the extended family or the Greek Orthodox Church. In Helsinki, however, mental health problems were accepted, but because of the structure of services, and the long distances involved in travelling to treatment centres, young people tended to be admitted to inpatient beds when there were worries about them. As we have said, hospital admission was against the ethos of the study. We did not want to include admissions, since we felt that working with the young person within his or her family would address both the difficult family issues and the young person's internal problems.

## *Support and supervision*

Overall, as the chapters in this book will show, the families, children, and young people recruited to the Project had severe and complex problems. In the light of this, we needed to build close support and supervision into both arms of the Project to support the professionals working with them. We also needed the expertise of the multidisciplinary team, together with the skills of the wider community network, to think about a range of social issues: parenting, schooling and educational support, and health and mental health issues for both parents and children.

While we set out in this book to describe a research project exploring the nature of childhood depression, the chapters describing the clinical work convey both the essence of the families, their despair and their courage, and the skills and emotional resources needed by the professionals to carry out the work.

## *Outline of the chapters*

The chapters set out to illustrate the range of voices and perspectives involved in the research project. In the main, the clinical studies included here are from the London arm of the Project. Alongside the research team, the clinicians included both systemic family therapists and individual child and adult psychodynamic psychotherapists. The Project thus involved a broad range of cultures and techniques, with the use of both quantitative and qualitative research approaches, coupled with the opportunity both to learn more about childhood depression and to compare the outcomes of systemic family therapy and individual psychotherapy. The chapters in this book reflect this diversity and the range of work that took place within the Project as a whole.

Following this introduction to the Project, Judith Trowell addresses in chapter 2 the historical and theoretical background for the nature and recognition of childhood depression, looked at from both a medical and a psychoanalytic point of view. What is striking in her account is how it is only in relatively recent times that it has been recognized that children can be depressed. She outlines previous research studies considering the incidence and nature of childhood depression. She goes on to give a brief introduction to both psychoanalytic and family therapy approaches as a background to the accounts of the clinical work that took place on the Project.

Part II contains three case studies from London and one from Greece, written by the clinicians working with the children in individual work on the Project. While the writers have chosen their own themes in presenting their work with the children, strong common themes emerge with regard to the work on the Project. Knowing the extent of the difficulties presented by these children/young people and their families, all the writers began with serious misgivings about the ethics of offering them time-limited short-term interventions. These misgivings continued throughout the time span of the research, and were the stuff of international research meetings. Similarly, they struggled with the research demands, such as the presence of tape recorders in the room. However, what emerges from these case studies is the use the children/young people made of the help offered and the interesting part played by the research demands in the therapeutic work. Within this short-term work, all these authors highlight the importance of attending to transference and countertransference elements within the therapeutic work, though another key theme was the importance of mirroring.

Agathe Gretton (chapter 3) takes themes from her work with three young people within the Project. She gives vivid clinical material, describing how she set out to provide a therapeutic space, involving her in a constant struggle to understand and respond, guided by the young person's unconscious communications. She stresses the importance of listening to the patient, particularly with this group of such troubled young people, and how she often had to rely on her own responses in the room, her countertransference. She addresses the implications for her of involvement in the research and the consequent difficulties she anticipated, for herself and the patient, in terminating the work at the end of 30 sessions. However, despite her initial misgivings, she learnt from the experience that the young people had been able to use the therapeutic space and the therapy to move on with their lives.

Jane Cassidy (chapter 4) also writes from her experience of working with three of the young people. In doing so, she also discusses her initial apprehension about the research issues involved for the therapists. However, she felt in retrospect that there had been considerable gains from the work, both for the children and their families and for herself in thinking about her practice. She considers the research demands, the short-term work, and the use of the tape recorder. She presents her experience in the light of these demands and, in so doing, highlights the importance of attention to the use of projective identification, to the therapists' countertransference, and to the dangers of enactment that she experienced. Despite her initial reservations about the time-limited work, in practice she found it a valuable additional focus, alongside working in close collaboration with the parent worker and with access to the help of outside agencies. She has interesting reflections on the use of the tape recorder, which was there for research purposes but gave her surprising and valuable information about her own responses to her patients. Notwithstanding the difficulties of the work with these very troubled children, Jane also discusses the advantages she found in working within the defined structures of the Project, and she underlines both the importance of the regular supervision and the close working relationships developed with colleagues.

Jackie Hall (chapter 5) takes her experience of supervision on the Project as her theme, writing about one particular case. She describes in detail the process of her work with a 10-year-old boy, about whom there were also child protection concerns. Over the same period, the parent worker meeting with the boy's mother held a considerable amount of the anxiety aroused by the case and maintained contact with the concerned professionals outside the Clinic. Together with a description of the work with the boy in the room, Hall gives a commentary on discussions that took place in supervision. These discussions guided the progress of the work and focused centrally on the framing of therapist responses. We also see the therapist struggling at times to contain negative projections and feelings of rejection and, within the short-term contract, having to handle the pain of what felt to her, too, to be a premature ending to the work. However, she ends by visiting the research data, which certainly indicated that whatever the future in terms of his care, her patient had gained considerably in self-esteem during the therapy.

The fourth in this section of chapters about the individual work with the young people comes from Greece (chapter 6). The authors begin with a discussion of the literature concerning short-term psychoanalytic psychotherapy and, in so doing, outline the content of the Project Manual for the workers with the individual children (Trowell, Rhode, & Hall, 2010). They describe three stages of the work: engagement, a middle stage working within the transference on issues that have emerged, and a final stage addressing issues of separation and loss invoked by termination of the therapy. In doing so, they talk of their experience of working in the Project and of the impact of the brief therapy and the research demands on the therapeutic work. They go on to illustrate these stages in short-term therapy with material from two cases. This case material centres on work in the transference, which they feel draws heavily on their previous training and experience in long-term psychoanalytic work. They demonstrate the use of the countertransference in this short-term work and stress the importance of providing a therapeutic relationship that can survive negativity. They also describe their initial misgivings about working in brief therapy with these very depressed young people, but they felt impressed by the use the young people made of the opportunity.

Gillian Miles (chapter 7) writes about the work with the parents in parallel with the individual work with the children/young people. She begins with an overview of the complex nature of parent work, with its shifting focus on the child, parenting issues, family and parental dynamics, and both inner and outer worlds. In this context, she describes the troubled families and the intense parental anxiety and sense of hopelessness with which they came to the Project. She draws particular attention to the fractured, broken, and conflictual parental relationships, and the consequent absence of a strong third voice alongside the mother–child dyad. She describes the surprising effectiveness of this short-term intervention, often with the help of the school and outside agencies, facilitating a crucial shift in the family and freeing the child/young person to return to a separate and more normal environment. She draws attention to the powerful projections of hopelessness, the stress on the workers, and the importance of colleague support.

All the individual therapists were offered fortnightly supervision of their cases. In the final chapter in Part II (chapter 8), Maria Rhode, a consultant child psychotherapist and one of the supervisors of the individual work, reflects overall on themes in the work with the children and young people, alongside thinking about what had been learnt, both about childhood depression and about therapeutic approaches, from the work with this group of depressed children and young people. She presents these themes, highlighting the children's own descriptions of their depression and their experience of existential anxiety. She considers the therapists' responses and the technical issues involved in the work, focusing on the importance of mirroring. What was striking about these children/young people was that the therapists' response of mirroring seemed evoked by the serious lack of such experiences in their lives. She recalls the profound influence on both therapists and supervisors of their work within the Project.

The chapters in Part III are by the family therapists who worked in the Project. Sue McNab, David Pentecost, Vicky Bianco, and Henia Goldberg (chapter 9) write from the perspective of family systems therapists about the families they saw, and they explore the families' experience of depression—both the child's depression and often that of other family members. They discuss their experience of the research context and the ways in which, at first, this approach felt foreign to them, beginning with a diagnosis of a particular individual family member. They describe the work and convey the impact of the family depression on the workers. In this context, they discuss the particular benefits of co-working and supervision in their efforts to keep hope alive, where hope seemed to have been abandoned. This theme echoes the struggles described in the individual work to keep hope alive and survive despair. In considering the powerful impact of the families' depression, they note the importance of self-reflection in undertaking this work.

Sara Barratt and Emilia Dowling (chapter 10) write from the perspective of the family therapy supervisors on the Project. They discuss the theoretical basis for the systemic supervision they provided and describe the different tasks that the systemic supervisor can have in different contexts, focusing particularly on the family therapy work within the Project, where the therapists were experienced and known colleagues. In this situation, they describe their supervision as contributing ideas within the discussion of the work with families. They also pursue the theme of hope and hopelessness. Undoubtedly, in the light of the previous chapter, the supervisory group discussions made an important contribution in holding the therapists who worked directly with the families, as they experienced the power of the depression and despair present in the families.

In the final chapter in Part III, David Campbell (chapter 11) considers a small sub-group of families from within the family therapy arm where childhood depression was also linked with high anxiety and where, in the course of the therapy, there was a striking and significant reduction in anxiety. He considers these families alongside a group where the changes had not been so great. Using discourse analysis, and with detailed extracts from the transcripts of sessions, he sets out to explore the therapeutic factors that led to these significant changes and to think about the implications for family therapy practice in work with depressed children and their families.

Part IV contains three scientific papers. The central research paper by Judith Trowell and Ilan Joffe (chapter 12) gives the overall scientific results of the Project across the three countries. Two further papers explore the findings of particular research instruments used in the assessments before and after treatment: Gerasimos Kolaitis and colleagues from Greece write in chapter 13 on the preliminary findings on the effects of social adjustment and functioning; Finn Ferdinand Garoff and colleagues from Finland discuss in chapter 14 treatment outcomes and changes in family functioning in individual and family therapy. Given the present emphasis on evidence-based practice, these chapters are an important contribution. They demonstrate that the young people did well with these short-term focused interventions; their depression lifted, and they remained well at the six-month follow-up. The attempt to measure change scientifically using two previously unvalidated psychological therapies proved fruitful, in terms both of increasing our understanding of the nature of childhood depression and of exploring the effectiveness of the different therapeutic interventions. Now that the usefulness and possibilities of research in this area have been demonstrated, the hope is that more studies will be generated in the future.

In Part V, Judith Trowell and Emilia Dowling reflect on the learning from the Childhood Depression Project, about the nature of childhood depression, the effectiveness of the two different therapeutic interventions, and the issues arising for professionals for the recognition and treatment of childhood depression. They also consider the many research issues involved in setting up a study of this kind: the work involved in devising and running an international project, and the dilemmas arising for clinicians around standardized treatment measures and in recruitment—for instance, when random allocation is necessary. Their hope is that the positive research outcome described in the scientific papers in Part IV, alongside the clinical accounts in earlier chapters in this book, will prove useful for practitioners in their understanding and work with depressed children and their families. They are also hopeful that further such studies will follow on.

CHAPTER TWO

# Background: a short history of the recognition of childhood depression

*Judith Trowell*

Not too long ago, it was thought that children did not become depressed, then that, anyway, it was only a small number of children who suffered with depression. Only recently have adults begun to recognize the fact that children and young people do indeed suffer with depression, although the way it presents may be different from the typical picture of adult depression.

William Parry-Jones (1995) has written an excellent historical review of childhood depression. Childhood melancholia was described by Maudsley (1867), and at that time it was thought to be a constitutional defect, which might be linked to inherited syphilis. However, Maudsley went on (1879) to relate the type of melancholia to the level of development reached by the child at the time of onset. This was a developmental sequence that differed from that proposed by other authors (Maudsley, 1895).

Guthrie (1909), speaking from a paediatric perspective, was one of the authors who drew attention to functional nervous diseases in children—for example, fretting and homesickness while hospitalized—and Spitz (1946) went on to study this in detail. Puberty and adolescence were recognized quite early as the time when there was mental disturbance with a major physiological cause (Clouston, 1892).

Historically speaking, the causes of depression in children and adolescents were seen as many and various. There were physical causes such as infections; there were psychological causes such as shocks and traumas, bereavements, and losses; and there were other causes such as faulty education and parental brutality. Adverse early experiences were also recognized as of concern, whether there were harsh or over-indulgent parents. However, the role of inherited predisposition was widely accepted, with these other factors acting as triggers.

In the 1940s, psychoanalytic writers (e.g., A. Freud & Burlingham, 1944; Spitz, 1946; Winnicott, 1945) began to explore childhood depression, particularly focusing on deprived and institutionalized children. These authors developed the concept of depression following a child's separation from its mother and saw this in terms of misery, withdrawal, and apathy. In developing their thinking, they linked childhood depression to the work of Abraham (1911b) and Freud (1917) on adult depression following the loss of a loved person.

Bowlby (1960) drew on the work of James and Joyce Robertson (1971), and that of Robert Hinde (1976), to develop his ideas on separation and loss and thence onto his attachment theory. At the same time, some writers still doubted the existence of affective disorders in pre-pubescent children (Antony & Scott, 1960; Mahler, 1961). However, in the 1960s Sandler and Joffe (1965) looked at the records of 100 children and drew out from these records the features commonly associated with depressed affect. In doing so, they confirmed the presence of depression in children, characterized by sad affect, withdrawal, discontent, rejection, passivity, and insomnia.

Later, the understanding of childhood depression was greatly helped by recognizing the concept of "masked depression". Somatic complaints, behaviour problems and delinquent behaviour, school phobia, and learning difficulties in children and young people began to be seen as possible symptoms of underlying depression (Glaser, 1968). However, alongside this, it should be noted that depression in children was not mentioned in the medical categories of *DSM–II* (APA, 1968). Its recognition in the *DSM* is still fairly recent (APA, 1994).

Within a medical framework, Kolvin and Sadowski (2001) have considered the phenomenology and classification of depression. Ramani and Paykel (1992) drew up criteria for the diagnosis of depression (both inclusion and exclusion criteria), and these formed the basis for the *DSM–IV* classification (APA, 1994). They stated that for children and adolescents to be seen as depressed, they would have to have at least five symptoms over a period of two weeks, and that this should include being depressed or irritable for most of the day and losing interest or pleasure in their lives. The other possible symptoms might include change of weight, sleep problems, agitation or retardation, fatigue, feelings of worthlessness or guilt, a diminished ability to think and concentrate, and recurrent thoughts of death and suicide. To be seen as childhood depression, these symptoms should not be due to the taking of substances or to related medical conditions. Within these definitions, depression is divided into the categories of Major Depressive Disorder (MDD) and Dysthymia. Dysthymia involves low mood for at least a year alongside two significant symptoms.

Kovacs and colleagues (Kovacs, Akiskal, Gatsonis, & Parrone, 1994; Kovacs, Fenberg, Crouse-Novack, Paulauskas, & Finkelstean, 1984) have provided a detailed description of Childhood Depression and Dysthymia. In 1998, Kovacs and Devlin reported that the medical categories then in use, *DSM–IV* and *ICD–10* (WHO, 1992), did not fully coincide in their descriptions of depressive disorder, and that *ICD–10* did not envisage the existence of Double Depression—that is, a combination of Dysthymia and MDD. However, in 2001, Kolvin and Sadowski developed and supported the dual diagnoses of MDD and Dysthymia, both as distinct entities.

In 1986, Kovacs wrote at length about problems inherent in the presentation of childhood depression, because children may not be able to experience or describe symptoms such as self-denigration, worthlessness, hopelessness, or feeling of guilt, self-blame, and shame. They may have neither the language development nor the cognitive ability to register or describe these emotions in early stages of their development. Kolvin and Sadowski (2001) conclude that depression in childhood and adolescence resembles that in adults, similarities being greatest between adolescents and adults, and least so in the pre-school years. However, distress and negative affect may be expressed in externalizing symptoms.

They go on to consider at length how depression in children and adolescents should be defined and classified: first, through a clinical approach; second, through a statistical approach using multivariate procedures. Using this latter approach, Kolvin and colleagues (1991) identified two components: an endogenous type and a depressive cognitions type.

They further consider concurrent co-morbidity, common in depressed children and adolescents. Levels range from 70% of depressed children in the United States (Kovacs, Fenberg, Crouse-Novack, Paulauskas, & Finkelstean, 1984) to 90% in the United Kingdom (Goodyer, Herbert, Secher, & Pearson, 1997); the co-morbid symptoms are separation and anxiety disorders, conduct disorder, and dysthymia. There has been considerable recent work looking at childhood depression with anxiety (Cole, Peeke, Martin, Truglio, & Seroczynski, 1998); it is suggested that this co-morbidity increases the severity and duration of the depression, making it more difficult to treat. Again, where a child or adolescent is depressed with co-morbid conduct disorder, the depression may remit but the outcome may be worse, with lower social competence (Renauf Kovacs, & Mukerji, 1997). Where the child or young person has MDD together with dysthymia—that is, double depression—then the depressive episode is longer and more severe, and there is more likely to be suicidal behaviour and psychosocial impairmentl; together, these makes the depression more difficult to treat.

## *Prevalence: how big is the problem?*

Angold and Costello (2001) looked at studies of children and adolescents using the *DSM–IV* and gave an estimate of 1.6–8.9% of individuals under 18 years. They go on to state that around 2% of school-age children and adolescents have severe unipolar depression and another 4% have mild to moderate unipolar depression. It seems that in pre-pubertal children, the rate of unipolar depression is at the same rate for boys as for girls (Angold & Rutter, 1992).

However, rates of depression rise for girls in adolescence (Angold, Costello, & Worthman, 1998, 1999) after the age of 13 years.

More recent studies have shown more boys and girls under the age of 13 years (pre-pubertal) to suffer from depression (Angold, Costello, & Worthman, 1998, 1999). It remains unclear if there are ethnic differences in rates of depression. However, it is definite that co-morbidity is a real characteristic of the phenomenology of child and adolescent depressive disorder (Angold & Costello, 2001).

## *Family: genetic issues*

It seems likely that young people become depressed from a mixture of underlying genetic factors and environmental factors, underlining the importance of the family in both these aspects. Studies have shown that MDD is three to four times more likely in children of adults who themselves suffer with unipolar depressive disorder (Strober, 2001).

Rates of dysthymia also show an association between parent and child, the risk to children of unipolar adults being 8–32%,whereas controls (i.e., children of parents not suffering from unipolar depression) show a rate of 0–6%. Non-affective disorders are also more common in children of affectively ill parents. However, it is not known whether this is related to genetic factors or due to environmental disruptions and difficulties.

Are there specific risk factors for depression? The severity and chronicity of parental depression, together with marital disorder and other demographic variables, lead to greater overall functional impairment in their children. Children were more affected by a depressed mother than by a depressed father (Keller et al., 1986; Kovacs, Devlin, Pollack, Richards, & Mukerji, 1997; Kovacs & Sherill, 2001; Todd et al., 1996).

Studies where relatives of depressed children and adolescents have been interviewed (Harrington et al., 1997; Kovacs, Devlin, et al., 1997) have shown that these relatives are more likely to develop affective disorders than individuals in the general population.

However, it remains unclear overall how much childhood

depression is due to genetic factors and how much it is the result of environmentally adverse circumstances.

### *The influence of psychosocial events*

Goodyer and colleagues (Goodyer, Kolvin, & Gatzanis, 1985; Goodyer, Herbert, Tamplin, Secher, & Pearson, 1997) have looked at particular adverse circumstances and life events and have explored their impact on children and adolescents, bearing in mind their developmental status. Life events are divided into four groups:

1. Danger to self, such as accidents or community disasters.
2. Danger to others, such as siblings or parents.
3. Personal disappointments, such as examination failure or relationship break-up.
4. Loss, as with death or permanent separations.

It seems important to look at longer term as well as recent events when thinking about the impact of these on depression; early difficulties seem to predispose the individual to a depressive response to difficulties experienced later in life (Bifulco, Brown, & Harris, 1987). It is also thought there may be a genetic susceptibility to the development of a depressive response to more recent events (Silberg et al., 1999). But there is no overwhelming support for the suggestion that events in early life lead to major depression if there are then similar events later. Rather, what predisposes to current depression is the low mood state of the individual, which may have been brought about by previous events (Berney et al., 1991; Goodyer, Kolvin, & Gatzanis, 1985).

Lewinsohn and colleagues (Lewinsohn, Gotlib, & Seeley, 1995; Lewinsohn, Rohde, Klein, & Seeley, 1999), in a large longitudinal study, showed that major life stress is more associated with a first episode of depression, whereas low mood and negative thinking was more associated with recurrent depression. This carries the implication that an underlying pathway or mechanism is set in trend by the first episode, and this raises the question of resilience to difficulties or vulnerabilities and speculation about the reasons for these differing outcomes.

Goodyer, Herbert, et al. (2000a, 2000b) have shown in a recent study of young people between 13 and 16 years old that almost all episodes of depression occurred in individuals with a high level of depressive symptoms prior to the depressive episode. These young people were also at high risk with two or more psychosocial factors, such as parental psychiatric disorder or disharmony, deaths, or separations.

The events that seemed to have most impact, leading to depression, were personal disappointments and losses—that is, permanent separations or deaths.

Danger to the self or others did not seem to provoke depression in the same way. Nor did there seem to be a gender bias when considering recent precipitating events, although girls retrospectively reported more such events. But not all depressed adolescents have experienced difficult life events. About half of these depressed young people had experienced difficult life events, but the other half had not; the latter had slower onset depression, without event provocation.

Psychosocial events may influence the duration of a depressive episode. Recovery is influenced by family functioning; problems with communication and criticism delay recovery. The friendships that individuals are able to sustain during their depressive episodes may strongly influence recovery (Goodyer, Germany, Gowrusankur, & Altham, 1991; Goodyer, Herbert, Secher, et al., 1997; Goodyer, Herbert, Tamplin, et al., 1997). Peer relationships seem to be particularly important.

## *Psychotherapy issues*

It is important to note (Kovacs, Gatsonis, Paulauskas, & Richards, 1989; Kovacs, Paulauskas, Gatsonis, & Richards, 1988) that early-onset depression is often associated with co-morbidity, anxiety, or conduct disorder. Alongside this, there are often significant family problems, and the depressive episode itself is often prolonged and prone to relapse (Kovacs, Obrosky, Gatsonis, & Richards, 1997). It has therefore been suggested that a brief course of treatment may not be adequate. Additionally, young people suffering with dysthymia may develop MDD, and a small number develop bipolar illness.

Kovacs and Devlin (1998) showed in clinical samples that comorbid anxiety disorders were at least twice as common as comorbid conduct disorders. Both lead to functional impairment and make the depression more difficult to treat. In the families, high levels of marital conflict and conflict between parent and child also make treatment more difficult.

## *Psychoanalytic thoughts on depression*

As previously mentioned, psychoanalytic writers from Freud and Abraham onwards have been concerned about depression. Freud worked with clinically depressed adults whom he considered to be suffering from melancholia. He felt the depression was characterized by guilt feelings leading to a sense of worthlessness, a lack of zest for life, self-accusations, and frequent suicidal thoughts and impulses. He described it as similar to mourning, in that it followed the loss of a significant object, usually a loved person. But instead of a gradual letting go of the missed relationship, and an internalization of the memory, there are feelings of hostility and aggression. At the same time, the individual takes in the lost object and becomes identified with that person (becoming rather similar), and then the hostility is turned in on this aspect of the self. The guilt then arises from self-reproaches and is a form of aggression (Freud, 1917).

This internal process can be seen in those young people who have lost a parent by divorce or death, or who live in the crossfire of severe marital friction. Young persons either lose the loved parent in reality, or loses him or her from their daily experience, and then direct their feelings of worthlessness, hostility, and anger upon themselves. They may become withdrawn and have thoughts of death, or at least of wishing they did not exist. Their internal world is overwhelmed by rage and aggression turned inward upon themselves, alongside feelings of guilt arising from the superego.

The energy expended is often considerable, and for Freud this came from the instinctual source, the death instinct (Freud, 1920).

Abraham (1911b) writes about anxiety and depression as fear and grief. He describes "neurotic depression" when an individual has to give up his sexual aim without gratification. The individual then feels cut off and incapable of loving and therefore despairs of life and the future. Abraham felt that this state lasted until the individual was able either to experience an actual change or to find a psychological modification of the displeasurable idea. He goes on to consider the differences between this neurotic depression and psychotic depression, which may be part of a bipolar disorder (manic-depressive disorder) or a major depressive disorder (melancholia). He likens the depression in these cases to obsessive compulsive disorder, where the conflict between love and hate prevents development—that is, "The tendency . . . to adopt a hostile attitude towards the external world is so great that his capacity for love is reduced to a minimum" (p. 139).

The young people in our study, aged between 9 and 15 years, were pubertal and were at the stage of needing to move on from intense involvement with their parents to look outwards towards their peer group, needing to relinquish sexual investment in their family and to see the external world as of interest, with potential for satisfying relationships. This would seem to be the developmental task they could not achieve. Seen in this way, their depression can be understood as their failure to let go and move forward.

In her paper "A Contribution to the Psychogenesis of Manic Depressive States" (1935), Klein discusses the formation of the superego, and its relentless severity in the melancholic. She describes the bad internalized objects that attack both each other and the good objects, leading to feelings of persecution—the very strict and cruel demands of the good objects, and the attempts in the internal world to keep apart the good and the bad. She explains the problems to which these demands and the associated anxiety can lead—that is, feelings of paranoia and depression. The individual makes desperate efforts to avoid the threatened disintegration and destruction of his or her internal as well as external objects (relationships in the outside world).

Feelings of guilt and self-reproach follow the failure both to protect and to achieve perfection. Depressive anxieties and paranoid anxieties arise from this failure, as the hatred produces further disintegration. Klein's development of the concepts of the paranoid-schizoid position and the depressive position—a constant part of psychic life from infancy to old age—can be confusing; the "depressive position" here is the term used by Klein (1935) for a developmental state and is not to be taken as indicating that depression (clinical depression) is healthy. The importance of the development of symbol formation in the development of the ego, and its delay or lack of this capacity, is a valuable concept in understanding childhood depression.

Klein further develops her thinking in her papers "Love, Guilt and Reparation" (1937), "Notes on Some Schizoid Mechanisms" (1946), and "Envy and Gratitude" (1957). The oscillation between the paranoid-schizoid and depressive positions is central to our understanding of mental functioning, but the "depressive position", with its developed capacity for compassion, concern, sadness, and reparation, is not clinical depression.

The mechanisms described in relation to these early psychic processes—splitting, denial, projection, and projective identification—have proved essential when working with these young people and their parents. Again, it would seem that the clinical depression described and treated in this study could be better described psychoanalytically in terms of existential anxiety, with its problems located within the early paranoid-schizoid position.

Winnicott (1945), while recognizing the depressive position as a part of normal development, considers that it is loss—and a failure to manage its associated grief and sadness—that leads from the depressive position to depression. Since hate is in the ascendant, persecutory elements increase and benign ones are weakened. He also describes how children can somatise their negative feelings of badness and worthlessness and become ill, or have accidents. He suggests that clinical depression lies between the neuroses and schizophrenia. He sees depression as a wide concept, ranging from a near-normal state to near-psychotic. If the individual is supported, mild depression can lift or remit, as the underlying conflict is resolved or worked through, following, for example, a death or life event. Winnicott associates psychotic depression, with its feelings of de-personalization and de-realization, with loss, but not necessarily loss of a person or connected to any significant event; the loss is often unrecognized, a disruption or a displacement leading to a feeling of disorientation that could not be processed and managed. He felt that the role of the mother in this situation is usually crucial (Winnicott, 1954).

Bowlby (1980), in Volume 3 of *Attachment and Loss*, discusses sadness and depression. Following Abraham and Klein, he considers loss experienced early in life to be crucial. Failure to process or mourn loss or the threat of loss in childhood can be seen as pathogenic when the intensity of the distress persists, and it may be split off and denied. However, Bowlby views the child in the context of the family and sees the outcome as, in part, dependent on how the family responds. He considers the child's relationship with the mother as crucial throughout the early years, and it is the loss or the threat of loss of this relationship (attachment), or perhaps other central relationships, that predisposes to depression. He sees a secure attachment with a secure base as protective, and this should be in the context of a secure and stable family. Here Bowlby considers relationships in the external world to be as significant as those in the individual's internal world.

## *Background to family therapy*

Bowlby and others were involved in the development of family therapy, which included attachment theory and systems theory. This approach is based on the knowledge that family members are intimately connected, and that there are patterns of interaction within families. Problems in a family are seen as inappropriate adaptations, and understanding and focusing on these may be a way to promote change. In this context, change is seen to involve consideration of the presenting problem together with relationship patterns.

Family therapy focuses on altering interactions and sets out to improve the functioning of the family as a unit. It usually involves seeing the whole family together, but at times an individual can be the sole representative. Family therapy looks at diversity, transitions, disruptions, and changes that are occurring.

Systemic thinking in family therapy derives from the concept of mutual causality or mutual influence, the inter-relationship of events within a given framework. A system consists of a network of interdependent and coordinated parts that function as a unit and contribute to the coherence of the family. The relationships that form within these systems are taken in by children as mental representations (Gorrell-Barnes, 1994).

The family therapist, therefore, does not identify an individual patient but sees concerns as arising from dysfunctions in the family system. Family therapists observe the patterns of interactions and responses within the family and work with these patterns in the therapy. They are also interested in what is carried forward, what is adverse, and what is protective in the family patterns. These are called Internal Working Models (Bowlby, 1980)—that is, mental representations of the self and others used to guide behaviour and to interpret experience. Families are considered to have both a boundary and sub-systems within the larger system, which is important to be considered when working with the family. Homeostasis in the family works to reduce stress; life events that involve change may require reorganization or else may lead to fragmentation within the system. Where change is induced either by life events or by therapeutic intervention, this may arouse resistance to protect the coherence of the family system. Working with families in transition during divorce or post-divorce, where new family groupings are being formed and there is a need to consider the responses of different family members, is a large field, in which both children and parents are frequently depressed. In these situations, family therapy can be very helpful in managing painful change. (Dowling & Gorrell Barnes, 2000). Family therapy is also helpful in work with lone parents and in situations post-divorce or following separation. In these situations family members may be depressed, but the individual's depression is not the focus; rather, again, the focus is on the functioning of the family unit. These issues are explored further in Part II, on family therapy.

PART II

# INDIVIDUAL THERAPY

*Trainees and newly qualified child psychotherapists worked with the young people. Supervision was provided by very senior consultant child psychotherapists, Maria Rhode and Anne Alvarez. The parent work was undertaken by Clinic social workers, psychotherapists, and a psychoanalyst/child psychiatrist. This work required considerable liaison, internally with the child workers and externally with a range of professionals.*

*Agathe Gretton, Jane Cassidy, and Jackie Hall have written about their clinical work with the young people. Gillian Miles considers the complexity of the parent work alongside the work with the young people within a research project. Maria Rhode then describes her experience of providing supervision.*

CHAPTER THREE

# The wake-up call of adolescence: time-limited clinical work with three young people

*Agathe Gretton*

> *"Je ne trouve rien dans ma memoire qui soit en meme temps aussi enchante et aussi desenchante"* [I can't find anything in my memory that might be at the same time enchanted and disenchanted].
>
> Alain Fournier, *Correspondance*

> "Despite it all I feel strong: I have my mother's backbone inside."
>
> *The 25th Hour*, directed by Spike Lee, from the original novel by David Beniof

As we all know, adolescence offers the possibility of reworking some of our earliest conflicts. The hormonal changes in the body lead to a redefinition of the young person's sense of self and identity. The new sexualized body gives immediate reality to the possibility of intercourse and reproduction, thereby remembering and making possible the taboo of incest (the longing to have sex with a parent) and, at best, promoting some degree of resolution of the Oedipus complex. It is noticeable that this reactivation or reworking of our deepest sense of identity should be rooted in our body, just as in the very beginning of life our sense of self was defined by our body ego; we may here want to recall Freud's statement that our ego is first and foremost a body ego.

A number of artists have attempted to tackle this rite of passage between childhood and adulthood. In his emblematic novel *Le Grand Meaulnes* (1966), Alain Fournier describes the turning point of adolescence by means of the concrete arrival in his young 15-year-old narrator's life of a new body, a 17-year-old boy nicknamed *"le grand Meaulnes"*. Fournier goes on to associate the turmoil of this arrival to that of the young narrator's original loss of his native country at the age of 5. Thus *le grand Meaulnes* is seen to originate from the narrator's lost childhood country, thereby reactivating, by his very presence, the forlorn memories of the native land, or mother's body, and the wretched sense of being torn apart from the once so familiar. Indeed, one could say that the whole novel deals with the difficulty of bearing the paradox of a memory or internal object that is, at the same time, enchanted and disenchanted. The quest for the beautiful lost domain in the novel thus mysteriously turns not only into a journey of self–discovery, but perhaps more literally into a work of appropriation or integration of a new self, or what Jung would call individuation, through the acceptance of the absolute fact of the end of childhood. I believe that the absolute aspect of this realization, incarnated in the loss of the child's body, is the first real intimation of mortality in the life span, an echo of the dread of dying experienced by the infant when separated for too long from his mother, emotionally or physically or both (Bion, 1967). This may go some way to help us understand why depression, suicidal thoughts, and various attacks on the body are so often associated with that age group, when the psychic task of integration just feels too overwhelming.

As Mo and Eglé Laufer (1975) have pointed out, this developmental view of adolescence should not be underestimated, as it also underpins the real possibilities for change that can be achieved when working with these young people. By re-actualizing in a different form the first struggle towards integration, the adolescent process can give the individual another chance to put it right, as proved to be possible in some of the work I am going to discuss.

I will present some clinical work I have done with three young adolescents between the ages of 13 and 15, who were locked in a state of depression: they just "hated life", as one of them succinctly put it. The work was undertaken under the auspices of the Childhood Depression Project. All three young people had been diagnosed by the Project researchers as depressed, some with dysthymia, some with "double depression", both conditions being recognized as very difficult to treat. One could say that, at one level, they had simply refused the challenges of adolescence. Not attending school, with minimal contact with peers, they presented as emotionally homeless, with neither any reference to an inner country or self they could call their own, nor giving any sense of having containment from the external world. They seemed to be drifting dangerously in a no-man's land of depression, spending most of their time indoors, often in bed with the curtains closed. As one of them poignantly put it:

> "I feel like a tramp; a tramp does not have a home, a tramp lives in the street, looks for shelter, does not have proper clothes. Nothing fits, I feel like a tramp, I don't belong anywhere."

Without a sense of identity she feels homeless, with no space to call her own. This lack of internal space, or inner self, is a notion that I will explore with all three young people with whom I worked.

## *The Project's framework*

I saw each adolescent individually for once-weekly psychotherapy, for a total of thirty sessions each, which roughly corresponded to an academic year. This was part of the overall Project framework, and the young people were seen by the Project psychologist regularly throughout the intervention to fill in research questionnaires. A parent worker was also allocated to each family and saw the parents/carers fortnightly.

I think that this framework was an important contributing factor to the progress and shift achieved in the therapy. It gave an external structure and containment to these distressed families. In the case of the child psychotherapy interventions, both parents/

carers and young people were given their own space in which to be and think, with separate therapists. This did seem to help them experience the possibility of surviving separation, which was a huge issue both for the parents and for the young people.

The Project also defined the length of the work. In effect, this essential requirement, though difficult to bear at times, came to provide one of the cornerstones of our intervention as therapists. The clear 30-session time limit could indeed be used as a therapeutic tool in its own right, a reality factor in the treatment, something with which both patient and therapist needed to work. The young people had been told about the number of sessions prior to seeing their individual therapist. We were therefore perceived from the start as being a part of a bigger ensemble, which I am sure had some repercussion on the transference; it diluted it somewhat, perhaps making it more manageable. Some of the frustration and anger experienced towards this rigid and unshakable boundary could be directed at the Project as well as at the therapist, thus lessening the blow. This aspect of the work offers a similarity with that of working within the boundaries of an institution. The painful aspect of the time constraint was somewhat mitigated by the presence of an overall containing structure that included, apart from the individual therapy sessions, supervision of the therapists, therapeutic work with the parents, and contact with the schools and relevant education workers when appropriate. It is indeed questionable whether the progress achieved with the individual children would have taken place without such parallel therapeutic intervention.

The last Project requirement was for the therapists to use a tape recorder in the room for each session. What seemed at first to be a rather persecutory demand turned out to be rather harmless and un-obstructive with the three young people I saw.

### *Setting up the work: some technical difficulties*

My three patients, Sarah, Samantha, and Michael, were very different in personality and social background, but they gave me the same challenge in the room—namely, that it was quite impossible to attempt any direct interpretation in the transference. Any reference to myself (therapist-centred interpretation) was fiercely resisted. Any such attempts would either be totally ignored or lead to outbursts of anger: "*Why do you want to refer to you, what has it got to do with you?*" I was left in no doubt that it was the wrong track to follow, if I wanted to reach them. What struck me, however, was the liveliness and vehemence of their outbursts. As a participant in the Project, I had been told in advance of the severity of these young peoples' depression. Consequently I had expected to find myself in the presence of withdrawn and rather speechless young people; I was prepared for long silences and for having to play an active role in the sessions. I was therefore surprised that all three young people, in their different ways, were extremely talkative. At times, they filled the room so completely with their words that it made me feel rather superfluous.

I started to wonder whether part of this dynamic was around the possibility—or impossibility—of having two separate people in the room, two people and two minds in the same place at the same time. My experience was of being faced with a powerful invasion of my own internal space and capacity to think; it seemed that I could only exist on their terms. I had to adjust to their presence, without being allowed to have my own state of mind. Slowly I came to understand that it was not so much they trying to colonize the space, thereby trying to erase my very existence, but that the dynamic was that of reversal. They were perhaps simply letting me know about their own experience with their primary objects. Indeed, the rigidity or one-way-only aspect of the emotional tone in the room made me think of a mother–baby dyad that somehow could not get going. The rhythms were all wrong; there was no synchronicity, no room to experience being both alone and together (Winnicott, 1965).

To an extent, these young people were not sufficiently built up internally to be able to function within a more elaborate type of relationship, one that could acknowledge and tolerate a degree of otherness. I was left wondering whether the experience of the other had perhaps happened too early for them or, if not too early, had been experienced as a flood, a breaking down of boundaries, an intrusion, rather than as facilitating the slow development of a core self, through repeated introjections of feeling understood.

Frances Tustin (1972a) refers to what she calls a premature psychic birth in cases when such basic rhythms could not be established at the beginning of life, either through the infant's difficulties or through over-projection on the part of the carer, or often a combination of both.

Indeed, the degree of deficit in these young peoples' backgrounds also pointed to some intergenerational issues. Two of them were being brought up in single-parent families, following traumatic events—domestic violence in one case (Samantha), the death of a pregnant mother in the other (Michael). The family life of the third, Sarah, was plagued by serious ongoing marital difficulties. Whatever the aetiology, these youngsters were quite unable to face the bid for adolescence; they were stuck in a bad place internally, a place where voices (Sarah), ghosts (Samantha), and endless ruminations (Michael) were their daily companions.

In such a context, it seemed premature, at first, to attempt anything else apart from remaining in an alert state of observation, staying with the flow while getting to know the invader, as it were. Slowly, as to some extent I accepted the part I was assigned to play, the rigid aspect of our emotional encounter started to modify, at least for Sarah and Michael. Having agreed to be part of their script, I was then able to begin to describe my position, thus allowing a kind of third position to develop. I was both a participant and at the same time a witness of our interaction, thus showing the young person that it is possible to experience a situation and think about it at the same time (which may well be what Fonagy, Gergely, Jurist, & Target, 2002, calls "mentalization", and Bion, 1967, "binocular vision"). Winnicott (1965) has described this as a mirroring function, a process in which the mother is both an emotional participant with her baby and also able to name the experience at the same time. In this particular type of play or interplay, the young person can begin to experience him/herself as being both together with the therapist and separate—that is, alive. This was expressed by Sarah's touching exclamation in the middle of an intense play: *"Wicked, you are an artist aren't you?"* She was expressing gratitude for being given the space to play.

Out of the three young people, Samantha was the one who missed most sessions. She attended 15 out of the 30 sessions on offer. Her mother proved unable to bring her on a regular basis, perhaps having a vested interest in Samantha not developing independently. This mother, unlike the other parents, could never fully engage in the therapeutic process offered to her by the parent worker. For her part, Samantha had not yet developed enough of an inner self to take the risk to come to her sessions of her own accord. However, she was able to develop a strong and positive relationship to her social worker who happened, like me, to be French! It seems that this family was too deprived to make a difficult journey to the Clinic on a regular basis, but this social worker (unlike the parent worker and myself) was able to visit them in their own home. Samantha scored well at the two follow-up research sessions after the treatment; she was not depressed any more. This would seem to indicate, among other things, that these missed sessions (experienced by me as very frustrating, but not an attack on the treatment as such) had had a function, perhaps representing a lack, the unspeakable deficit in her background.

## *Clinical material*

### *The toy box*

As they were young adolescents, I decided to provide each of them with an individual box in the room, despite my concern that they could also react negatively to this, feeling too old for it. As it turned out, they took to using their box, and it became a precious therapeutic tool for me. It allowed for a degree of distance between us, when too much closeness could feel claustrophobic. This particular type of play also gave me some access to early, nonverbal, or unverbalizable states of mind.

The use of the box can be seen as an illustration of the particularity of working with young adolescents who are still close to their childhood and to more infantile ways of mental functioning. Melanie Klein (1955), for instance, thought that children's play with toys could be interpreted in the same way as dreams in adult patients. The German-born psychoanalyst Gisela Pankow (1981) has also demonstrated with remarkable results how the use of play-dough helped her adult schizophrenic patients to structure their internal world. Indeed, two of the young people I saw were greatly helped by the use of the toys. Playing with the fences allowed Michael to begin to represent his difficulties with his internal space, away from his constant ruminations. Being provided with a box gave Sarah permission to use the whole room as a giant toy box, in quite a concrete way. By allowing her to rebuild the room according to her specifications, I got to know her phantasies, and this helped us to begin the task of differentiating phantasy from reality.

## *Clinical presentation 1: Michael*
## *Unintegration—the internal world is not fully constructed*

Michael, who was 13 years old, was locked in a state of rumination, mostly uttered as arguments against his father. The sessions often started with him telling me how many arguments he had had with his father during the week.

Father and son were living alone together since the death of Michael's mother when he was 4 years old. At home, Michael's bedroom did not have a door, something I saw as illustrating his difficulty with having an internal space, or sense of self. Without this sense of an inside or core self, he could not properly tolerate any experience of the outside world as being separate from him. At times he was talking to me about his father as an extension of himself, which made it very difficult for me to understand what he was saying. Was he telling me about his feelings, or about his father's feelings? Who was angry? Who had started the fight? I spent quite some time telling Michael how confused I was about who had done or said what. I also wondered with him whether he too felt confused sometimes, with just the two of them, him and his Dad, and no one in between to help them.

One of the first signs I was given that our work was effective was when Michael let me know, in a casual sort of way, that his bedroom did *not* have a door, that it was an open space. He was, of course, beginning to have a concept that bedrooms are perhaps meant to have doors, and, indeed, four months later he told me that his bedroom now had a door. This seemed concretely to represent the beginning of the possibility of Michael establishing his own inner world, or, to put it differently, that he could begin to have an internal object rather than to live permanently inside the mind of his father.

Both he and his father had been unable to mourn the death of Michael's mother. They had been stuck in an endless cycle of grievances, reminiscent of the recriminations of the ageless male couples in Beckett's plays: "I cannot go on, I will go on." I also think that the door, or lack of it, stood for a generational gap between them, which had not been properly established. Consequently, the onset of adolescence in Michael had increased the level of physical violence between them, to a point where it was doubtful that they could have carried on sharing a house together.

I cannot help speculating that at least for Michael, the impossibility of mourning, progressively to let go of his mother, was rooted in an unresolved primary relationship to her. He had not reached a basic level of separation from her when she died, which made it difficult for him to mourn her as a separate person. His sense of his inner self was not sufficiently developed, and consequently he was often confused and rather paranoid. For example, he would ask me why his father would tell him one day that he (Michael) should water his mother's rose bush once a day, only to tell him the next day that he should water it twice a day. Was his father out of his mind, or was he doing this on purpose, just to confuse and annoy Michael?

### *The first few weeks*

During the first few weeks of the treatment, I felt rather hopeless about how I could help this boy. He talked non-stop in a toneless voice about the arguments, giving endless details in a rather obsessional way. He presented as a small boy with fine but rather underdeveloped features. His clothes were too big for him and hung loosely around him. He had a way of letting his jacket slide from his body, which I found rather unnerving. I was concerned by his lack of concern and his detachment, both of which I experienced as chilling.

He had only used his box once, in the first session, painstakingly producing the drawing of a farmyard with a tractor that looked distinctly like a funeral hearse. The sky was blue, he drew two rainbows inside the puddles, the animals were there, so was the farmer, but the drawing had a lifeless quality, a stunning stillness, which reminded me of Pompeii. The box had been disregarded since, closed and useless, seemingly a symbol of the impossibility of moving on.

In the following vignette I reflect on my decision actively to bring the box back into the picture.

*EXTRACT FROM SESSION 6*

The other day when he came back from school he felt that the house was so empty and sad, even though his Dad was there. . . . His Dad was in the middle of boarding up the window that he (Michael) had smashed the other day, and it made the room look even gloomier and he got angry at his Dad for doing this.

I ask him whether it feels better to be angry at his Dad, better than feeling so sad and depressed, and he says yes, it does.

He says that he often feels sad when he is just coming back from somewhere. It strikes him then how lonely the house is.

I say that he is telling me that it seems that it is the transition between ending something and starting something that makes him aware that something is missing. He says yes.

I now have a feeling that we could go on talking in this way forever, and that nothing would ever happen. I straighten my back on the chair. I feel stuck, and there is a long silence.

I tell him that in the room with me, here, it seems to be difficult for him to use his box AND talk to me at the same time. I suggest that it is like being either all sad or all angry, with nothing in between. He says yes, in the very definite way he has.

He opens his box in a rather awkward sort of way and carefully starts taking the fences out.

*Commentary:* When Michael comes back to the house, he feels that it is so empty and sad, despite his Dad being in it. He lets me know that it is *in* the gap between comings and goings that he is caught unaware by his depression. His father does not function at first as an external agency; his presence does not modify Michael's powerful feeling of depression. It is only when he notices that his Dad is repairing the smashed window that Michael can project some of his anger at him. Similarly, in the room with me, Michael is talking at me, rather than to me, and I experience the dread that things could go on in this way forever. I am also wondering how I could perform the function of the repairing-window type of father-therapist to allow Michael to be more actively engaged with me.

He is a keen observer of himself, and at one level he appears to respond well to my comments. However, my sense that we could go on talking in this way forever indicates that there is an emotional quality missing in his communication. Earlier in the session, I had noticed the different qualities in his eyes as he was glancing at me; one eye seemed cold and calculating, the other more benign or ordinary. I was aware of having to attempt to engage these two aspects of Michael, in order to avoid a one-track-only intellectual contact. I come back to the here-and-now of the session, and I bring the box into the picture, with the hope of engaging both sides of Michael directly, to occupy or focus the wandering eye as well. I could have made an interpretation about this other eye, but at this point it felt premature to try to mobilize this more symbolic level of functioning.

The following section of the same session is quite instructive, in that it confirms my sense that Michael was not sufficiently built-up internally for a more traditional interpretive type of work.

### *EXTRACT FROM SESSION 6 (CONTINUED)*

He spends quite some time with the fences, first putting two fences side by side, hesitating. I comment on his concentration and his hesitation. He slowly and tentatively makes an enclosure with four fences, forming a rectangle, but disregards it. He tries again to construct a rectangle; he creates three sides of the rectangle using a ruler, the side of the box and one fence, and he leaves the fourth side open.

I comment on how difficult it seems for him to complete the enclosure, and I wonder aloud whether it is as difficult as experiencing oneself as complete.

*Commentary:* Michael becomes very engaged in this struggle to define a space. For many of the following weeks, he will start the sessions with this play, using the fences in different combinations, but never able to complete a shape.

The first completed enclosure he managed was a triangle formed by two fences, with the toy box as the third side. It was interesting that he could not yet use the three fences to form the triangle; he had to use the side of the box as the third side. I understood this to be an indication of his need to lean on a third party in order to be able to conceptualize a space. One could say that he used the side of the box as the backbone of his construction, a backbone that he had not yet quite internalized.

Genevieve Haag (1991) has written extensively about what she calls the construction of the body or the body ego, reminding us that the body is not a given, it has to be constructed progressively in parallel with the mind. In particular, she demonstrates in her work with autistic children how the body can be experienced as two separate sides, one side staying with the mother when she leaves too abruptly, either emotionally or physically, or both. She shows that the establishment of a core self comes together with the realization that one still remains in one piece when the mother goes, a realization that is built up over time, with layer upon layer of experiencing and re-experiencing the coming and going. This she calls the primal bodily–psychic interchange or "relational rhythm".

It seems that Michael could not complete the building of his inner self because he had experienced, and continued to experience, the absence of his mother as like a piece of himself missing, the missing fence perhaps. My troubled sense of his two eyes with different looks in them seemed related to the expression of a binary bodily split in Michael, an un-integration between different parts of himself, which left me feeling uneasy. Only one half of him was with me in the room; the other half, the missing half, was "somewhere else", possibly looking down on us. Similarly, my sense of unease at the way he let his coat slide from him in a detached way was, I believe, a reaction to his own disowning, or split-off, aspects of his experience.

It is important to be aware of the autistic aspect of a "psychotic" depression and not to interpret at an oedipal level what could in effect be a terror of different aspects of the self getting together in a violent rather than integrating way. I think that the work with the fences offered Michael a way to represent his struggle with his sense of identity. The completion of a shape or enclosure can be understood as standing for experiencing oneself in one piece as a separate bodily entity, and this was precisely what seemed to this boy too dangerous to achieve. The function of not completing the shape (echoing that of not accepting the challenges of the new adolescent body) was that of protecting him from the phantasy that in so doing his aggression could become out of control There was, indeed, a poignant quality to his game with the fences, and I was often moved by it, at times suggesting to him that he seemed to be struggling with the notion that two arms, two legs, two hands could actually equate with one finished person or body.

### *Later stages*

In the fourth month of our work, Michael started to bring dreams to his sessions, and this coincided with no longer using the toy box. He had completed the work he had to do at this level, and he never went back to using it. The therapy had entered a different phase. One can also perhaps wonder whether it was precisely his work with the fences, in my presence as a witness to his attempts, that had enabled him to make this psychic leap.

I would now like to give an extract of a dream towards the middle of the treatment at seven months. I chose this particular dream because, among other things, it shows the link between the emergence of sexuality and the concept of an inner space or container:

#### *EXTRACT FROM SESSION 17*

The dream: *He is in a supermarket and decides to buy seeds. They have put them in a pot for him. There is a window where you pay for the seeds and a sort of room behind it, a bit like your room here, he says, and something happens, and the whole room gets flooded. He insists that the water does not go beyond the room. It just fills it.*

In the dream for the first time Michael is able to name me as a transference object. He associates the therapist with a space; "a sort of room a bit like yours", he says. The transference is to my room, the room I give him, in which he could feel able to grow like a seed. The French psychoanalyst Didier Houzel, who has worked extensively with autistic children, has written of the importance of transference to a container (Houzel, 2002); he describes this as an earlier level of transference than the infantile transference described by Melanie Klein. One could think of this as a preconception of a space available for emotional containment. I see the work with the fences as an illustration of such a preconception. What the dream makes clear, in the beautiful way dreams have to express different elements at the same time, is the anxiety that such a space could be flooded and destroyed. It seems that adolescence and its emergent sexuality—ejaculation in this case—reactivates the early anxiety about the original container, a mother who died when she was pregnant; the deadly danger of seeds. The dream helps us to understand Michael's struggle with the fences: how could he complete his own space when his original object had been flooded and died? The dream also indicates how, in the transference, he is beginning to experience me as a new object, one that hopefully might be able to cope with his seeds and contain the flood.

In fact, from this point on, Michael started to dress in a smarter way and began to put gel in his hair. I also noticed that his father was looking smarter in the waiting room, where they both sat, side by side, hidden behind their respective newspapers. I was moved by his bid to grow up, and it was difficult to stop the work with him when he was just beginning to develop. This feeling was mitigated by a sense that a real shift had been achieved in the work. The boy I first met kept on telling me that "he was thinking to himself", and he had began to experience the possibility of thinking together with someone else.

In conclusion, it is necessary to stress the importance, in the overall progression of this case, of Michael's father's meetings with the parent worker. It provided a separate space for him. The paternal function—that of establishing boundaries and quite literally bedroom doors—needed to be nurtured in its own right in the external world, as it was of importance in the development of the young person's inner life.

### *Clinical presentation 2: Sarah When too much is not enough*

I shall now present the case of Sarah, who was 13 years old. Everything about her was oversized, including her body and the tales she brought to her sessions. Indeed, she gave me a sense that she was living in a television soap opera. At 13 she looked more like 17, wearing heavy make-up and having been offered a paid job on the pretence that she was 18.

Hers was a family where emotional drama between all four members (she had a brother), and particularly between the parents, was the daily bread and butter. The level of anxiety was high, and emotional explosions the norm. Sarah had been out of school for over ten months when I started seeing her. She spent her days at home, in her room. There had been several suicide attempts; I also knew that she was terrified by a number of voices who told her to put needles in her body. The overall picture was a worrying one. She had seen a number of professionals already, and inpatient treatment had been considered prior to involvement in the Project.

My very first impression of Sarah was one of dislike. I experienced her as a rather unpleasant sort of girl, cold and unfeeling, when I saw her shuffling down the corridor in her flip-flops. In fact, this first impression turned out to be one of the first indicators of the power of this girl's projections. She hated having to come to the sessions, at least initially, and it seemed difficult for me not to respond to this projected hatred with dislike—and perhaps a wish to retaliate? Thus, the intensity of the projections made it difficult sometimes for me, as a therapist, not to feel driven to act-in during sessions. For instance, I was often aware that my interpretations, and not just interpretations of the transference, could be an expression of some acting-in on my part, an avoidance of staying with more intense and unbearable feelings, thus turning me into an as-if therapist.

Not surprisingly in such a context, the first thing that Sarah brought to her session was a concern about something fake.

*EXTRACT FROM SESSION 1*

> She sits on the chair opposite mine, in a rather floppy way, holding an empty cup of hot chocolate.
>
> She is silent for a while and looks rather uncomfortable, so I suggest that she may find it difficult to be with someone like me that she does not know at all.
>
> She says that her father and her uncle think that she is a fake.
>
> When I ask what she means, she says that they don't believe her. She speaks in a rather strangled voice, coming from deep inside herself, and rather inaudible.
>
> She then says that she hates life.

*Commentary:* I am worried for Sarah, lost in her huge body, with a voice that does not quite emerge. Who is she? Where is she? She gives me the impression of someone who has been experiencing the onset of adolescence and sexuality as catastrophic. As a result, she has opted for living in a rather un-differentiated state with her mother: they look very similar, and they wear the same type of clothes and make-up. Sarah's bid to jump the queue and become a pseudo-adult woman has not been successful, and her unease is located in the male members of her family: they are the ones who think that she is a fake. It seems that her hatred of life stems from the hatred of having to face a real identity crisis.

As I have said, I often had to face my own identity crisis as a therapist in the course of this particular treatment. Who was I in the room with Sarah? Was I a play therapist, a child minder, a fellow drama student, a cognitive behavioural therapist? Was I stupid, unable to do my job, colluding with her? With hindsight, it seems that it was precisely my tested ability to bear being a blank canvas for this child's projections, and a degree of tolerance for not quite knowing what could be the appropriate level of communication with her, that created a possible therapeutic space for Sarah.

At first, it was difficult for her to accept the fact that she had to be on her own with me when her parents were being seen by the parent worker, or were waiting for her in the waiting room. The second time I saw her, she had a very severe panic attack in the room. She was screaming. She wanted to see her Mummy. At one point she could hardly breathe. I therefore agreed to take her back to the room where both her parents were being seen that day. The five of us stayed in that room for the reminder of the session.

Slowly it became possible for Sarah to enact some of her emotional dramas in the room with me, while actively enrolling me as a protagonist in a sort of role play in which she took charge. This proved to be a first step out of her stuck and depressed state of mind. I use the word "enact" rather than "dramatize" because it seems to better describe a much earlier form of play. This is not yet a symbolic level of functioning. We are in a transitional space where the protagonists or characters are hardly separate from their creator. The following vignette illustrates such a realm, where inside and outside are not quite differentiated.

### *EXTRACT FROM SESSION 3*

Sarah had spent the beginning of the session comparing me to the other doctors she had seen and telling me off because while they had asked her many questions, I had not, and she thought it was very wrong.

She goes on to say that she feels sad, but then she always feels sad, so she has got used to it.

She then asks me in a very lively voice: "Is this your office?" And then: "No I don't think it is; there are no folders in here."

I say that she seems to be wondering what sort of place this is, and what sort of person I am to take her to such a place.

She says that she was wondering whether it was my office, because if it was, I should do something about it. The lights are too bright, the desk is ugly, I should have different curtains and a different cover on the sofa.

I smile and tell her that it seems that the room is not up to scratch and that she would do a good job at refurbishing it. She says that she wants to be an interior designer.

She continues to talk in an increasingly manic way about the redecoration of the room.

*Commentary:* Sarah is responding to the fact that I am different from the other doctors. She rightly picks up that I am not in a psychiatrist's role, and she complains that I am not giving her a clear enough structure as it might perhaps make it easier for her to hide. The redecoration of the room can also be seen as a projection of her own sense that she had not been a good-enough baby for her mother: it had not been love at first sight. Thus I am made to feel what it is like to be at the other end of a redecoration process.

At this point in the work, I was not yet aware enough of the importance of fully playing the part that has been assigned to me, in order to explore the phantasy in reverse, so to speak. For instance, I do not complain in a play-mode way that someone does not like me and wants to redecorate my space, taking time to reflect on this predicament. Instead, I put it back to her that she is a good decorator. Sarah therefore gets more and more carried away in a manic way, and the manic aspect of the redecoration takes precedence now over the possible meaning it could have; it becomes a thing in itself.

I am now going to introduce another moment in the session, when she can respond directly to a feeling of being understood

*EXTRACT FROM SESSION 3 (CONTINUED)*

She asks me whether I like the colour blue. As I do not give a straight answer, she says that the ceiling looks like a school dining-hall. I silently think of this communication as her telling me that I am too institutionalized for her at this point.

She says that she has answered my questions, so why can't I answer hers?

I say that it seems she wants me to be just like her, she wants us to be equal. I then add that perhaps she feels it would be easier for her to talk to me if she knew a bit more about me.

She says, "Can you repeat this, please?"

In this exchange, one can see that Sarah is touched for a moment when I show her that I can understand her frustration, as she perceives me as an impenetrable therapist. She asks me to repeat what has made sense to her, as if unsure whether she can hear something good properly. Here, one is reminded of the fact that she is a bulimic girl, someone who cannot quite believe that she has taken in enough, someone for whom too much is never enough. This difficulty in introjecting a good experience properly is also demonstrated by the fact that she cannot sustain for long this feeling of being better understood, and she spends the rest of the session reverting to asking me in an obsessional way whether I like the colour blue.

A transitional space is a complex space where the patient starts to emerge from a more fragmented, or un-differentiated, state but is not quite ready for full symbolization or separateness. Throughout my work with Sarah, the technical difficulty was to be attentive and vigilant about the level at which we were actually communicating, to be able to understand adequately the move back and forth, between early undifferentiated states, transitional, and more symbolic ways of functioning. It is interesting to note in this respect that for Sarah, too, just as for Michael, doors were not to be taken for granted, precisely because a more symbolic way of functioning was not fully established. The boundaries between inside and outside were not firmly set. But whereas Michael had successfully gone from having no door to having one, the passage proved more complicated for Sarah. Doors were far from straightforward entities for her. For instance, she described her bedroom door as hollow inside, with all sorts of bizarre objects hidden in this hollow, thus illustrating how problematic the barrier between phantasy and reality was for her.

### *Progression in the work*

As Sarah became more and more able to make use of me in her play, it became easier for me to engage fully with the exploration of her phantasies, while following her instructions as my artistic director. She started using her toy box from session five onwards, but in fact she really used the whole room as a giant toy box. Thus, the plant was actually one day cut into bits to make a soup for me, and she began to move the heavy desk sideways in order to turn it into a bank counter, where she, the Manager, would receive me, Mrs G, who desperately needed a loan.

I shall now present an extract from Session 23 (ten months into the work), as I think it illustrates the notion of transitional space, which I have mentioned earlier. This is also a poignant *mise en scene* of the impact of ending the work.

#### *EXTRACT FROM SESSION 23*

I tell her that we have a limited number of sessions left, which is sad because she and I have started to work together and have come some way. I suggest that it is like our credit-card game, where there is a woman whose card has been blocked when she wants to buy more goods.

She gets up and says: "Let's play now. You have to sit on the couch because now you are in the waiting room." She moves the desk between us and gives me my credit card. I thank her.

She tells me that Mrs G (me) needs a loan because she cannot unblock her card.

I say that I need extra help because the Project has blocked my card and it would be nice to have extra help.

She asks me whether I would like to sign the request, and then adds in a small and sad voice; "Do you think that it will be enough, Mrs G?"

I pick up her anxiety as to whether the Project would have helped her enough.

*Commentary:* One can see how it is slowly possible to explore more difficult feelings from the realm of the transitional space. The tone of her voice in her last question revealed the full impact for Sarah of ending the work. Much affect has become available, and the play is used as a means of communicating the painful feelings raised by the imminent ending. By that time, Sarah had been able successfully to return to school, just as our play had also successfully replaced the voices that she had described to me at the beginning of the work.

However, as we ended the sessions, I was concerned about whether we had advanced enough with our work really to help her out of her depressed and undifferentiated state. In the room with me, she could take on board more of my comments, but she still needed to be in charge, in an omnipotent way. For this reason, the ending proved particularly traumatic for her. However, Sarah did well in the two research follow-up interviews. I think this was due to the fact that she had experienced some real contact with me in the room, which had gone some way to helping her out of the fake identity with which she had started. Alongside this, much work had taken place with the parents, and with the relevant school authorities, to enable Sarah's return to school.

### *Clinical presentation 3: Samantha*
### *The enduring power of projections—transgenerational issues*

Samantha nearly got lost from this chapter, which seems to reflect the tentative quality of her presence in the room, notwithstanding the fact that she missed half her sessions. Furthermore, I was surprised that in her research follow-up interviews she was no longer depressed. Thus the lightness of her presence, or what I had experienced as her insubstantiality, was powerfully reflected in my own lack of belief in the impact of our contact on her state of mind.

A pretty, slim 15-year-old, Samantha looked totally different from her mother, who was struggling with overweight. In the waiting room her mother always addressed me in a proprietary way, as if implying that I was *her* therapist. By contrast, Samantha would disappear against the wall, so that I had to look around to find her. When she followed me in the corridor, she seemed to be floating behind me like a shadow. In the room with her, I often experienced my own body as ugly and overweight, as she talked to me about her sense that the world was split into two parts, between fat and thin people. She reported that her mother was on a diet to lose weight, and that she (Samantha) had to share this diet, as there was not enough money for two diets. She spoke in a soft voice with a melodic quality to it, more conducive to sleep than to thinking. Her delivery was easy and fluent; she could verbalize a wide range of feelings, from rage, hatred, anger, sadness, even happiness at times, but I was usually left with a sense of something unsubstantial, if well formed. She was positive about our contact, and she told me that she often felt better for a whole day after our sessions and then the good feeling just vanished. Similarly she felt that she was not putting on weight despite all the nourishing food she was taking in. She reported that, on the other hand, her mother ate little and put on too much weight. My own sense of being fat in the room with her (despite all appearances), illustrates the power of the delusional eye projected into me by this girl. In Samantha's internal world, there was no room for two of the same, only opposites; thin/fat, black/white, trendies/townies, children/grown-ups.

In this either/or realm, one can understand the meaning of the missed sessions. It seemed that if she could allow herself one live session, she had to offer another one to the dead. She did tell me that her life was populated with ghosts and that three of them visited her regularly. I found it nearly impossible to make any transference interpretations, as I was made to feel that referring to myself in this way would be the equivalent of taking all the room for myself, at her expense. This gives some indication of her fear of being born, as, for her, being born or separate from the mother seemed to be equated to a hostile act. The last months of our contact were taken up with her realization that she needed a passport in order to be able to go abroad. The acquisition of the passport became the representation of being born to the world, which meant, too, that she could begin to let go of her ghosts. They were replaced by the emergence of some historical perspective. Samantha was able to let me know that her mother had been given up for adoption by her mother, along with her sisters, whereas this mother (Samantha's grandmother) had kept all her boys with her. As the youngest of her mother's children, Samantha seemed to have been the carrier of the unspeakable and undigested emotional inheritance of the previous generation, a world literally divided between the haves and have-nots, which made her feel "emotionally homeless, like a tramp".

The work with her was different from that with the other two young people whom I have presented. Samantha was two years older than they, and at one level she was more fully developed as an adolescent. She never used the toy box, but the missed sessions seemed to provide a concrete way of letting me know of her difficulties in fully joining the living. As I have said, my own peculiar resistance to recognizing the actual positive results achieved in this therapy can be seen as a testimony to the persistence of the power of transgenerational projective processes. Thus, in a near repetition of past history, this particular story was nearly not told, nearly not given the same legitimacy as that of two of her siblings in the Project.

## *Conclusion*

All three young people were profoundly depressed at the beginning of the work. They all lacked a sense of a core self, or inner space. The parental couple was not well established as a benign entity for any of them, internally, and as a result, they were fragile and ill equipped to meet the challenges of adolescence.

Michael used his ruminations—or, as he astutely put it, his "thinking to himself"—as a hard-core envelope, an obsessional defence against the engulfing sadness of the lack of his mother. The onset of adolescence felt particularly dangerous to him, as it was challenging this basic defence—cracking the shell, one could say.

Sarah had opted for a false self, a fake identity. Her more hysterical defences, in the form of voices or omnipotent play, had got in the way of being able to develop her own inner resources. Thus, faced with having to experience her own sexualized body, rather than borrowing her mother's identity, had proved quite catastrophic and had led to a retreat from the outside world, including school and peer relationships.

Samantha had never been able to take the risk of a psychic birth; claiming a passport felt heroic, as in this "either-her-or-me" type of world, there seemed to be no room for two of the same. Any journey felt unbearable, a reminder of what she perceived as the deadly danger of separateness. Emotionally homeless, she presented defensively in a way that was as unsubstantial as the ghosts that visited her, but the strength of her unprocessed emotional luggage was powerfully projected into the therapist's mind.

It is remarkable to think that this short and focused therapeutic work was able to take these young adolescents out of the very pathological states in which they found themselves. The fact that the intervention not only focused on the individual treatment for the young people, but equally addressed through the parent work the context in which they were living, seems to have made an important contribution to the overall therapeutic gain for the young people. Within the Project, this was further confirmed by the equally striking results achieved by the family therapists. These results do seem to demonstrate that the context of the work needs to be taken seriously in order to achieve therapeutic effectiveness, especially so in the case of deprived families. At a technical level, I would like to stress that with each of the young people I have described, it proved essential to provide them with a containing space in which they could begin to experience being with another free from projections, before any full-blown interpersonal transference could be explored. Thus the relative neutrality of the containing space, and the time-limited aspect of the work, were particularly useful therapeutic tools in the treatment of these young people, who had been the recipients of such powerful projections in their lives.

CHAPTER FOUR

# Lost boys: aspects of projective identification, countertransference, and enactment with three boys

*Jane Cassidy*

As a child psychotherapist, I took part in the Childhood Depression Project over a period of three years and worked with three different young people. All were boys, all were living with their lone mothers, and the mothers were struggling with their own serious issues, alongside their real concern for their children. The children/young people were all very depressed, in and out of school, and were often isolated at home.

Although the Project was primarily a comparative one of individual psychotherapy and family therapy, it highlighted several specific areas for me personally. These were, that:

» time-limited psychotherapy is effective

» parental and childhood depression is often enmeshed and is muddled with transgenerational aspects

» the recognition of countertransference and projective identification are important, as a means both of communication and of understanding the internal world

» tape recording of psychotherapy sessions can be extremely useful, both for the therapist as a method of increasing

self-awareness and as an additional tool in understanding a child's way of relating
- close work with colleagues is important in this work, either through supervision or through peer-supervision groups.

At the time of writing, the way in which I work has evolved considerably from the time when I first participated in this Project. The Project itself had a great influence upon this development, and my participation in the Project and knowledge of its research findings marked the start of this development in my thinking.

At the beginning of the Project, there were various unique features linked to its research requirements that caused me concern with regard to the risk of "diluting" the way in which we, as child psychotherapists, work. The first was that the therapy was time limited to 30 once-weekly sessions for the children, alongside 15 fortnightly sessions for the parents. This seemed a totally inadequate amount of therapy to attempt to help these worrying and very depressed children. In fact, the task seemed quite hopeless. In addition, the research criteria required us to tape-record all the therapy sessions. Both factors seemed to detract from our normal way of working, and I certainly held the opinion that the benefit of the sessions would be diluted, both by such time limitations and by such apparently intrusive external requirements. With hindsight, I have changed my mind. Much of the work was successful, and many of the families were able to move on from a very stuck and depressed position, both psychologically and in their living circumstances.

During the Project, I became more aware of myself as a therapist and more conscious of how I worked. This was largely due to listening to the recordings and hearing the exact content of the session after the event. There were many times when I was surprised by my interpretations or responses, and I was able clearly to identify episodes of my "acting in". These moments were different from the times when my colleagues or I found ourselves working in a way that went beyond the boundaries one would normally associate with the pure role of psychoanalytic psychotherapist, when we became involved with outside agencies in order to help these very paralysed and stuck parents and children/young people. In fact, in my opinion, *these* practical interventions certainly helped some of the shifts to occur, and they were very different from the episodes of "acting in" that I describe later in this chapter.

The structure of the Project also played a part, with close and regular supervisions and the opportunity for discussion with colleagues, so that despite these episodes of "acting in", we were able to sustain our way of thinking and to use these experiences to contribute to our understanding of the individuals and their relationships.

## *My three young people*

As already mentioned, all three were boys living with lone mothers. One was an only child, and the other two both had siblings. All of the mothers had issues of unresolved loss, and they either had no relationship with the absent father or, where contact was maintained for the children, there had been an acrimonious divorce.

### *The boys*

I have described the boys as "lost children" because there was a quality of "lostness" about all three which communicated a sense of deprivation and a need for emotional nurture. They all had difficulty attending school, and yet on the whole this seemed to have gone unnoticed; they had slipped through the net, and their difficulties had not been picked up. In each case, there was a significant degree of enmeshment between the boys and their mothers, which may have developed as a means of avoiding separation but, at the same time, prevented a more real medium for nurture that would have ensured that their emotional needs were met. The child's needs were in some ways lost in the parent's minds, not present in their awareness. All three boys seemed to have little sense of their own identity and direction. They all spoke about themselves carelessly, as though they were okay. They had a defensive carapace to protect their vulnerability and distance themselves from their own feelings of despair and hopelessness. I think they were also defended against a sense of failure. My initial impression for each one was that 30 sessions of therapy would be insufficient.

Throughout the therapy, my countertransference was strong and, at times, overpowering. I frequently reacted to this, rather than being able to contain the projections and think about what was happening. When I was able to think, rather than react in this way, there were moments of meaningful contact and closeness. I discuss this in further detail later.

I will call the boys Richard, Roger, and Sam. Roger was 11 years old and Richard and Sam both 12 when they entered the Project. All three often spoke to me in a belittling manner, Richard and Roger in a more sneering fashion, while Sam could be quite patronizing. They all treated me as though I was a rather stupid, untrustworthy adult. However, whereas Richard and Roger were more hostile and aroused my annoyance, Sam was extremely reasonable, yet dismissive, and treated me as though I was the one in need of therapy. I felt inadequate and useless with him, a sense his mother also conveyed to her therapist. Sam was more sophisticated and used manipulation in a seductive way. All three boys were quite suspicious and mistrustful, and regularly checked on my memory, often showing surprise when they discovered that I had not forgotten.

## *Richard*

Richard was referred to the Project by an educational psychologist who had diagnosed a specific learning difficulty and was very concerned about his depression, his lack of school attendance, and his isolation at home.

Richard lived with his mother and elder siblings. His parents were divorced. His father was erratic in keeping in touch, his contact with the children being minimal and inconsistent. Following the divorce, the family's lifestyle had changed significantly over the last few years. Richard struggled with his learning problems, and he was being bullied and finding it difficult to go to school. His mother was depressed, very angry about their situation, and she and Richard were enmeshed. He was quiet, softly spoken, and generally slow to respond. During the initial family meeting, his mother consistently answered for him, often speaking just as he seemed about to speak. She allowed him little space to talk.

*Richard's mother.* Richard's mother was difficult to engage, with a tough exterior. She adopted an intensely angry and independent stance throughout the therapy.

She was an unhappy woman, whose anger was directed at one faceless institution after another, and it became apparent that she needed to be locked in a battle and appeared to use anger as a defence against emotional pain. On the rare occasions when her vulnerability was expressed it was conveyed through psychosomatic illness. She was frequently unable to acknowledge painful experiences of her own, and when she did, she tended to deny their significance. Her other children were coping well at school and had no difficulties. She saw Richard as the needy, depressed, "problem" child and could articulate his difficulties, but she appeared unable to connect with any emotional understanding of his position.

Initially she was wary and suspicious of her therapist and quite afraid of criticism, but she gradually seemed more able to let the therapist know about her own difficulties. She remained resistant to the idea of help for herself, but there seemed to be the beginnings of a sense that she could have an experience of someone understanding her without feeling attacked.

### *Sam*

Sam was referred because of his difficulties in going to school. His parents were divorced. He lived with his mother and elder sibling, and his mother herself described their relationship as "enmeshed". Here, however, there were close links with a caring but erratic father, to whom Sam was close and with whom he stayed regularly. Sam was depressed, without friends, and was finding school attendance difficult.

*Sam's parents.* Sam's mother was an intelligent, able, but vulnerable young woman. Like her son, she used an intellectual arrogance and superior distance to protect herself. Sam and his mother seemed locked together in an oedipal relationship; she was ambivalent about their closeness, as she also needed her own life. Her own separation anxieties came to the fore as she found it progressively more difficult to feel shut out of her son's therapy and frequently questioned the way the work was continuing. She was very defensive in relation to the Project generally, usually leaving her therapist feeling somewhat useless and inadequate (probably also a reflection of her own sense of inadequacy as a parent).

## *Roger*

Roger was referred by the school because of his erratic attendance. He was intelligent, but his work was poor, and when at school he seemed tired and unable to concentrate. He was a bright and chirpy boy, always looking on the bright side. He tried to be helpful and was popular with teachers at school. There was a quality of neglect and deprivation about him. He clearly found his sessions helpful, as he managed to get himself to them on his own, despite a long journey. He had no contact with his father.

One of the initial questionnaires for the Project was never returned by Roger's mother as she continually forgot to post it, despite several reminders. After many phone calls, she came for a preliminary appointment with her son. She spoke freely about her own long-standing depression and about her concerns about Roger, his depression and temper outbursts, and the fact that she could not get him to school.

*Roger's mother.* Roger lived with his mother and younger siblings; his mother did not work, and there was no contact with the children's father. There was a real sense of poverty. Roger's mother had a history of clinical depression, and her attendance at meetings was erratic. Her poverty was very evident, and she often looked tired and washed out. Her absences were covered by a variety of guilt-ridden excuses, which we later realized were probably related to periods of addictive behaviour. When she did come, she was at times hopeful and thoughtful, full of plans to get out and engage in activities. At other times she seemed overwhelmed, fragmented, and persecuted. She seemed unable to maintain her boundaries, and Roger often seemed lost from her mind, and needed to look after himself in her chaotic confusion.

During discussions with colleagues about this family, it was always difficult to sustain thinking about Roger and not allow thoughts and discussion regarding his mother to dominate. He frequently slipped out of our minds and was too easily lost from our thoughts. Over time it became clear that he did not protest about being forgotten, but existed in a rather detached way, partly in a fantasy world of make-believe, punctuated by moments of danger. As we came to recognize this, we became aware of the importance of practical interventions, with both the school and the local hospital, to ensure that Roger's mother received the help she needed and that the school were aware that their concerns about Roger were justified.

## *The tape recorder and projective identification: how and what we learned.*

In order to record the sessions, we used small standard tape-recording machines with flat, round microphones. Although not large, they were quite noticeable in the room. Having no experience of being recorded while working, my response to the machine sitting on the desk was that I found it both intrusive and persecutory. None of the boys liked it, and all three reacted negatively, albeit in different ways. At times, to them, it seemed to represent my partner in a rather oedipal manner; at other times, it represented a part of myself that could be attacked more easily than by directly confronting me. It aroused suspicion and dislike.

None of the children ignored the machine. Roger flicked at it, surreptitiously knocked it, complained about it, and thought I was only interested in him to "get stuff for my tape". Sam also disliked it, but true to his usual form was quite reasonable, although simultaneously damning—I needed it because I probably wouldn't be able to remember without it, and also because of the research project. However, he would often surreptitiously push his box against it and crush it into the wall. Richard articulated how much he loathed the tape, and he was extremely suspicious of its use. He told me on one occasion that he thought I wanted to tape his stuff so that I would be able to make lots of money blackmailing him later when he became famous. He also asked, in a somewhat paranoid fashion, about where the tapes were kept and how safe they were.

Over time I myself became more interested in the usefulness of the tape-recording machine. It had provided certain opportunities for discussion with the boys. I did not listen to my recordings at all during the first three months of the Project, but on one occasion I wanted to hear exactly what I had said, and took out the tape. As I listened, I was highly surprised to find how the actual session was, at times, quite different from my overall recollections.

I noticed quite quickly, and with some alarm, that I kept talking and not waiting long enough to allow Richard time to speak, such that I said to myself: "For goodness sake, let him speak, give him some space!" I was saying to myself exactly what I had thought about his mother during the session when we had all met together; listening to the tape, I realized that I had begun to relate to him in the same way as his mother. This awareness was most helpful in future sessions, and I continued to listen to the tapes to monitor my work. One of the most significant issues for me was the degree to which I had been unaware of the change in my way of working during the session. My recollections and session notes did not convey the atmosphere in the room as accurately as when I heard it live on the tape. Then I listened to tapes from another case and noticed that I did not do this with another child; it only appeared to happen with Richard. My reactions when listening to the tape outside the consulting room and the session were my "normal" ones, in keeping with my usual clinical approach.

The concept of projective identification was introduced by Melanie Klein in 1946 as a way in which, in the paranoid-schizoid position, remote from the conscious mind, and as a defence against anxieties and impulses, parts of the self are projected into the object, in a way that weakens the sense of self. This influences both the perception of the object and its subsequent introjection as well as the behaviour of the object, who begins to behave as though he or she were actually characterized by these projected thoughts and beliefs.

Betty Joseph (1987) describes the different types of projective identification:

> Splitting off and getting rid of unwanted parts of the self that cause anxiety or pain; projecting the self or parts of the self into an object to dominate and control it and thus avoid any feelings of being separate; getting into an object to take over its capacities and make them its own; invading in order to damage or destroy the object. [p. 65]

She goes on to say that the infant or adult who continues to use these mechanisms powerfully can manage to avoid awareness of

> separateness, dependence, or admiration; or awareness of the concomitant sense of loss, anger, envy etc., but in so doing sets up persecutory anxieties, claustrophobia, panics and the like. [p. 65]

All three boys were suffering from persecutory anxieties and panics, and, as the work continued, claustrophobic themes emerged in the sessions with Richard and Sam. In the work with the mothers, similar defensive mechanisms were observed.

Bion (1962) describes the process thus if projections cannot be contained:

> If the projection is not accepted by the mother the infant feels that its feeling that it is dying is stripped of such meaning as it has. It therefore reintrojects, not a fear of dying made tolerable, but a nameless dread. [p. 116]

With hindsight, it is clear that my countertransference, the projection of Richard's nameless dread, was too powerful for me to contain and think about. What appears significant is that when I cannot tolerate his communication, it is then that I behave in the same manner as his mother, become irritated and impatient, and reject him by leaving no gaps or space for him to speak.

Hinshelwood (1994) describes projective identification as an interpsychic process that is central and crucial when making emotional contact with another. From the beginning of an infant's life, projective identification functions as a preverbal and pre-symbolic means of communication. I believe that Richard was attempting to communicate his very early anxieties by projecting something preverbal and pre-symbolic that he could not bear, and which I also found intolerable. I filled the space with words and hurried on through the session, thus rejecting his projections rather than containing them.

The tapes, alongside discussion with colleagues, brought a whole new dimension to the understanding of my own work, and to seeing the power of such projections. With my new awareness, as the therapy continued I was more alert to different reactions in myself, and more able to tolerate and reflect on such difficult feelings in the countertransference. As this happened, there were more moments of closeness between us, and Richard began to talk more freely and bring dreams to the sessions which were full of persecutory and claustrophobic imagery. As the therapy went on, he was able to talk about these feelings and images relatively easily. It also became apparent that his fear of school was not entirely misplaced; his school was rough and violent, and frightening events had occurred from time to time in the classroom. Later, he was able to return to school, and his hypochondriacal tendencies began to disappear. With the assistance of supervision and the use of the tapes, I had become more able to contain and consider Richard's communication via my countertransference, which contributed enormously to my understanding of his internal world.

As his mother's sessions continued, it became clear that she was herself depressed, with many issues of unresolved loss. As she was able to make a closer contact with her therapist, she began to allow herself to become more vulnerable and to talk a little about her past; unfortunately, her therapist had to leave the Clinic, and she found this loss very difficult to manage. Although she resumed sessions with another therapist, she became more defended again. However, she did manage to understand more about Richard's difficulties in relation to her own.

Sessions with Roger were difficult to recollect and keep in mind, and I was frequently unable to remember the content immediately afterwards. During sessions my mind would wander, and I had to make an effort to concentrate on what he was bringing. He would sometimes rock backwards rather dangerously on his chair, raising my anxiety regarding his safety. He told me stories about spending time out at night with friends, activities that seemed inappropriate for his age. He conveyed a sense of a rather neglected, forgotten, and lost child, with no one capable of keeping him in mind.

Roger articulated his dislike of the tape machine, but he often tried to "help" by fiddling with the microphone or the controls, stating that he understood how to work it better than I did. Interestingly, what then happened frequently was that the tape machine would stop during the session, or it would not restart, so that the session was not recorded. However, when I tested the machine later, it would work perfectly. On several such occasions when I thought I had managed to record properly, when I listened later there was only silence. The tape should have provided me with the means to recover the lost material, and to recover Roger in my mind, but either by my own muddling up of the recordings or Roger interfering with the tape machine, it was irrevocably lost. This seemed symbolic of the impossibility of keeping Roger in mind, alongside the occasion when I forgot to take his toy box to the room with me, so that he arrived to an empty room, something I had never done before. Roger always appeared to accept these situations with calm pragmatism, perhaps because he was used to being forgotten and not heard. As I have said, he frequently spoke in a manner that suggested his expectation of being forgotten. In this situation, the lack of recordings on the tape machine was helpful in thinking about him and the "dropping out of mind" that always occurred.

In terms of sequence, Sam was the final child I saw in the Project, and by now the parent worker and I had worked together for some time. Here, it was the structure of the Project itself that helped us to see what was being acted out in the therapeutic process. In the work with this family, the powerful feelings of need and unbearable loss were so great that we both became caught up in an enactment of something with the family, rather than being able to contain and think. The context concerned the issue of ending the therapy, and one of the main themes throughout for mother and son had been the issue of separation.

Sam had a pseudo-maturity and the ability to converse in an adult manner, discussing things with me like a colleague. Towards the end of the therapy, there was a dispute between Sam, his mother, the parent worker, and myself about dates. Sam complained to me in such a reasonable and persuasive manner that I began to agree with him, and I found myself deciding I should alter the boundary and the structure of the research project.

At that point in time, with Sam struggling to get back into school, this decision seemed to make perfect sense, and in my discussions with my colleague I had begun to behave like Sam, manipulating and persuading her that this was a good idea, to which my colleague responded by considering an extension to the number of sessions Sam should have. She was also under a similar pressure from Sam's mother to extend his sessions. Our behaviour was clearly reflective of the ways in which mother and son were enmeshed together, with both workers being unable to bring in a boundary and keep to the limits. As mentioned above, a particular theme for this family was a difficulty with separation and letting go, which was at the root of many of their problems.

My colleague and I finally questioned ourselves and discussed our dilemma with the case supervisor, whose immediate reaction was clear and firm: we must reinstate the original boundary. The situation was rescued, and I was able to talk with Sam about what had happened. We were able to use the last few sessions to concentrate on the ending and on his anger about saying goodbye and not having had as much help as he would have liked, rather than colluding with the idea that he needed more and that we could both ignore the reality of the time limit and avoid separation. We had been able to call upon the supervisor to be the regulator who helped to effect the separation. Sam both finished his therapy and managed to return to school before the end of term.

This was an interesting example of the power of projective identification in the therapy room. Both therapists responded in the same way to their patients and then went on to enact the situation together. In John Byng-Hall's (1986) family therapy terminology, we had become involved in the "family script" and reacted to the "need" of the family, rather than being able to contain their desperately anxious projections and both tolerate and understand them.

## *Unresolved loss and transgenerational patterns*

As discussed above, in all three families we began to notice similarities in both the behaviours and the ways of relating between each mother and son. We also noted how similarly we felt being with mother and son and how similarly we responded to them.

While being very different in many ways, the parents all appeared to be living with unresolved conflicts and issues of loss.

In my interaction with each of the children, the particular form or pattern of my acting in was the same as that of their individual mothers, not the same with each child. In trying to understand this, I have considered Fraiberg, Adelson, and Shapiro's (1975) description of "ghosts in the nursery". These are the bogeymen from the parents' own childhoods, recalled, half remembered or forgotten, which return to haunt their children's mental landscapes and relations. The power of these bogeymen or ghosts is proportional to the extent to which the memory and affects of their terrors have been repressed, leading to the children, when parents themselves, ridding themselves of them by further unconscious transgenerational psychic bequests.

Fonagy, Steele, Moran, Steele, and Higgitt (1993) have demonstrated how toxic these poisoned legacies can be to the development of the younger minds by tainting and undermining an integrative mental paradigm whereby it is safe to enter and experience another's mind. Again:

> The child's capacity to develop a model of the mind that can contain and make sense of their own experience entails feeling that it is safe to know the mind of another. [Barrows, 1990, p. 549]

When I was unable to tolerate the child's projections, I reacted to these in the same way as their mother did, unconsciously following the family script (Byng-Hall, 1986), or at that moment using that family's pattern of relating. The child would have learned the pattern from the parents and would now, influenced by the way in which others respond to them, continue the pattern of relating and create a cycle whereby there would be pressure to repeat and continue relating in this way. This indicates the importance of parallel work with parents in order both to support the therapy and also to make space for new patterns of relating that the child is developing through therapy.

## *Outcomes of the therapy*

I have listed in Chart 4.1 the difficult areas and significant patterns of relating for each of the boys, alongside the changes following

**Chart 4.1. Outcomes of the therapy**

*Difficulties and patterns of relating*

**Richard**

Bullied at school
Easily drew me into reacting to him and arguing—difficult to stay in role with him
Inability to articulate angry feelings
*World made up of unreliable, untrustworthy objects*
*Tough, self-sufficient, cut-off and not-caring attitude*
*Little eye contact*
*Lonely and isolated*
*Withdrawn and difficult to engage*
*Little faith in therapy as helpful; belittling*
*Disappointed, angry, and let down by father*
Hypochondriacal—convinced he had terminal illnesses—very pessimistic—his mother only showed vulnerability through illness, so maybe an attempt to evoke sympathy from her
*Dismissive and contemptuous as a way of distancing from emotions*

**Sam**

Bullied at school
*Intellectual and clever—able to twist words and things around to suit him/herself*
*Self-perception as the clever, knowledgeable one who always knows best*
*Manipulative behaviour*
Psychosomatic illnesses
*Loved mother/son but wanted to get away from her/him*
*Used to feel dissatisfied all the time and thought that things were over when they had only just begun; found it hard to enjoy things*
Invented other things to help him instead of therapy

**Roger**

Delighted and surprised when I appeared to remember something
Never stayed in my mind, I could not remember the sessions
*Tried continually to maintain that he/she was okay and my/our concern misplaced*
*Didn't want to acknowledge his/her need for help—communicated need, but rejected the idea of support*
*Frequently gave me/us cause to be alert to his degree of risk and issues of safety*
*Under a coping exterior was disappointment, hopelessness, and despair*
*Not really trusting adults/professionals as helpful*
*Always alone—neglected and abandoned*
*Spoke as though he/she didn't expect to be heard*
*Did not expect to be listened to, and expected to be forgotten*
*Seemed to be able to make him/herself invisible*

*Changes*

Developed a more reliable, resilient internal sense of who could, to some extent, be trusted

Opened up and was able to articulate and express emotion—particularly of loss, disappointment, and anger—in a more direct way

Able to let go of a sense of responsibility for the family problems and its associated guilt

Not so hypochondriacal, and rarely spoke of terminal illness

Able to feel angry with his father for being unreliable

Lighter, less stuck, and wanting to go to school

School phobia lessened, and this became more his mother's issue, as she was not happy with the school

His mother had become more depressed but was more aware of her need for help to cope with her own emotional difficulties

---

Became more separate from his mother

Became more open and talkative, yet less grandiose

Able to show his vulnerability and ask for help

Acknowledged his sadness about his parents' divorce and did not feel so guilty.

Stopped feeling ill all the time

Became more confident

Started attending school and making friends

Began to enjoy life, going out and doing things with friends

Mother was able to move on and begin to develop her own life.

---

His awareness of his own needs had developed, and he determinedly attended the sessions on his own

He was more able to speak out for himself.

He became more aware of danger and less accident prone, therefore less at risk.

He acknowledged his need for help, both with home life and at school

His school attendance improved, and school were able to make suitable provision for his needs.

Mother was able to allow professionals to help her in a more stable and sustained way the therapy. Statements in italics refer both to the son's difficulties and to those of the mother.

## *Discussion*

All three boys had suffered major losses in their lives; their parents had divorced and their fathers had left the family home. All three mothers had also suffered unresolved losses, which they appeared to manage by shutting off or detaching emotionally. Our work, both during sessions and in our discussions afterwards, contributed to our awareness of how the parent–child related, which in turn helped them to separate from their enmeshed state. Although not part of this discussion, throughout we had many examples of how the creation of a triangular space (Britton, 1989) provided room for thoughtfulness and reflection, which led to the possibility of change.

We were very aware of absent fathers. Frequently the mothers appeared to relate to their sons as their lost partner, rather than as separate, different individuals. As therapy continued, all three boys appeared gradually to become freed from the claustrophobia of the emotional burden that weighed them down, as their mothers began to take back into themselves and experience the appropriate feelings of sadness and loss that were theirs. The mothers became more able to acknowledge their own emotional difficulties and painful unresolved losses and to accept that the difficulties were not solely located in their children.

## *Conclusion*

To conclude, while I am not suggesting that anything here is new, what is striking is the similarity between the "symptoms" of the mothers and their sons and the powerful quality both of the countertransference and of the use of projective identification. Chart 4.1 also illustrates the improvements gained after the therapy and how much freer the children became, relatively quickly, once their mothers were receiving the appropriate help.

The use of the tape recorder meant that it was possible to capture those moments when something important in the interaction was taking place, out of the awareness of the therapist, and which became crucial knowledge available to be used in the ongoing work.

Personally, I found the structure of the Project containing in itself, with a co-worker, a supervisor, and clear time boundary. Close communication between workers allowed a greater degree of containment for mother and child, as well as providing a means of understanding the complex inter-family relationships in a way that cannot happen if one is working solely with a child. The opportunity for discussion and thinking about the families in this detailed way added significantly to the work that took place during the psychotherapy sessions. Both the tape recordings and the work with colleagues prevented me from becoming lost in a labyrinth of projections and the resultant acting out. The case supervisor was able to provide a perspective that was involved and yet separate, thus bringing an informed yet more objective view.

As I mentioned at the beginning, my involvement in the Project has had a great influence on how I work currently, both with the involvement of co-workers and using time-limited therapy. In my opinion, when work is undertaken with parents alongside the individual work with the child, there are enormous benefits to be derived, and the parallel parent work certainly contributes to the effectiveness of individual child psychotherapy.

## *Note*

I would like to acknowledge the contribution to this chapter of my colleague who undertook the parent work.

CHAPTER FIVE

# Affirming a sense of agency: the influence of supervision in once-weekly, time-limited work with a depressed child patient

*Jackie Hall*

## *Background*

This chapter describes individual time-limited therapy with a 10-year-old patient, as part of the Childhood Depression Project. As has been described elsewhere, in the Project the children were seen for 30 weekly sessions, with parent work alongside, following on from a research assessment. There was fortnightly supervision for the child psychotherapists as part of the Project. As a requirement of the research, all sessions with the child had to be recorded, so there was a tape recorder in the room.

As a child psychotherapist in the latter half of my training, one of the main areas of interest to me in embarking on participation in the Project was whether there would be a specific way of working with depressed children and in what ways, if any, this would be different from more generic way of working, when the diagnosis is not so measured and precise. Despite some preparation and discussion about the relatively "brief" nature of the work (for a child psychotherapist), at the beginning I did not register or comprehend the impact that the time constraints would have on the treatment and the way I would feel about it. This became particularly significant because, early on in the work, child protection concerns were raised in relation to my patient, which made adhering to this structure unusually difficult and painful.

My supervisor was Anne Alvarez and, as is fitting to a piece of work about supervision, this chapter is resonant with her voice, and the distinctive grammar and syntax of her insights. Although I was familiar with her work (Alvarez, 1992) and her enormous contribution to the development of psychoanalytic ideas and practice (Edwards, 2001), I had not anticipated how this thinking could apply to the particular experience and demands of working with a depressed young person in a time-limited way. However, although the influence of the supervision was manifold on the experience of working with the child, the emphasis on holding negative projections and paying attention to a sense of agency when it appeared in my patient's communications and behaviour stand out as particularly important. As she helpfully observed sometime early in the work, the purpose of the therapy was not simply to get my patient into the "depressive position"; he was already depressed. Although logical, this required a rethinking on my part about the differences between depression and the "depressive position", and it also required a greater tolerance for receiving communications in the therapy without making precipitous interpretations that could return my patient's feelings in a premature and unprocessed way. The containment provided by fortnightly supervision supported me to do this. Alongside this, there was the Project Manual for child psychotherapists, to explain and provide guidance for this work. (Trowell, Rhode, & Hall, 2010). My purpose here is to describe the application and effectiveness of such approaches to time-limited work with a particular depressed patient, as well as to consider some of the inevitable questions and tensions that can arise when child protection concerns come to light in the process of the therapy.

## *Case study*

Thomas was a boy of mixed heritage who was the oldest of three children: he had a sister who was 7 years old and a brother aged 3 years. He had a long history of behavioural problems, with reports of aggression, stealing, swearing, and lying. In the research assessment meetings, Thomas's mother said that they had attended family therapy a couple of years before at another local clinic, but she had not found this helpful and did not continue.

When Thomas was 7 he was sent to live with relatives abroad, where he stayed for eighteen months. He returned to England for holidays and eventually asked to come back because he wasn't happy. He said that he liked the freedom but was lonely. Thomas's mother said that she had missed him during that time, but she had also felt things had been easier at home. His time away from his family coincided with the birth of his brother.

When I first saw Thomas he had been back in his family for nearly two years. However, his parents had recently separated, and his father had moved out of the family home; the children had had little contact with him for some time because of the demands of his work. Thomas's problems were felt to be the cause of rows and difficulties at home, and, in the assessment, Thomas spoke of feeling guilty about this, particularly towards his mother, but he was also angry. He had described himself as feeling "fairly sad, with worse patches when something goes wrong in the family".

At the time of the assessment, there were constant difficulties with Thomas's behaviour at school. His mother had said that she wanted Thomas to have therapy because she was keen that his behaviour should become more reasonable before the onset of adolescence. There were no reported concerns about her other children. Thomas shared a room with his siblings, and one of his complaints in the assessment was that he was rarely allowed out with friends. The result of the research project baseline assessment was that Thomas met the criteria for dysthymia, and he was randomly allocated into the individual therapy arm of the Project.

## *Therapy*

Thomas was a well-built, strong-looking boy, quite mature in appearance, with a distinctive and stylish mode of dress. There was a strong feeling of independence about him, like being with a person much older than his years. Although supervision was expected to run at fortnightly intervals in parallel with the work, for various reasons the supervision of Thomas's therapy began quite late into the work, at Session 7. In the early sessions, Thomas expressed powerful resistance. He didn't want to be at the Clinic. He didn't see the point as he said he didn't have problems any more, and he would rather be at school. He complained that the sessions were boring and interfered with playing with friends and break times. Nevertheless, Thomas liked his toy box. He played with the cars—often violent, smashing-up games—and also drew a little. He would greet the teddy bear when he opened his box and would hold him and adjust his bow-tie, and he would often said goodbye to him as he put him away at the end of the session. Originally I felt he would be contemptuous and dismissive of the bear, but he used to talk to him as if he were alive. He questioned me about whether these toys were just for him, and when I said they were, he couldn't seem quite to believe it.

I wrote up Session 7 for supervision, using a transcript of the tape for the first and only time, as I had left quite a gap between seeing Thomas that week and making my notes of the session. Between writing up the session and seeing my supervisor, I received a phone call from a social worker to say that there had been a report of Thomas being severely punished at home. I was also told that there had been reports of similar concerns about physical chastisement in the past. I attended a network meeting at the local Social Services office and a Child Protection Investigation was initiated. In the light of this history, Thomas's depression seemed understandable.

## *Technique*

In this first session that I took for supervision—the one I transcribed from the tape—Thomas was in a flat mood. I had commented that he seemed to have "come with quite sad feelings today".

> We discussed the use of the word "sad", and whether "low" or "fed up" would be better in the future, as Thomas might not know that he was sad. This might feel less heavy, besides

giving Thomas more space, allowing room for angry feelings as well as sad ones.

Thomas had played a very violent game with the cars. The cars were in a "cage of terror": they were blown up and there were terrible fires.

We discussed my possible responses to these actions, maybe to comment on how terrifying they were, for example, to try to carry and contain the feelings a little. We also thought about the discrepancy between the excitement evident in this play and his underlying mood, and that maybe he was trying to excite himself.

Thomas played with a car, and had it say "I'm the fastest . . . roughest . . . wickedest."

We thought here, too, about the contrasting affects, and whether one might comment on the fact that he might be trying to feel like that, but seemed to be feeling fed up.

Thomas's depression lifts in this session when he shoots a car off the table and it unexpectedly lands in his box, which surprises and pleases him.

This prompts us to think about depressive moods and about the importance of affirmation when something good and effective happens.

At the end of the session, Thomas is tired and becomes quite silent and cut off, rejecting my attempts to make contact. I interpret this as Thomas blocking me out and not wanting to think, pushing this at him in a determined and persistent way. I hadn't remembered this sequence when I transcribed it from the tape, and I was quite shocked when I heard it.

We discussed how difficult it might be to remember what one doesn't understand, and that this underlined a need to go more slowly and perhaps acknowledge that Thomas had done enough thinking for today.

At the end of the session, Thomas asked me if the Clinic is "open all night," and the issue of Thomas needing more therapy than the planned 30 sessions for the Project already begins to be an issue in our minds.

In the next session, Thomas makes a "Keep Out" picture and wants to take it home and put it on his door. I suggest that now he has made one at the Clinic, perhaps he could make one at home. Violent play with the cars continues to be a regular activity. In the midst of one of these games, Thomas suddenly stands a felt tip on end. He builds a "palace" of these for the first time, with internal struts, rather like a Roman temple. It is so precarious I hold my breath. He puts a sheet of paper on top as a roof. There is an enormous feeling of suspense. His dexterity is exceptional, but there is an inevitable collapse.

> This led us to think about the precariousness of his world and the delicacy and effort required on his part not to precipitate a collapse, letting me know what hard work it was being him.

Later on in the session, he tells me the soft ball is a "stress ball", and I get hit a couple of times when it rebounds around the room.

> We think about the possibility of remarking that I need to be "a good stress ball", and understand that I have to be an object that can withstand attacks.

In an earlier session Thomas had told me he was "not going to tell me about being hit".

> We thought about how I might respond to this, and I am encouraged to comment, saying that perhaps Thomas wonders whether I remember what he said. We think about Thomas's entitlement to feelings of anger, and the difference between a grammar of wishes (in working with neurotic patients) and a grammar of needs (in deprived and depressed patients), where recovery is facilitated when there is a recognition that the object should change, should be different.

In sessions that follow there is a theme of useless police cars. When I comment on this, Thomas sings a song about the police turning up too late to deal with a violent incident and someone dying as a result. The police disperse the crowd and are kindly and sad but ineffectual.

As the sessions progress, it was obvious that Thomas was a very thoughtful, able boy and that he seemed to be beginning to respond to the experience of being thought about in the therapy. In the same session as he sang the song about the police, he referred to his trousers being too big for him, and I talk about two parts of him, the "tough boy part" and the "younger boy" part, that perhaps we could also think about. Thomas asked me questioningly if I meant "the baby?" When I said yes, Thomas commented "I would like to be that".

In the last session before the Christmas holiday, Thomas drew space ships with fire coming out from underneath them. He hadn't come the week before, telling me that neither he nor his mother had wanted to come, and I interpreted these fiery feelings as maybe having been connected with this missed session, which Thomas hotly denies.

> In our supervision discussion I am alerted to a pressure to overwork, partly because of my awareness of the limited time Thomas and I have together, and that I need to go more slowly. We think about the imagery of the session in a different way, wondering about the fire in a leisurely, more open-ended way, rather than jumping to the "why" or "who"; I need to filter my comments through the levels that Thomas can take. We think of his feeling of exposure, coming out of school for therapy, together with the exposure of the problems in his family.

I had given Thomas the dates for the Christmas break, and in this session he asked if he could take his pictures home when the therapy ends. I think this was his first reference to the ending. He also tells me that he and his sister will be spending the holiday with their father, and this is the first time he has referred to his father living separately.

Thinking about time-limited work, and specifically working with depressed patients, I was beginning to realize that as a matter of technique, it was particularly important to be able to hold very uncomfortable feelings/projections and not give them back too prematurely. This seemed more possible with regular supervision, when there is a regular time to think together about the session material, and one feels one is thinking as part of a couple. These thoughts crystallized for me when I was not able to hold feelings of rejection and anger before the break, when Thomas told me he didn't know why he came and that he found the sessions boring. I found his rejection and the related sense of my deficiency very uncomfortable. Instead of accepting what he said, I responded by suggesting that his comments might cover more uncomfortable feelings to do with the upcoming break and his anger at feeling rejected.

> We thought about this in our supervision session, and agreed that it would have been better to accept what he had said, acknowledging that he might find the sessions boring, and perhaps adding something like, "So that's how you feel at the moment. Perhaps it doesn't help yet; maybe we have to get to know each other a bit better before it can help". I could begin to see that I didn't need to work so hard to help this patient into a depressive position by trying to evoke depressive feelings, as "he was depressed already".

### *After the break*

In the first session back, Thomas said "hello" to the tape machine. His relationship with the machine had grown gradually over the sessions. Later on he will turn it on frequently, which raises the theme of recording and remembering. He tells me he didn't think I would collect him. He thought I might still be on holiday. He asks again how long it will be until the end of the therapy. He tells me it's better than school, because he's missing something he doesn't like. In this session, Thomas spins a chair and then worries that he is disturbing people underneath. When I talk to him about feeling worried about this, he tells me he has to be very careful at home or else he gets into trouble. He then asks to go to the toilet. When we return, he shows me his new trousers and enacts a conflict of his feelings. He puts a hand into each of his two pockets and tells me they are mouths: one mouth says to the other that he talks too much.

> In our supervision session, we are struck by his considerable skills, and the need to notice and affirm them, and perhaps to comment on how hard he works to be good at things. We also reflect again about how the time-limited nature of the work stirs up his sense of deprivation.

In the following session, Thomas was the most weary and depressed I had seen him. He could barely lift his head, and he rested it on the rim of his box while he drew in a desultory way, starting his drawings of people with the trousers first, then building upwards to the head. His pictures were of people doing sports. Following on an earlier discussion in supervision, I commented on this discrepancy of feeling—that Thomas was tired, and how he seemed to be putting his liveliness into the people he was drawing. There was a very delicate atmosphere, and I was aware of how easily I could bruise him with words, even inadvertently. I then said that perhaps he wanted things quiet today. Thomas looked up and smiled for the first time.

He repositioned a head in the drawing so that the character looked more animated and was pleased with this; indeed, the picture and the session moved from a dead to an alive feeling. He linked up the pictures so that they told a story: somebody scores a goal, a supporter cheers, somebody else is skateboarding. He attached them to the wall and said that they are part of a series. He wanted to take them home and it is hard not to let him, but he accepts this. He says he'll do more next time. There's a feeling of recovery and a sense of a future.

In a subsequent session, Thomas seemed very fed up when I collected him from the waiting room, where his mother had already left with the parent worker. He told me that he is missing valuable time at school, and he screwed up a number of important pictures he has done to make a "ball". He drew an abstract picture of the mouths of cannons exploding and then a shoal of piranhas, and he said he wants to leave these on the wall of the room (he later sticks them on his box). Just as the session is ending, Thomas told me that he thought I was late in collecting him from the waiting room.

> In the following supervision session, I was able to see that I was being put through something via his projections, and how important it was to recognize this with him. On the one hand, there were Thomas's disillusioned and cynical feelings and destructive actions; on the other, the despair and impotent outrage that I was feeling. It was important to pick up these feelings with him, to comment on the picture being destroyed or on the fact that he was making me feel quite desperate and hopeless. It also seemed important to differentiate between feelings in the session; how anger is different from bitterness and hatred.

In the next session, he rewound the last few minutes of the tape and listened to it. He told me that he wants to record over it. In a previous session, when he had tried to do this and I had told him not to, Thomas had told me angrily that "It was his tape, his voice on it". This time I acknowledged that the tape was about him. Thomas commented that he just liked listening to what we said.

> Thinking about this in our supervision session, we thought how important it might be to reflect back with him on this interest, how it was a record of us talking to each other: "How did we get to where we got in the sessions?" It also helped with thinking about what to say about leaving the pictures behind, the importance of holding on to what had happened in our minds, "wanting to be sure that something lasts, that Thomas and I remember that something important happened here".

After this session, I heard there was a threat of Thomas being sent to live abroad again permanently with his extended family. I was also informed by the social worker that the Child Protection Investigation has been inconclusive.

In the last few sessions leading up to the end of the therapy, there were mixed feelings and some more paranoid material. In Session 25, Thomas suspected that cars had gone missing and that items from his box had been changed. He cheered when he heard that there were only five sessions left, but then asked, jokingly: "Can't I keep coming?" and added that "I will miss it a bit". Things started to be hidden, or appeared to be missing, and there was now a lot of activity at the window, where there were repeated threats and charades of objects being dropped out. (Very few did actually get dropped, but Thomas was good at tricking me, and I had to go through feelings of uncertainty again and again that objects have may have been lost, dropped, or left behind.)

> At this point in the supervision, we reflected again about the importance of recognizing the difference between wishes and needs in interpretation; that for neurotic patients a wish for things to be different is alright because they can bear the alternative, but that for a very despairing patient a "wish" can be weakening, adding to despair. With the end of therapy approaching, we thought about Thomas's right to be remembered and acknowledged, maybe with something like "I had better make sure I won't forget you", which is more assertive and upbeat.

In one of the last sessions, Thomas sang a song with the refrain, "What future? I have no future"; when I tried to speak to him about this, he told me dismissively: "It's just a song". I commented that somebody would talk to his mother at the end of his therapy about what might be best for him, but I remarked that he might well feel rejected about this part of the work coming to an end. Thomas said quietly, "Yes no, Yes no".

> In the following supervision session, we think about Thomas's eloquence and how he is almost too reparative for his own good. I am encouraged to think about his entitlement to more therapy and to be straight with him about this, to tell him how I think he has used the sessions very well, that at times he has liked it, and that I would like him to come back after the end of the Project. I am still being hit by the soft ball from time to time in the sessions, seemingly inadvertently. I am encouraged to acknowledge his right to be angry that the therapy is com-

ing to an end, and "how he might feel like giving me a bit of a bash".

Games and activities that we do together now dominate quite large chunks of our sessions—for example, noughts and crosses. In another session, Thomas read a long passage out loud from a book that he has brought with him. During the course of the therapy, a Portacabin has been put up in the car park outside the window, and increasingly Thomas takes on the persona of a private detective in the sessions, noticing that things "are strange . . . why is that building there . . . what's going on?". My supervisor points out that this is the "paranoid underbelly of separation".

In the penultimate session, Thomas is concerned that his mother is not being seen that day (the parent sessions are fortnightly). He reports that his mother has said that she will be relieved not to have to bring him to his sessions anymore. We play noughts and crosses. I talk to him about it being a way of us being together without us having to think directly about the sad and difficult feelings of ending. A little later he tells me he is going to fall asleep, and there is an enormous feeling of fatigue. When I link the wish to sleep in a similar way to the ending, Thomas says "like playing noughts and crosses not to think".

In our supervision session, we think about the soothing nature of these games, how they are being played at a symbolic, transitional level and that they are not "a symbolic equation", or a turning away. We felt that it would be appropriate to recognize this with him, with a comment such as "At least we can play and be friendly together".

Although I was still being hit with the ball from time to time, there was a sense that Thomas felt he had to protect me from sad and difficult feelings. We thought about how I could be a receptor who would allow him to feel outrage at the ending, and how to put this into words, maybe saying something like "You feel I shouldn't be leaving" or "How dare they finish". In putting his projective identification into words in this way, I would be allowing and giving Thomas permission to handle his feelings in this way (Alvarez, 2000). We also recognized

> Thomas's ordinary need to play or to go to sleep and that it might be helpful to comment on how he might be "tired of thinking about all this heavy stuff"; we were also reminded of Rosenfeld's observation that "patients can only take so much" (Rosenfeld, 1987).

The last session felt quite desperate and broken up, an enactment of things being thrown, or pretending to be thrown, from the window. Thomas's mood and behaviour were very unsettled, with rapidly changing thoughts and tricks; although I tried to gather these and he remained for most of the 50 minutes, he could not stay and ran from the room before the session ended.

## *Conclusion*

Following the ending of the therapy, Thomas's mother was invited to the Clinic to discuss the possibility of further therapy for Thomas, but she did not take up this offer. In her final session with the parent worker, she had disclosed her own experience of being physically abused as a child, and this may have made it difficult for her to return. As we knew, too, Thomas had already made a comment shortly before the end of the therapy about his mother's fatigue in bringing him to the Clinic. In any event, there was no further contact with Thomas and his mother, although ongoing treatment would have been available to him following the end of the Project.

Not being able to continue to work with Thomas felt very difficult, especially in the light of the uncertainty about his future. Nevertheless, the time-limited therapy had provided him with an experience of regular focused work, which had been actively chosen by his parents and which he and his mother had been able to complete, unlike their previous experience of family therapy. The short-term 30-session therapy model had offered a choice to which Thomas and his mother were able to commit, despite the difficulties that emerged, when more open-ended treatment may not have been taken up. The changed circumstances in the family, with the separation of Thomas's parents and the departure of his father from the family home, may have placed additional strain on Thomas's mother to support the therapy.

The termination of contact in this way, however, was unusual in the parent cohort who took part in the Project. Alongside the marital difficulties and break-up, it may have been hard for Thomas's mother not to feel responsible for his difficulties on some level, and hard for her to bear her identification with him, as the events of physical chastisement and abuse that had come to light in Thomas's life resonated powerfully with the experiences she had suffered as a child. Analysis of parental histories within the Project did suggest transgenerational patterns of difficulty in many of the children who took part (Maria Rhode, personal communication).

At the time of writing, a preliminary look at the research data in the Project would seem to reveal some shift during the course of therapy in Thomas's sense of responsibility for the difficulties he had experienced. In the Moods and Feelings Questionnaire, which he filled in with the psychologist at monthly intervals, there are a number of changes that seem relevant. This questionnaire contains 16 statements that concern feelings of sadness, loneliness, and responsibility for difficulty, as well as states of sleeplessness and restlessness, which the child was asked to rate in relation to how he or she had been feeling or acting over the past month. All these statements are negatively weighted—for example, "I felt miserable or unhappy" (Question 1), for which there are three possible categories of response: "True", "Sometimes True", or "Not True". For Thomas, there was overall improvement across all items during the course of the treatment, although there was a reversion on five items in the final questionnaire, at the end of therapy. To some extent this reaction would be anticipated, as the child is likely to experience the loss of the therapy with a mixture of feelings, including a heightened sense of being left on his own. Three of the statements that were more negatively rated in Thomas's responses in the final questionnaire were to do with feelings of loneliness and rejection, one with restlessness, and one with self-esteem ("I felt I was no good any more"); this was the first time Thomas had rated this as "True" since the measures had been taken before the beginning of therapy, over eight months previously. On other items in the questionnaire, however, there was a softening of Thomas's sense of self-blame—for example, he rated as "Not true" that he was "a bad person", which he had rated as "True" at the beginning. Also, he did not think he "did everything wrong", which he had rated "Sometimes True" at the beginning of the therapy, and he thought it was only "Sometimes True" that he "could never be as good as other kids", which he had rated "True" at the start of treatment. Generally, the trend observed in Thomas's self-rating on this and other questionnaires (e.g., Battle, 1981) suggests that the therapy had helped to improve his self-esteem and helped him to gain a more positive sense of his own capacities. More detailed and systematic analysis of individual research data is required, but these positive changes in some of Thomas's answers would seem to reflect the general improvements that were found in the individual psychotherapy cohort in the Project as a whole, as a result of this intervention (Trowell et al., 2007).

Although as Thomas's therapist it felt hard not to be able to continue the work with him, the fact that there was some shift in his view of himself and his difficulties, and a more conscious recognition on his mother's part of the cause of his sadness and behaviours, suggests that the short-term intervention had been valuable. The fact that further working-through of these feelings was not possible certainly made my experience of the ending particularly painful, in addition to the natural sense of responsibility that I felt as a professional in relation to the child protection concerns in this case. Any continuation of work with Thomas's mother would necessarily have involved greater focus on her identification with Thomas, requiring her to be more in touch with her own childhood pain, and it seemed likely that these feelings were too much for her to cope with at this time.

CHAPTER SIX

# Brief psychodynamic psychotherapy in adolescent depression: two case studies

*Stelios Christogiorgos, Eleni Stavrou, Marie-Ange Widdershoven-Zervaki, & John Tsiantis*

Depression is thought to affect up to 20% of adolescents (Lewinsohn et al., 1999). This is not surprising as the adolescent stage of growth and development is beset with emotional vicissitudes. The inner turmoil of adolescence may be accompanied by intense affective reactions, considerable moodiness, feelings of depression, and fleeting suicidal wishes; sometimes this stage cannot be managed without serious disruptions such as clinical depression. Moreover, dealing with any type of loss can be very difficult for the adolescent and may result in depressive feelings and suicidal preoccupations, which obviously contain a plea for help.

Given the serious nature of adolescent depression it is necessary that the treatment is provided promptly and performed by skilful therapists, but one challenge facing mental health services is the high rate of depressed adolescents who do not receive any help—up to two-thirds in one epidemiological study (Rey, Sawyer, Clark, & Baghurs, 2001).

In this chapter we would like to present two case studies of adolescents who were treated with a focused short-term psychodynamic psychotherapeutic treatment, as part of a research programme aiming to evaluate the effectiveness of short-term psychodynamic psychotherapy in childhood depression within the NHS (Trowell, Rhode, Miles, & Sherwood, 2003; Trowell et al., 2007; Tsiantis et al., 2005).

This programme assessed the effectiveness of two different forms of psychotherapy for major depression in childhood/adolescence: (1) focused individual psychodynamic psychotherapy with a focus on interpersonal relationships, life stresses, and dysfunctional attachments; (2) systems integrative family therapy with a focus on family dysfunctions, but without specific attention to unresolved intrapsychic conflicts and early childhood.

The outcome study provided evidence supporting the use of focused forms of both individual psychodynamic therapy and family therapy for moderate to severe depression in children and young adolescents (Trowell et al., 2003, 2007; Tsiantis et al., 2005).

Although psychoanalytic approaches have not fared well in the current climate of evidence-based practice, there are in fact a number of studies supporting their effectiveness. Abbass (2002) highlighted the wide use of short-term psychodynamic psychotherapy in the clinical practice of the NHS and concluded that variants of short-term psychodynamic psychotherapy are potential first-line treatments for adult depression. More recent meta-analytic studies found that short-term psychotherapy is effective in the treatment of more general psychiatric symptoms and that it adds significant benefits to the use of medication in major depression (Leichenring, 2004). In a later study the same author found that the outcome in short-term focused psychodynamic psychotherapy is related to the therapeutic techniques, to the therapist's skilfulness and accuracy of interpretation, to the degree of adherence to the therapist's intervention plan, to his or her competent delivery of expressive—but not supportive—techniques, and to the development of a therapeutic alliance. On the other hand, it was found that there is evidence that long-term psychodynamic psychotherapy is more effective than shorter forms of psychodynamic therapies (Leichenring, 2005). The effectiveness of short-term psychoanalytic psychotherapy in treatment-resistant depression was nevertheless also examined by Abbass, who found this form of treatment to be effective (Abbass, 2006). Short-term psychoanalytic psychotherapy appears to be feasible, cost-effective, and beneficial in his study, but it should be noted that this was an uncontrolled study of treatment-resistant patients.

Much less research has been carried out in the field of child and adolescent psychotherapy. There are fewer meta-analytic studies looking at the effectiveness of short-term psychodynamic psychotherapy for children and adolescents with depression. Muratori et al. (2002) evaluated the efficacy of an original model of brief psychodynamic psychotherapy for children with emotional disorders within the NHS. Emotional disorders were characterized by anxiety or depression without the characteristics of a special syndrome. They were broadly termed "internalizing disorders". The experimental group showed improvement in global social functioning, which suggested that brief psychoanalytic psychotherapy is efficacious in emotional disorders. The results of the study of Horn et al. (2005), who evaluated the efficacy of short-term psychoanalytic psychotherapy for the treatment of depression in children and adolescents, provided further support. Nonetheless some of the children required more intense treatment.

In 2007 the research programme we have been involved with added to this existing literature. The therapeutic approach used by the programme was individual brief psychodynamic psychotherapy. It entailed 30 weekly sessions of 45 minutes each. All participants were referred to the study from Community Children's Mental Health Services. Supervision played an important role in supporting the therapists in their therapeutic work (Trowell et al., 2003).

A Manual provided guidance on the approach, and the sessions were taped. Supervision was conducted every two weeks. The parent(s) attended one session every fortnight, and the therapists were supervised twice a month in accordance with the research protocol (Tsiantis et al., 2005). The short-term therapeutic approach was based on the model of Malan (1976) and Davenloo (1978). This model, while serving as a guide, also allowed the flexibility and freedom that are indispensable conditions to establish a working relationship between therapist and patient. The research study also included administering questionnaires at regular intervals, which was done by the research group, in collaboration with the patient and his or her parents.

The 30 sessions were divided into three stages. The first stage, Sessions 1–5, was the initial stage (described in a later section of this chapter) in which work moved on slowly and painful issues were often avoided. In the middle stage, Sessions 6–20, there was an intense involvement with issues regarding relationships, separation, and loss. The last stage, Sessions 21–30, was the stage in which the termination of therapy was worked through, with issues of separation and loss actively kept in focus.

The therapeutic techniques of brief psychodynamic psychotherapy can be seen as elaborations of more general principles of psychoanalytic psychotherapy. Short-term psychodynamic psychotherapy is characterized by the following features: brevity, focus, activity, and selectivity (Groves, 1996). The therapist is usually relatively active and aims at the development of a therapeutic alliance and a positive transference.

Short-term psychodynamic psychotherapy focuses on specific conflicts and specific topics that are formulated early in therapy. Attention is paid to the focus, the setting of achievable goals, and termination issues (Gurman & Budman, 1996). The main topics discussed are the patient's experiences in the here-and-now, including the patient's symptoms, but pre-existing conflicts are also addressed. With regard to transference, the emphasis is on the present relationship between the patient and the psychotherapist and it is not necessarily traced to the past (Leichenring, 2004, 2005).

A focus is not determined in a narrow manner (Schacht, Binder, & Strupp, 1984). In patients with depression, it is formed on the basis of the psychopathology of the major depressive episode, which is usually based on feelings of loss, low self-esteem, and inward-directed aggression. It is through the exploration of these areas that the focus of each patient is clarified. In most cases of adolescents suffering from depression, the focus can be pinpointed to one of the following difficulties: (1) unresolved mourning over a significant loss, (2) low self-esteem, (3) maladaptive patterns of regulating stress or aggressive drive impulses, (4) inability to cope with the emotional demands of everyday life, and (5) poor object relations.

### *Brief psychodynamic psychotherapy during adolescence*

The limited time prearranged for brief psychodynamic psychotherapy constitutes a crucial factor, as it diminishes both the patient's regression and dependence (Mann, 1973) and the time used for therapeutic working through, a process that starts during therapy and continues after therapy is over. It is based on the individual's ability to continue the experience of gaining insight after the therapy has been terminated.

The therapist assumes a more active role during the therapeutic process without dispensing with the analytic therapeutic framework (Tsiantis et al., 2005). Although the therapist and the patient enter a therapeutic relationship that entails several limitations due to its brevity, the patient is encouraged to make use of the method of free association, and the therapist uses his or her free-floating attention to the material the patient brings into the therapy session. The predetermined number of sessions shed light on matters of attachment and can trigger feelings of emotional detachment and loss—primary issues to be worked through both during adolescence and during depression. These qualities of a brief psychodynamic psychotherapeutic intervention appear to meet—in a way—quite a few of the adolescent's needs. According to many clinicians and researchers, fear of regression and the adolescent's identity confusion, as well as fear of dependence along with a wish for autonomy and authenticity, call for a psychotherapeutic approach that places emphasis on vigour, clarity, clearly defined targets, and empowerment (Golombek & Kozenblum, 1995).

It is suggested that the developmental fluidity that characterizes this age group allows for better therapeutic results in shorter time periods. The aims of brief psychodynamic psychotherapy in adolescents include a remission of symptoms, the attainment of affective and mental insight leading to forward development, the elimination of the defences that prevent a healthy development of personality, and the strengthening of one's ability to establish interpersonal relationships (Golombek & Kozenblum, 1995).

The duty and the role of the therapist in brief intervention is a lot more demanding: the therapist needs to understand the patient's communication patterns quickly and properly and has to decide how to react at a much faster pace (Mander, 2000). It is also imperative that the therapist regulates his or her own psychic sources sufficiently, with sensitivity towards his or her countertransference movements. He or she makes full use of the countertransference in order to understand the patient more profoundly (Mander, 2000). Thus, the therapist must be experienced and competent, open and flexible, assuming an empathetic stance. She or he is to be neither prescriptive nor exclusively supportive (Tsiantis & Trowell, 2010; Tsiantis et al., 2005). She or he uses the psychoanalytic methods: the interpretation, the clarification, and the confrontation of the patient's defence mechanisms, anxieties, and drive impulses. This approach, of course, constitutes a strong challenge for the therapist who has been trained to hold the traditional role of the patient's observer, and who has the opportunity afforded by open-ended therapy to bide his or her time. He or she can wait for the defences that the individual has developed in the course of her or his difficult life to be gradually exposed; and then, while the difficulties are being relived in the transference situation, new and more effective defences can be discovered.

The therapist's chief objective is to maintain the analytic framework. This framework, according to Winnicott (1965), fulfils the same function for the patient as the maternal holding environment does in the development of the child's ego. The framework is a locus of holding and offering, as in the primary maternal environment, but also of deprivations and frustrations.

In both of the following case studies, an effort is made to distinguish the three stages of the therapeutic process, as described in the Manual, with the corresponding issues that emerge in each stage of therapy. These case studies were, of course, not the only ones in the research programme. They were selected among the 11 cases in the Greek sample as they are the ones in which the authors of this paper were involved as psychotherapists.

Before proceeding with the presentation of the case studies, we briefly review the Manual and the way it describes the three consecutive stages of this brief psychodynamic intervention (Tsiantis & Trowell, 2010). These stages will then be illustrated in the presentation of Maria and Peter's case studies.

### *The initial stage of therapy (Sessions 1–5)*

As early as the first meeting, it is of the utmost importance that the framework of the therapy is clarified—especially the basic characteristics such as the objective, the duration and frequency of the sessions, the need for systematic and constant observation, as well as issues of confidentiality. Of course, later on, the emotions evoked by the framework have to be explored as well. Moreover, it is significant that the therapist does not state, nor even imply, that all the problems, the conflicts, and the anxieties can be resolved. The patient may harbour such expectations, combined with the prospect of arriving at "immediate solutions" aiming at the defensive elimination of every original anxiety. If the therapist becomes aware of such phenomena, he or she must intervene in order for the patient to elaborate on it. Furthermore, in this initial meeting, it is imperative that the reason why the therapist's help is asked, as well as the time at which this occurs, are explored. It is possible that there are major life events that should be discussed, and it might prove quite helpful if these are understood. This will pave the way for a therapeutic dialogue with the patient aimed at the establishment of a viable therapeutic alliance, a determining factor in therapy (Gray, 1994).

### *The middle stage of therapy (Sessions 6–20)*

In the middle stage, and after the therapeutic alliance has been established, the therapist will work on issues raised by the young patient, focusing on what is happening during the sessions, in the here-and-now, and connecting them to the material discussed in the initial sessions.

Ambivalent emotions may manifest themselves in the therapeutic relationship. Painful issues regarding relationships, separation, and loss are discussed; they become items to be worked through in the relationship, because they are connected to the next stage: the termination. The ineluctable desire to continue the relationship must be indicated, along with the ambivalence it causes. This is a transitional phase during which the working through of separation anxiety, related to the end that approaches, can result in maturation. The development of the relationship with the therapist is the key. The therapist's ability to cope with negative feelings that are manifest both inside the patient and in his or her attitude towards the therapist is of importance; being able and capable of discerning pain, anger, destructiveness, and self-destructiveness, as well as putting them into words and withstanding them, is especially crucial. This is pertinent to the theoretical psychoanalytic model of depression, according to which the problems—or the fear stemming from them—in regulating aggression within an interpersonal framework may lead to turning this aggression inward, against the self.

In this stage changes begin to take place, while, simultaneously, it is possible that crises may occur and serious clinical situations may emerge, such as a relapse of depressive symptoms with intense suicidal disposition, school denial, violence or drug abuse, repeated failures to attend sessions, or late arrivals—all of which may put the therapy and/or even the patient's life at peril. In this stage, it is essential that the adolescent's therapist communicates regularly with the parents' therapist; moreover, the adolescent's therapist has to be at the parents' disposal, should it be so required. It is important to be able to foresee such crises, allowing time to reflect on them and verbalize them. Should a crisis occur, it has to be dealt with thoughtfully: the therapist may have to discuss with the young patient the need for a meeting with the adults responsible for him or her, even if confidentiality cannot be fully guaranteed. These crises may result in the termination of the therapy. In such a case, it is important to clarify whether this was the child's or the parents' decision.

### *The final stage of therapy (Sessions 21–30)*

The final stage offers the opportunity to discuss and work through crucial issues of separation and loss in the here-and-now, as this is a scheduled termination. Previous experiences of loss and separation may be relived. Distress and anxiety are common. Furthermore, an important characteristic of this stage is the fact that both therapist and patient reflect upon what has happened so far, what has been accomplished, and what remains to be worked through.

The patient will be prepared, in the last 10 sessions, for the parting from the therapist. At the end of the therapy, it is important to contact the parents once more, for a meeting with all the parties involved in the therapeutic process. This meeting is a kind of review of what has occurred, what has been achieved, and what more might be accomplished.

## *Two case studies*

Maria, a 14-year-old girl and the firstborn of a divorced couple, who had created new families during the last few years, lived with her mother, her sister, and her mother's new husband. At the time of the therapy contract, the mother was pregnant. Maria was regularly visiting her father at the town where he and his new family (after a second marriage) were residing. The father agreed with the evaluation of Maria's condition and consented to her treatment, but this was the extent of his involvement with Maria's therapy. Maria's maternal grandmother was the one who facilitated the continuation of the therapy when Maria's mother could not bring her to the sessions.

Maria was referred due to learning difficulties. During the diagnostic evaluation, aside from learning difficulties, Maria showed signs of serious depression, which proved to be the reason for her learning difficulties. In addition, it was revealed that she had experienced sexual harassment from her uncle (her father's brother) at the age of 9 years, soon after her parents were divorced. This information was given by her mother during the diagnostic process and by Maria herself during the third session. She was guilt-ridden regarding the sexual harassment, especially because her father did not believe her. She seemed to have low self-esteem and poor school performance, even though she had high mental abilities. She was overwhelmed by feelings of helplessness, which resulted in isolation and led to a very meagre social life. She described how she had no close contacts, not even with members of her own family. She felt responsible for her parents' divorce and blamed herself for it. She was toying with suicidal ideas, although they were not organized. Her relationship with her mother was highly conflictual. Maria appeared to be divesting her life of anything creative and alive in order to maintain a kind of affective security, something that she managed to express physically too. It was decided that Maria fulfilled the necessary presumptions—a strong ego, a good intelligence, and the right age—to be part of the research programme. The fact that both Maria and her family would have difficulties in supporting a long-term psychoanalytic psychotherapy made this therapy model more suitable for Maria.

Peter, a 12-year-old boy, was the first child in a family with another son, aged 2 years. The family faced grave communication problems, with intense conflicts among its members. The father, although he initially agreed with the diagnostic evaluation process and consented to Peter's therapy, kept his distance for a significant amount of time. He was judgemental, and he eventually became more actively involved in the therapy after the fifth month, following the persistent intervention of the therapist who worked with the parents.

The mother, while seemingly in favour of the therapy, was intensely rejecting of her son, whom she quite often characterized as the root of all the family problems. Peter, during the diagnostic evaluation, showed signs of depression, which worsened in the last six months, with persistent notions of worthlessness, withdrawal from social activities, and deterioration of school performance. He was described as a bad student and fostered only a slight interest in sports.

### *The initial stage—introduction to therapy (Sessions 1–5)*

When the therapist first met Maria, she was impressed by her slimness and by the way she seemed to carry a tremendous burden. She thought that this must be her way of expressing her psychic burden, which later on she referred to with the next remark: "It is like I carry a ton of bricks." From the very first meeting, Maria was suspicious towards the therapy, towards the use of the tape recorder, and towards her therapist. The discussion about the duration of the therapy exacerbated her already great difficulty in communication, in expressing any thought or feeling, and in trusting—or relating to—the therapist. On the other hand, it seemed that, through her intense eye-contact, she really wanted to have a relationship with her. The therapist's acknowledgement of this situation and the subsequent discussion of it within the transference relationship helped Maria to gain enough hope so that a therapeutic alliance could be forged. In this manner, Maria managed to articulate her difficulty in relating to others, her conflictual relationship with the rest of her family, and her feelings of guilt with regard to her parents' divorce.

Typically she says: "I feel very alone, I can trust no one, because I am afraid that they will talk about me and I am afraid about what they will think about me." When she talks about her parents' divorce, it seems she feels responsible and says: "Sometimes I think that I would have done things better if I could go back in time." When the therapist asks her what she could have done better, she answers: "I don't know what exactly, but I could have done something to prevent my parents from divorcing." When the therapist comments on Maria's feelings of responsibility for her parents' divorce, Maria immediately responds: "Yes, once I believed that my father left because that same day I had an epileptic seizure, because I had forgotten to take my medicine." (At this point it has to be noted that Maria had used anti-epileptic medicines for about two years, but at the time of the therapy she was free of seizures and medicines.)

She also talks about her difficult relationship with her mother, because she feels confused by her behaviour. In Maria's own words: "Sometimes I feel that my mother is very good, but the moment she gets angry she is like another person." This is in accordance with the opinion of the mother's therapist, who sees her every fortnight, but also with Maria's therapist's impression, after the first meeting she had with the mother, before the start of Maria's therapy.

Maria did not report anything nice in her life. The only good moments seem to be the ones where she could play or talk with her dolls and animals. She mentions this in her first session, when she sees some of the toys in the therapy room. She says:

> "I feel ashamed about this because I know that I am a little bit too big for this kind of game, but I talk to them because I have no one else to talk to. I feel that I am able to express my real

> self when I talk to them. I do not dare to show this real self to anyone, because I am afraid that I will make a mistake."

Maria does not trust anyone and is afraid what people will think about her. All these thoughts, fears, and reservations were directed towards the therapist in the transference relationship. The acknowledgement and the interpretation of these feelings in the here-and-now had a positive result on the therapeutic relationship, and it was obvious that Maria wanted to relate to the therapist, in spite of her fears.

Based on past traumatic life experiences, Maria expected her therapist to be harsh and judgemental towards her, just as her father was. The interpretation of such transference phenomena supported her hope, brought her hidden mental strength out into the open, and revealed her desire to rid herself of at least a part of the psychic burden that she had been carrying. In the fourth session, Maria was able to discuss these feelings, because she started trusting her therapist and she felt that there was a therapeutic alliance. The moment that Maria talked about the sexual-harassment experience and about how she felt in relation to her parents' rejection of her, a harsh superego and an intense feeling of guilt were brought to the surface and were noted by the therapist. This was the moment in which Maria had revealed that deep in her mind she thought that "she could have done something about her parent's divorce". She talked about this part of herself that felt that everything depended on her and, while she could do something positive, she did not do this. When the therapist verbalizes these thoughts and the fact that she feels she possesses such a big strength, then the atmosphere in the session changes. The revelation of this omnipotent part of her made her laugh initially, but afterwards she stopped laughing and stayed thoughtful. When the therapist comments that it seems that what she said made her think, she answers: "I don't know, I think about it . . . (*silence*). I think about something else now . . . for me to do something, someone else has to tell me that I can do it. I need someone else to tell me first."

After this fourth session, Maria tells the therapist that although they have had only a few sessions, she feels better already. In this stage Maria showed signs of improvement. She mentions that she has stopped talking to her dolls and animals: "I don't feel the need any more to play these games . . . this impresses me." She agrees with the therapist when she comments that "maybe now you are starting to show your real self to me".

As a result, she moved on to checking the therapist's patience towards her own disguised aggression, appearing in the form of rejection due to a missed session (with no apparent reason). The missed session (as well as one of the following ones), instead of destroying the continuation of the therapy, functioned as a tool that facilitated understanding: the negative feelings regarding the therapy were revealed. These emotions, after being initially understood through the countertransference feelings of the therapist (who felt angry and forgotten), were verbalized in the relationship: Maria's endeavour to communicate both her own experience of rejection and her need to keep a safe distance from the therapist—having experienced a close contact with her—became evident. This unconscious communication could afterwards be comprehended and discussed more readily. This initial profound understanding gave Maria the chance to go on with her therapy, irrespective of her ambivalence.

Peter came to therapy imbued with a feeling that everything is futile and that life has no particular meaning. The issue of the therapy's limited time played an important role, and he attended all the sessions from the first onwards. While he was playing with a small toy car from his box, he banged it violently on the table and smashed it. "It broke", he says. "The force and the weight I used against it made it break. Do you understand?" He promptly replies to the therapist's comment. "This is exactly how I feel, too; that I will break, I will come apart any minute now, and you are telling me about 30 sessions all together. What good can 30 sessions do? Of course, you know what you are doing, but for me, the way I see it, the best outcome is that I will be able to think differently by myself, when we will not be meeting anymore." As it was stressed at the beginning of this chapter, there is less time for therapy work at our disposal, but, at the same time, the process that starts within therapy also continues after it, because the patient has the ability to internalize this experience.

In the second session Peter was crying, saying his life is not worth a penny and that at times the idea to end it has crossed his mind. His therapist remarks that Peter sometimes seems to direct his anger towards himself. Peter then adds: "I see you are cool. I thought you would run like hell. I have never said this to anyone. I feel much better now, as if a weight has been lifted off my shoulders." Alongside the attainment of empathy, another significant therapeutic factor is that the patient feels there is someone (in this case, the therapist) who can endure and contain his otherwise unbearable thoughts and feelings. The therapist establishes and reserves a caring environment for the patient, within a secure therapeutic framework. This internalizing of a good correctional emotional experience is a result of both the therapist's ability to endure the patient's pain and anger, and the patient's ability to experience the therapeutic relationship as something helpful, dealing with crises, and working through loss and separation.

### *The middle stage of therapy (Sessions 6–20)*

A stabilization of the initial feelings of trust was necessary in order for both young patients to proceed to the challenging part—that of the main therapy.

For Maria, external factors such as the arrival of a newly born baby in her house and her grandmother's illness instigated feelings of loss and anxiety, and fears of rejection and replacement. In this difficult middle stage of the therapy, the therapeutic relationship was tested by Maria's aggression, which she could now express freely.

Maria misses two more sessions, and this makes the therapist worry about the continuation of the therapy, especially because her mother declares that it is impossible for her to bring Maria to the sessions from now on. In spite of this information and although the therapist does not expect Maria in the next session, Maria comes and says: "I thought about calling you to tell you that I will come, but I did not." She continues: "maybe I wanted to test you, to see if what you said is true . . . that you would be here waiting for me, because we have an appointment." She thought the therapist would be seeing another client in her hour. When she rejoins the sessions, she describes that "it looks as if we are starting again" and expects the therapist to be angry with her. This becomes obvious through something she recalls; while she was looking into the therapist's eyes, she says: "I remember when I was smaller I had to look my father in the eyes when he was angry with me and he wanted to reprimand me." The recognition and containment of her mixed emotions by the therapist, hard and painful though it was, offered her relief. The therapist also facilitated her verbalizing these mixed feelings towards the new baby. It was obvious that Maria found it difficult to integrate the positive and negative emotions she felt. "When my mother gave birth to the baby, my grandmother cried, my sister danced, while I felt nothing. I think that maybe I was jealous, but it can't be that I felt jealous, because when I feel like that about someone, I hate him, and I love the baby." The therapist remarks that maybe she feels that these two positive and negative feelings cannot coexist, and Maria answers: "To me they cannot." The birth of the baby and the feelings of safety in the therapeutic framework allowed the recurrence of primitive needs, wishes, and defences as well as fear of abandonment. When Maria missed two more sessions, the therapist felt it was becoming more difficult to keep up the hope of continuing the therapy.

Having experienced the feelings of lost hope on behalf of Maria, and being able to reflect on them, the therapist managed to get in touch with Maria's feelings. This empathic stance, along with the understanding of the negative feelings involved in the therapeutic relationship, helped Maria to maintain a secure bond, with a reliable and supportive therapist, who could survive her attacks without being destroyed and, simultaneously, sustain his interest in her. Thus, Maria was led to experience that her aggressive impulses were not that catastrophic, and that there was room for reparation. She then was able to transfer this experience onto her relationship with her mother and to understand that expressing negative emotions does not have catastrophic results: "When I get angry with my mother now, I tell her. She also gets angry with me sometimes, but afterwards it is alright. Sometimes my mother is right and I can understand this; but mostly I am right, and when my mother is calm, she apologizes to me. We have both changed." She stays silent for a while, and when the therapist comments about this silence she says: "I just remembered how I felt with my father in the past. Many times I got angry with him because I felt he did not pay enough attention to me or to my sister. Once, with a lot of courage, I talked to him, and we quarrelled, but afterwards things got better." When the therapist asks her about her thoughts regarding this memory, she replies: "Well . . . that time I felt all these things like a big burden, I felt that all was destroyed and nothing could be repaired. Now I know this was not true."

During this stage, Maria's appearance started to change: she became prettier and began to dress like a girl of her age. Her school performance improved, and she managed to make some relationships with her peer group at school. On the other hand, it seemed that Maria's mother, who had a similar therapeutic experience with her therapist, was more able to see Maria's needs as well as her efforts. A correctional process followed, on both Maria's part and that of her mother.

For Peter, too, a stabilization of the initial base of trust was necessary in order for him to move on to the second stage of therapy. He was now a lot more motivated in his relationship with his therapist, and asked him about his habits and desires, and Peter seemed to start feeling that he existed and that he could now express his own desires as well.

It is clear that the presence of a tape recorder during the sessions was also the source of intense emotions. Peter frequently addressed it as if it were a person: "You, stop listening to me now. I am talking about very private stuff." Often, near the end of the session, he would approach the tape recorder, say something in a loud voice or scream, and after the session was over he would ask to listen to what he had yelled into the microphone.

At the beginning of therapy, he was extremely angry at the tape recorder. At one time he even used it as a target, throwing his ball at it. It fell on the floor, but he was relieved when it did not stop working. At first, remarks on this issue did not appear to suffice. Nonetheless, in the course of time, the tape recorder became an integral part of the therapeutic framework: Peter looked after it himself; he wanted to be the one to turn it on and off, and in one of the last sessions he said: "I finally got used to it, and I even like it when I think that when we are not together, you listen again to what we have said."

Our goal was the development of the ability to tolerate feelings of frustration, to deal with anxiety and loss, and to transmute the unbearable numbing emotions into thoughts that encourage the patient to trust his own psychic outlets.

In one session, half way through the therapeutic process, Peter persistently asked the therapist to play a knowledge game with him. Although the therapist successfully commented about Peter's need to confront him, to compete with him, still Peter insisted. The therapist accepted, and they agreed to play the game three times.

It is evident once again that, in Peter's case too, the way the relationship with the therapist evolved was the key. The therapist's ability to deal with the anger, the rage, the desperation, the desire for conflict and competition, and—most importantly—to verbalize these feelings was the crucial point.

Once more, the changes that took place in this stage were impressive. Peter's interest in his schoolwork improved, and for the first time he said that it would be a great disappointment if he was left behind this school year. At the same time as his school performance was improving, his social skills and relationships with the rest of his family, especially with his mother, improved as well.

### *The final stage of therapy (Sessions 21–30)*

Approaching the final stage of the therapeutic process, and having appreciated the positive aspects of her relationship with the therapist, Maria appeared to find it difficult to accept that the therapy was ending. She expressed this difficulty mainly by looking stunned each time she realized the number of sessions that were left. Her underlying feelings of anger about the fact that the therapy was about to finish became more evident on the occasion of a missed session.

This fact provided, again, the opportunity to reflect on the negative emotions stirred up by the impending loss. The missed session, once more, played an important role in the therapeutic process. It became a useful way of expressing anger and handling loss instead of being regarded as a waste of session time. Maria seemed not to attack her relationship with the therapist, but to express rage against the loss of her contact with the therapist, thus recognizing—and keeping within her—a more capable, determined, and supportive internal object whom she could turn to every time she needed and/or desired it. The question that reasonably arises is whether this good internal object was stably settled. Maybe it was not, but for sure we can say that even in the event of Maria losing this good internal support, she would know the way to ask for it in another therapeutic experience.

For Peter, too, this final stage was both painful and creative. In one session, Peter confessed to the therapist that in the questionnaire, which was used for research reasons, he had thought of describing his mental state with very dark colours. He hoped that through this very worrying description, he could persuade his therapist to change his mind and give him the opportunity to continue the sessions after the scheduled end of therapy. After this confession, he started laughing and told the therapist that in the end he decided not to do it, because he felt that there was another part of him that was happy with ending the therapy.

On the other hand, it seemed that the therapist had his own emotional reactions towards the scheduled end of brief psychotherapy, and these emotions became clear as the end of the therapy approached. A characteristic example of these reactions was as follows: on the morning of the one of the last sessions (which was to take place in the early afternoon), the therapist had an accident. He had stumbled, fallen down, lost consciousness, and was taken into hospital, where he was examined. Luckily there were no pathological findings, but the doctors advised him to stay one day in the hospital for monitoring. The therapist did not accept this advice. One of the reasons he did not was related to his afternoon appointments, which he did not want to cancel all of a sudden. Afterwards he realized that he did not want to cancel Peter's session especially, because it was such an "expensive" session, being one of his last sessions.

In one of the last sessions, Peter remembered the knowledge game he had played with the therapist and said: "You might think it strange, but whenever I remember that game we played, I feel wonderful." He asked to take with him the piece of paper on which they wrote the results of that game. When the therapist remarked that Peter wanted to take with him something tangible, as a reminder of this relationship, tears welled up in Peter's eyes. He counted the remaining sessions one by one, sometimes with surprise, other times in anger. In this process of termination of the therapy, his emotions were mixed; anxiety, and anger, at the loss of his therapist, and—at the same time—relief and a sense of pride over the fact that he could now try and make it on his own.

Considering the outcome of both case studies in retrospect, we were surprised that it was a lot more positive than we had anticipated.

Maria's appearance changed for the better, she became more attractive, and she started to take more interest in what she looked like. Her school performance improved considerably, and she managed to form a few good peer-group relationships. This was acknowledged by Maria and was also discussed both by Maria, during the last sessions together, and by her mother, in the final review meeting.

Peter showed great signs of improvement, both in his school performance and in his relationships with others—inside and outside his family. These significant changes were acknowledged by both his parents at the end of the therapeutic process.

## *Discussion*

Our experience of working with these two young patients suggests that the important process that underpinned their improvement was that the therapy provided them with a space within which they managed to express their negative emotions—their destructiveness—realizing that these emotions could not actually destroy something, either internally or externally.

These patients were representative of the young people seen as part of the larger research study, which, we suggest, illustrates the relevance of brief interventions for adolescents within the National Health Sector. With the new discussions about cost reduction and effectiveness in child psychotherapy, it seems that, especially for this age group, short-term psychoanalytic psychotherapy and brief interventions are important ways of delivering therapy.

More specifically, the research study suggests the following:

1. There is evidence supporting the use of individual short-term psychoanalytic psychotherapy with this age group.
2. It may be possible for trained therapists to deliver effectively this focused form of therapy, with the help of a Manual.
3. Treatment also appears to be exportable to wider settings with culturally diverse populations (Trowell et al., 2007).

The basic clinical training of the psychotherapists who took part in the research study was that of an open-ended psychoanalytic psychotherapy. Short-term psychotherapy was only used as a treatment in a few clinical cases during their clinical work within the NHS. Having the training and the experience of open-ended psychoanalytic psychotherapy, we thus entered into a relationship with these depressed adolescents with some anxiety, asking ourselves whether by offering them a brief intervention we might deprive them once again. The fact that both the limitations imposed by the suggested psychotherapeutic method and the requirements of the research programme (questionnaires, tape-recorded sessions) were known to the therapist and the patient (and that their relationship commenced only after they both agreed upon it) does not mean that there were no disruptions in the framework. The therapist, the patient, and—by extension—the relationship between the two were never free from intense emotions and difficulties. The therapist was preoccupied, especially at the initial stage of the therapy, with the question of whether psychotherapeutic work, and the creation of a reliable, secure environment that would allow the relationship to function, was a feasible task.

Therefore, right from the start, all these doubts were the subject of observation, discussion, and processing. There were frequent feelings of suspicion, lack of trust, and a negative transference towards the research framework, for both therapist and patient.

In our experience, this type of brief work, and the demands it places on the therapist, is best supported by a core psychoanalytic training, which will enable the therapist to carry out this demanding work. Only with these qualities will the therapist have the ability not to overlook the existence of the limitations and the disconcerting elements that invade the framework. It is important that these limitations are not denied but discussed, worked through, and contained in a fruitful and creative manner in the therapist's relationship with the patient. Only in this way will the therapist be able to preserve the necessary "stable" structure of the psychoanalytic framework. The therapist reaches this goal by quickly understanding the patient's communication, by actively intervening, and by using empathically his or her own countertransference. With this approach he or she provides the required facilitating locus where the patient's psychic world may unfold, past experience and the developmental deficit may be relived, and, thus, by way of the interpretation of the transference, modifications and development can be made possible.

CHAPTER SEVEN

# The work with the parents alongside individual therapy with the children/young people: present and absent parents

*Gillian Miles*

In recent years, the importance of parent work alongside child psychotherapy has been acknowledged and its many aspects discussed (Sutton & Hughes, 2005; Tsiantis, 2000). When children and young people are referred for treatment, it is certainly rarely satisfactory to treat children without some involvement with their parents, though this may not be the case for older adolescents. The child/young person brings with him or her a life-time history and present-day experience of living within his or her family with his or her parents and siblings. The young person's parents carry responsibility for his or her care and have their concerns about his or her current problems. Addressing parental concerns and family issues alongside the young person's therapy is therefore of great importance, and this was certainly so within this research study.

Parent work alongside individual work with the child or young person has many different aspects (Rustin, 2000) and can involve a complex moving in and out between these modes. The parent worker stands, as it were, on the cusp between our concerns with the inner world of the child and the outside world of family, school, everyday events, and outer reality. While the parent worker regards the parents as her clients, engages with them, and seeks to address their concerns, within the context of parent/child work the young person and his or her welfare need to be kept constantly in mind (Rustin, 2000; Sutton & Hughes, 2005).

The first aspect of the work is to support the young person's treatment, where all are agreed that this is in his or her interests. Sometimes this can become the central task, since if parents do not support the therapy, or take against the treatment, then it is highly unlikely to proceed. This underlines the central importance of creating a treatment alliance with the parent(s)—not always an easy task, especially when parents feel vulnerable or hostile. They may be reluctant to come to a clinic or to participate themselves, anticipating criticism or blame for their children's problems. At the outset, the worker needs to be in touch with her or his own countertransference, since it is all too easy to get caught up in powerful projections of hostility, rather than being able to recognize, contain, and acknowledge parents' underlying feelings of vulnerability.

Alongside the child/young person's therapy, the parent worker needs to keep in touch with day-to-day events within the family, thinking about family relationships and addressing parenting issues. Since parents may themselves have had difficult experiences of being parented, they may be at a loss to know how to respond, on the one hand, to adolescent challenging behaviour and, on the other, to silent despair. At times parental preoccupations, distress, and conflictual relationships may dominate the sessions, sometimes with the danger of losing sight of the young person's parenting needs. While addressing a parent's own issues can be an important part of the treatment, however complex the task our aim is to support and further "good-enough parenting" (Winnicott, 1965) and give space for thought about the possibility of changing relationships within the family as the young person's treatment progresses.

There are occasions when the parent's own past life experience becomes central, and it may well be appropriate for these themes to take precedence from time to time within the sessions. Often such past experience may be closely linked to present-day issues both for the parent and for the child/young person. Sometimes vulnerable parents can feel overwhelmed by past and present traumas in their lives, and they derive support and relief from talking about unresolved issues in their own experience. Here, judgement is needed about when to bring the session back to current concerns, providing a sense of boundaries, reinforcing parents in their parenting role, and acknowledging the separateness of the young person (Greene, 2000). Centrally, our dual role is to come alongside parents and to promote and support good parenting (Horne, 2000; Rushton & Miles, 2000). How we approach this task will be different in different situations, according to our assessment of individual parental strengths and vulnerabilities.

The parent worker is also the member of the team holding responsibility for links with other professionals in the outside world, mobilizing whatever support is available for the children/young people and their families. This has proved particularly important in the Childhood Depression Project, since we often needed to enlist the help of outside professionals alongside the therapy; also, our intervention was relatively short term, and many families needed both further help and ongoing support following the end of our contact. We have liaised with colleagues in the community and, on occasion, attended professionals' meetings, where thinking could be shared about the ongoing needs of the young person and his or her family. At times, enabling links with the community and school were key factors in promoting change and in providing continuing help for families after the ending of the work of the Project.

There remains the importance of the working relationship between the two workers—the child/young person's therapist and the parent worker. One of the advantages of the individual work with the child/young person was the provision of a separate and confidential space, both for them and for their parents. The two workers needed to find their own style of working together, protecting the confidentiality of the therapy, while enabling communication of key concerns to and from the parents, particularly where there were aspects of risk or where management decisions had to be made. Within this Project, where the young people were at times very worrying, the workers also derived considerable support from working together, and they experienced containment through working within the Project team.

## *The Project*

Within the overall Project, twelve young people were randomly allocated to the individual psychotherapy programme. They were aged between 9 and 15 years and had in common that they had all scored highly on the depression scales in the research tests. They had been referred by professionals who were concerned by reports of their unhappiness, in some cases by their failure to attend school, or by their lack of achievement in school. They were often the victims of bullying. There was a range of referrers: family doctors worried by parental reports of suicidal young people; fellow professionals in child and family clinics, aware of a young person's severe depression; and teachers and social workers concerned about a young person's struggles with school and school attendance. They were all extremely worrying young people.

The relatively short-term context of 15 fortnightly sessions meant that the work with the parents needed to be focused. The beginning engagement was rarely easy. The ending needed to be kept clearly in sight, though neither parent(s) nor worker found this easy to do.

## *The families*

Throughout the Project, we found very troubled families, where family structures had often disintegrated. Around half the children/young people were living with only one parent, usually the mother. At the time of referral, in only a third of the families were both parents still living together, or the mother with a new partner. As we came to know more, it became clear that very many parents were struggling against a background of chronic unhappiness, their difficulties of a long-standing nature. In the course of the Project, two couples separated and another was in the process of divorce. Of those parents who remained together, though living in the same house there was often poor communication and marital tension, with them living very separate lives. In other families, there was serious domestic violence, marital disharmony, and conflict. There were reconstituted families, mother and step-father. In several cases, although the parents had separated, the other parent (usually father) kept in contact with the children, sometimes with shared care arrangements, though communication between the adults could remain tense and difficult. Parental backgrounds ranged across class and culture.

The families came to the Project through concerns about their children's depression. However, in their different ways these were all families under stress, and there was a strikingly high level of hopelessness, anxiety, and distress in the initial interviews. They had already been seen for lengthy research interviews, and by the time they met the therapists they had accepted the random allocation. It is perhaps interesting to think how helpful it had been for these parents to know that there were others within the Project struggling with seriously depressed children, and that they were not alone. They had certainly found considerable relief in having their anxieties recognized, and, interestingly, none complained about the heavy research schedule, neither before, during, nor after the therapy. Engagement was not easy, but, once engaged, the attendance level was strikingly high throughout.

## *The clinical work: beginnings*

In the following sections, aspects of the work will be illustrated through vignettes from the work with five of the families.

In our initial meetings with the families, we were very struck by the seriousness of the young people's depression and the extent of parental despair. Problems seemed overwhelming, and anxiety flooded the room.

> *Alice*, aged 13, had been at home for several months unable to go to school, and, despite many efforts with different schools, her parents had given up. At home she was isolated from her peers, a constant focus of parental conflict and anxiety. She was self-denigrating, full of suicidal thoughts, picking fights with

her parents and siblings, and at times getting herself involved inappropriately in dangerous situations outside the home. Her parents felt helpless, hopeless, and demoralized, unable to support each other and out of touch with the wider family network. The mother, closely identified with Alice, was finding it difficult to bear her daughter's depression. She herself was on medication and in tears as she described what it was like at home. The father was present, but more detached. Alice and her therapist were present at the beginning of the meeting, before leaving to meet on their own. They returned after a short while, as Alice was suffering a panic attack, and the meeting was halted as Alice gradually calmed down, watched by her anxious parents.

*Richard*, aged 10, was referred by the school, where his attendance was erratic. When he did attend, he couldn't concentrate. His teachers were aware that all was not well, but despite many efforts they had been unable to make contact with his mother. Richard and his mother lived alone, and we too had difficulties making contact with her, despite many unanswered letters and phone calls. Eventually, the mother and Richard came for a preliminary interview, when it became clear that she was barely coping, overwhelmed by her own chronic depression and difficulties. While recognizing the school's concern for Richard, the mother had her own concerns about their constant rows at home. Her extremely low self-esteem and sense of shame were very evident. The interview was dominated by her difficulties and her long-standing struggles to keep going. Richard himself was silent, watchful, and non-committal throughout the interview.

These first encounters were dominated by parental distress and hopelessness. Parents seemed worn down over time by their children's problems, not knowing how to manage. Underlying these accounts, though in very different situations, was a powerful sense of parental feelings of inadequacy and bewilderment, trying to parent young people whose moods and behaviour they did not understand and which they knew were a very real cause for concern.

## *Engagement and emerging family issues*

Not surprisingly, the families came into the Project with considerable apprehension. The beginning inevitably focused on the young people and their difficulties, and the sharing of these anxieties seemed in itself to provide a sense of containment and relief. In these initial meetings, the workers were able to begin to establish a working alliance with parents, a necessary foundation for our continuing work together. In the one or two instances where it did not prove possible to engage in this way, the work with the young person was not supported and could not continue. Once a relationship with the parent worker had been established, the detail of sometimes very painful family situations could be shared and work could be done.

## *Generational issues*

Over time, we became aware of the difficulties that parents had experienced in the course of their own lives. It was striking how many had little support in their present difficulties from their extended family network, and how little contact there was with grandparents, parental siblings, or the wider family. Sometimes parents had died, or they were not in touch with the family. However, often there seemed clear links between this lack of family connection and their sense of parental failure, which appeared to leave them unable to acknowledge the extent of their children's difficulties, even within their own family. Most had come from backgrounds where there had been emotional deprivation. For some, childhood attachments had been severely disrupted, and there were distressing histories of parental abuse, neglect, or outright rejection. There were also painful accounts of the loss of key attachment figures in childhood and later life, when parental support would have been valuable.

> *Hazel*, aged 14, a slim, pale adolescent, was the youngest and now the only child living at home with her mother. Her parents had been involved in a violent relationship, and her father had recently had to leave the home after incidents that involved the law and Social Services. Hazel's mother was one of many

children in her family, and in her early years her own mother had given her up for adoption. She still carried a very real sense of grudge and deprivation, had little experience herself of good parenting, and was highly critical of all community workers and their agencies. Her elder children had moved away, only maintaining spasmodic contact. Hazel, left alone with her mother, was unable to go to school, despite many efforts from a school counsellor to escort her. At first Mother was wary, aggressive, and difficult to engage. However, over time she developed a strong attachment to the worker and to the Project, and the ending was inevitably difficult and painful.

### *Family constellations*

Within Hazel's family, a very central factor was the absence of a strong father figure. In some families, the fathers were not present, through separation or divorce. These situations varied, since some fathers remained actively involved with their children, while others had lost contact or maintained little interest. A father's absence from the home left the mother in a sole parenting role, often herself depressed and unsupported in the care of the children. In other families, where there was severe marital conflict or situations of chronic marital unhappiness, again it was difficult for parents to come together in a parenting role. Adult issues, which could dominate our meetings, gave a powerful sense of the atmosphere in the home. What was clearly missing was the presence of a third voice, able to intervene in the intensity of the mother–child dyad, or to give support in maintaining difficult boundary issues.

Alice's parents would begin each meeting with reports of their concerns about Alice and the events of the week. However, very soon the meeting would be overtaken by disagreements between them, or violent arguments about the positions one or other had taken in relation to Alice. Father would accuse Mother of taking sides with Alice against him, while Mother would accuse him of being too harsh; for the remainder of the session, Alice was in danger of becoming lost in the parental conflict, which usually left Mother in floods of tears. On each occasion, with difficulty the parent worker intervened to bring their attention to what was happening and how Alice had got lost to view. Over time these parents were more able to reflect and to own their own depression and difficulties, thus freeing Alice from being the focus of all family problems and anxiety.

Richard's mother's attendance was erratic, and Richard often brought himself to his therapy. When his mother came, she would become absorbed in thinking about her own sense of failure, her difficulties with neighbours and friends, and tearful accounts of her own early abuse. The impression one had was that Richard was either left to his own devices or caught in angry and uncontained conflict with his mother. With an extremely fragile sense of self, and very self-destructive tendencies, she seemed unable to hold Richard's needs in mind, and we needed to recruit the school to support Richard's school attendance and progress. The mother's need was such that the ending of the therapy was very hard for both her and her worker, and we were in touch with adult services to continue her treatment and support.

### *Parenting issues*

It was clear that many parents were themselves under immense emotional strain and were struggling with the difficult task of parenting depressed children/adolescents. Since they had themselves often lacked an experience of satisfactory parenting, they had no working model when it came to parenting their own children at this stage in their development. In addition, as we have seen, many were struggling, stuck in broken and conflicted relationships, or parenting alone. In many instances, in this short-term intervention the parent workers needed to become actively involved in offering a model of a parenting relationship, and supporting the parent in setting appropriate boundaries, and in thinking about their children's parenting needs. These interventions took place in a variety of ways, but it was sometimes necessary to be firm and very definite at times, and to make quite concrete interventions.

*Roger's* parents were divorced; he lived with his mother and elder siblings, and his father rarely made contact. Roger, aged 11, was not in school, having complained of bullying, and he was at home under the feet of his mother, herself angry about her situation and depressed. The mother was very overprotective and worried constantly about him, finding it difficult to think of his return to a rough school environment. It also emerged that Roger was sharing a bedroom with his mother, though there were other rooms in the flat. The parent worker addressed her concerns about the mother's own depression and was active in thinking with her about possible outlets for Roger, to create more space in what had become a suffocating mother–son relationship.

*Dominic's* parents were separated. An intelligent lad of 13, he lived with his mother; he was depressed and withdrawn, and erratic in his school attendance. With no close friends, he was living a very isolated life while his mother went out to work. Mother and son were struggling together, though in different ways, with the parental separation. The mother felt paralysed by Dominic's depression. Mother and son were thrown closely together in the father's absence and seemed locked in a mutual depression. It was not possible to see the parents together, as they were not on speaking terms, though Dominic saw his father on a regular basis. The parent worker needed to involve the father, to cut across the non-communication between the parents, and to think with them separately about how to move forward. Cutting across the adult conflicts in this way began to free Dominic from his sense of responsibility for his parents, alongside reasserting the importance of a third voice in the family.

## *The importance of fathers*

Where possible, it was important to involve fathers in the work of parenting. When parents were together, the workers engaged them both in the fortnightly meetings. These were worrying situations, where both parents needed support to intervene with depressed and sometimes suicidal young people. Often their anxiety or conflict had disabled them from setting appropriately firm boundaries, and they needed help both to recognize the appropriateness of boundaries and to find the strength to maintain them. When parents could work together in this way, the children/young people could often be helped back into more normal situations outside the home and given space to get on with their own lives.

> Towards the end of her therapy, Alice's therapist felt that she could manage to return into a school setting. Her parents worked hard to find a school, but both were aware that they would find it very difficult to get her there every day, when they knew she would panic and they would feel overwhelmed. The mother knew that she would find it too distressing to confront Alice's initial anxiety and resistance, and she feared her suicidal threats. It did not occur to either parent that the father might undertake this task. Here, the parent worker actively intervened to suggest the father's involvement and to help these parents support one another over a common aim, despite their own problems, mutually undermining each other and with very deep conflicts between them. In this way, with her father initially accompanying her, Alice did successfully return to school, where she gradually began to relate to her peers and find a life of her own. Following the end of their contact with the Clinic, the educational social worker agreed to be involved to maintain the school attendance.

### *The involvement of other agencies*

As we have seen, in this short intervention we set out to enable and support parental authority. However, there were situations where it proved crucial for the parent worker to liaise with other agencies, to enlist their interest in the family, and to ask for their involvement in helping the children/young people through difficult transitions. Through the time span of the Project, we made contact with many different professionals. We were in touch with family practitioners about medical issues, eating problems, and parental depression.

We liaised with Social Services and psychiatric services when there seemed to be issues of risk for the young people, or where parents could now acknowledge their own need for treatment or support. We made very particular links with schools and with professionals working within and alongside schools. We were impressed by the way in which educational professionals were willing, sometimes outside the normal run of duty, to give time to work with us and to use their skills both in ongoing family work and in making plans to help children back into a school setting. It was often helpful simply to draw attention to the plight of an individual young person who was in danger of getting lost to mind in a large and busy secondary school. Where other agencies already knew the family, making these links could also involve the parent worker's attendance at meetings of professionals, where all together could give thought to planning interventions.

> Dominic was still out of school towards the end of his therapy. Both parents separately knew that it was important to confront this hurdle, though Dominic remained extremely anxious and resistant to plans for his return. After discussion with mother, we contacted the Year Head, who visited Dominic and his mother at home to discuss a possible timetable for his return. He became actively involved in setting up a programme for the first weeks, including the possibility of time out in the library should school become too stressful, and continued to show interest in his progress. Dominic managed the transition and gradually established himself back in the school setting, much to his parents' relief.

There was ongoing concern about 14-year-old Hazel being out of school. A school counsellor knew Hazel and her mother well, and a social worker was already involved over both the issue of non-attendance and the domestic violence that had taken place before the father left the home. A professionals' meeting was called, which Hazel and her mother attended. The discussion at this meeting brought together many different views of the family problems and focused on ways in which Hazel and her mother might be helped. By this time, mother was less defensively aggressive and was able to acknowledge her own need for psychiatric help. In the past, much pressure had been put on her to get Hazel back into the school setting. However, following a tense discussion, the group recognized that Hazel was not going to be able to return to school. A therapeutic social worker was assigned to work with her following the end of her therapy, while the parent worker continued to support the mother in making links with a psychiatrist, to attend to her own needs. Hazel did not return to school but, following the end of her therapy, continued to work with the social worker, and later she attended a local college. In this way, the work of therapy was continued, and Hazel seemed able to separate out from her mother and to contemplate a future of her own.

## *The impact of the work*

At times, both therapists working with the family found the work extremely stressful, with the overwhelming nature of the problems, the depression, and the despair. There was the added pressure of the short-term work, when in the normal run of things these were families who would certainly be in long-term treatment. There was also the stress of being part of a research study, with a sense of the importance of "getting it right". In this situation, the co-workers with the families looked to each other to communicate about the ongoing work, for mutual support, and, at more difficult times, to keep hope alive. Endings proved particularly difficult, under pressure from families not to end the work, which indeed felt unfinished since many problems remained. However, there was no doubt that both parents and children/young people had moved on, and this was later confirmed by the research findings.

One of the additional benefits for the professionals working within the Project was the opportunity to participate in research meetings and discussions, shared by the researchers, family therapists, child psychotherapists, and parent workers. Interestingly, the young people made good progress within both parts of the study, and many common themes emerged. Thinking about this, while there were considerable differences in approach between the two treatment modalities, both had in common the fact that they set out to address both the young people's depression and the parental and family relationships.

## *Conclusion*

These were extremely depressed young people, whose families seemed stuck in their own often chronic problems. It often seemed that the young people had been inappropriately caught up in these adult issues, with a lack of separateness, and in many cases their difficulties had become the focus for family projections. Where parents were on their own, some were struggling with mental health problems, with little space available to think about parenting issues. Where parents were together, they had difficulty in acting together. There was high parental anxiety. Beginning engagement was difficult, but working with the parents proved a very important part of the therapy, both ensuring the young person's attendance, but also addressing the parental and family relationships and problems.

We were struck by the way these troubled families were endeavouring to cope with the young people's worrying depression and behaviour. It often seemed that appropriate boundaries could not be drawn because of a fear of the young person's self-destructiveness. Very many parents had considerable difficulties in their own lives, leaving them lacking in skills and confidence for the difficult task of parenting adolescents. Very many parents were coping on their own. However, it was striking how these comparatively brief interventions could be effective in promoting change. We were aware that many problems still remained as we ended our contact with the families, but for the most part there had been a critical shift both for the young person and the family, and where appropriate we had been able to make links with other professionals to carry on the work. There is no doubt that our engagement and work with the parents had not only enabled the young person's therapy, but also played a considerable part in enabling their separate lives and in supporting parents in their parenting role.

Nor would it have been easy for the workers to contain the very high level of anxiety within these families and to make active interventions without the mutual support of their fellow workers and without the containment provided by the Project, the supervisors, and the Project Director. There were certainly occasions when it would have been easier to maintain the status quo rather than confront the avoidance of difficult issues. Here we were helped by discussion with our colleagues, who could maintain an objective stance. It was a reminder of the important role of supervision and colleague support when working with such difficult and risk-laden situations under the impact of strong emotional projections.

To return to the research: a simple research questionnaire was devised to be filled in by all the parents at the end of the Project, asking them about both their own experience of the work and their view of the children/young people's therapy. Within this small group of families, there was a clear correlation between those families where the parents had felt positive about the young people's therapy, and those young people who had been able to make use of it. Overall, the parents' reports were positive about the help offered by the Project; they valued both the help offered to their children/young people and the support available for themselves. They valued and used the opportunity to think about the difficulties inherent in parenting worryingly depressed young people; also, by addressing their own family and parenting issues, this enabled the young people to move on with their separate lives.

CHAPTER EIGHT

# Some reflections on the individual therapy: themes and interventions

*Maria Rhode*

The three chapters by Jane Cassidy, Agathe Gretton, and Jackie Hall focus on work with the individual child. While Gretton stresses the overwhelming challenge that the developmental tasks of adolescence represent for depressed children, Cassidy's main emphasis is on "working through in the countertransference" (Brenman Pick, 1985), and Hall concentrates on the technical problem of phrasing interventions in a way most likely to support the child's sense of autonomy. Each of the young people we hear about comes over very much as an individual. What greater contrast could there be than that between Gretton's patients Sarah and Samantha—the one vividly present, larger than life; the other elusively always on the point of vanishing, both physically and emotionally? Add to these individual differences the cultural differences that emerged between treatment centres, as well as the inevitable differences in emphasis between treatment modalities and even between supervisors within a given treatment modality, and any attempt at generalizing from the clinical work in the Childhood Depression Project begins to look like a daunting task.

And yet, common features do emerge, both from the therapists' accounts and from Project discussions, both within and across

Centres. In what follows, I shall concentrate on three main aspects of the work: some recurrent themes emerging in the course of treatment; technical adaptations made by the therapists in response to the young people's state of mind; and the impact on both therapists and supervisors of working within a research project. In conclusion, I shall offer some speculations on the type of depression encountered in this study, and on the surprising degree of improvement achieved by these very troubled children and young people after a relatively short intervention.

## *Some recurrent themes*

Identifying recurrent themes across a group of young people treated by different therapists who were, in turn, supervised by different supervisors presents obvious methodological challenges. Workers in the family therapy arm of the Project (Campbell et al., 2003; see also chapter 11, this volume) addressed such challenges by identifying what they called "significant moments". Each therapist presented to a group of colleagues the video-recording of what they felt was a turning point in the treatment. These moments were then discussed by the whole group of family therapists, who analysed the context and generated the categories that Campbell lists in his chapter. While it would have made obvious sense to use a similar methodology within the individual arm of the Project, preliminary discussion with the therapists revealed that they did not think in terms of significant moments but, rather, in terms of the evolution of the therapeutic process. This does not in itself imply that "significant moments" were not a feature of the individual work; merely that the conceptual and practical framework of the individual therapists (including the absence of video-recording as part of ordinary clinical practice) did not favour the emergence of this shared way of thinking.

Apart from the therapists' clinical accounts, a preliminary overview of the work formed part of regular whole-Project meetings throughout the treatment phase. Second, based on the process notes of work with three of the children, a preliminary frequency count of themes and interventions was conducted (Trowell, Rhode, et al., 2002): some of the tentative findings concerning two of these children have been published (Trowell et al., 2003). Future aims include systematically transcribing the taped recordings of sessions and carrying out their analysis by means of grounded theory and interpretive phenomenological analysis (IPA). A comparison of those sessions so far transcribed with the process recordings of sessions suggests that these process recordings were an essentially accurate account of themes, sequence, and "orthodox" interventions, but that some of the less orthodox interventions were not included when the therapists wrote their process notes. As Cassidy has written, listening to the tapes allowed the therapists to become aware of aspects of the countertransference that would normally have escaped their attention. The role of the tape recorder as representing the research framework of the Project is discussed in Trowell et al. (2003).

Overall, what emerges from these various sources is the degree of existential anxiety that these children and young people experienced. Gretton's patient Samantha summed this up powerfully:

> "I feel like a tramp; a tramp does not have a home, a tramp lives in the street, looks for shelter, does not have proper clothes. Nothing fits, I feel like a tramp, I don't belong anywhere."

All the children and young people, to a greater or lesser degree, conveyed the sense that they did not feel that they existed, or that they had the right to exist. They suffered from a high degree of annihilation anxiety. Different aspects of their personality could not be integrated within a sense of self that felt reasonably coherent. They worried that their own development occurred at someone else's expense, typically at the expense of their parents; transgenerational issues were salient within the families. One could think of these themes as a cluster concerning the foundations of the sense of self. In my experience, this cluster is characteristic of children on the autistic spectrum, who are so centrally concerned with the problem of what Winnicott (1956) called "going on being". It may also be met with in the material of seriously ill children in hospital, who are literally under threat of death, and in the material of some looked-after children with a traumatic history involving many placements, whose sense of a continuing, rooted identity has been disrupted by the circumstances of their life.

The main themes that emerged from the whole-project focus groups are as follows:

1. Identity and sexual identity.
2. Having nothing of one's own/being a "have-not".
3. Living in a "black hole".
4. Living and growing at someone else's expense.
5. Being unable to perform.
6. Fear of damaging the parents' marriage.
7. Fear that aggression is unmanageable/intolerable.
8. Fear of being murdered by a Mafia-type gang (generally at school).

These themes are obviously interrelated: the central issue could be formulated as a conflict between the aspiration to a life and identity of one's own, and the fear that this would damage others, particularly the parents.

From Freud (1917) onwards, the way in which aggression can be managed, and its central role in depression, has been at the core of psychoanalytic theory. The phrase "living in a black hole" was a direct quote from one of the patients. Highly unlikely as it was that he would know about Frances Tustin's (1972b) description of the "black hole" experiences of children on the autistic spectrum, his choice of expression lends force to the suggestion that these young people were encountering elemental, "autistic" levels of existential anxiety. The degree of this anxiety was perhaps surprising to those working on the Project, but a language already existed within psychoanalysis to describe the phenomena: the sense of not existing, including the fear of falling (Bick, 1968, 1986; Tustin, 1986; Winnicott,1949), the vicissitudes of aggression and guilt (Abraham, 1911a; Freud, 1917; Klein, 1935, 1940; May, 2001), the fear of, or perverse reliance on, gang-like personality structures that were sometimes felt to be located in the outside world (Meltzer, 1973; Rosenfeld, 1971; Steiner, 1993), and the impact of transgenerational factors, or "ghosts in the nursery" (Fraiberg, Adelson, & Shapiro, 1975). However, these categories and the phenomena to which they refer are unlikely to be an artefact caused by the theoretical framework of the psychoanalytic psychotherapists. The family therapists developed categories that, though framed in very different language and based on a systemic theoretical framework, in fact described similar phenomena. This did not become clear until there was a presentation of the Project involving two supervisors—a family therapist and a child psychotherapist—as well as the Project coordinator, with enough time for detailed explication and discussion. The similarities between categories that had been independently developed then became compelling. "Living in a black hole", for example, could be seen to refer to the same phenomena as "the attractive force of sadness"; also, the importance of fathers' involvement, as emphasized by the family therapists in relation to "significant moments", could be related to the fear of damaging their parents' marriage that was expressed by so many of the children in individual treatment. This convergence of categories arrived at in differing ways by workers in different treatment modalities, and with divergent theoretical frameworks, strengthens our belief that the phenomena in question are central to the young people's experience.

A more detailed examination of the process notes for several of the children and young people suggested the possibility of some interesting patterns. First, an important deepening of the therapeutic relationship often seemed to occur around Sessions 12 to 15—that is, between one third and one half of the way through the treatment. It was as though entering into the middle phase of the treatment enabled the therapists to focus on the transference relationship, even while retaining a light touch in the way they interpreted (see below). Sometimes, though not always, this development was supported by the experience of the interruption of a holiday, bringing with it the young person's heightened awareness of feelings towards the therapist. Cassidy, for example, describes her increased ability to take up her countertransference experience with Richard instead of acting on it: this followed immediately on a holiday break.

Explicit references to the theme of identity tended to increase in the course of treatment. Some two-thirds of the way through, a number of the young people appeared in new clothes, as though giving concrete expression to a developing sense of self. The way in which aggression was handled changed significantly during treatment, though in different ways for different children. For example, Richard's material at the beginning of therapy was full of references to damaged people and to the explicit fear that he was to blame for his parents' marital break-up. By the end, he was able to say straightforwardly that he resented some of their behaviour, and his appropriate assertiveness did not need to be inhibited, as he no longer confused it with aggression. No doubt this development was supported by his therapist's ability to address his subtly contemptuous behaviour and to show herself as someone who could tackle hostility straightforwardly, and who reliably returned from holiday breaks in spite of it. Sarah was different, in that she hardly ever expressed any direct criticism, even at the end of her treatment. However, from the middle of therapy onwards, she began to use play for the purposes of projection and role reversal, in which her therapist was supposed to suffer a variety of experiences of being excluded, misunderstood, or tantalized. This role reversal seems to have served as a container for her aggressive impulses, as well as making it increasingly possible for her to cast off a negative self-image. In the last six sessions of her therapy, when this process was at its height, there was a dramatic drop in her negativity score on the Moods and Feelings Questionnaire. In the treatment of a number of the young people, it is tempting to link this development to the appearance of new clothes, or to a focus on having a room of their own.

Transgenerational issues manifested themselves in a variety of ways: in the parents' accounts of patterns of sibling relationships that were repeated in successive generations for instance, as well as in the young people's explicit statements. Richard, for example, was aware of parallels between himself and his father, in that they both lived with their mothers, and it was as though he felt trapped by the absence of an adult male role model, whose position he could aspire to, envy, and grow into. Sarah stated at the beginning of treatment that she was exactly like her mother, who in turn was exactly like Sarah's grandmother. She seemed to understand comments by her parents as meaning that her life was theirs to control while she lived at home, and she could not envisage helping herself, because of the bad consequences there might be for them. (For instance, if she stayed off school, where she felt acutely miserable and under threat, she thought that they would be sent to prison.)

In contrast to Sarah, who saw herself as exactly the same as her mother, Samantha presented as her mother's polar opposite, but she shared Sarah's feeling that what was good for her was bad for her mother, and vice versa, and that it was impossible to accommodate the needs of both. Another girl, whose treatment is not described, identified herself, and was identified by her mother, as the daughter who was unable to perform in areas where her sister excelled. This pattern, which modified in the course of the work, turned out to have been the family pattern in the previous generation, as well as applying to the maternal aunt's children. In other words, powerful emotional factors played an important role in the degree to which each of these children could claim their own identity and access their capacities.

## *The therapists' interventions*

Most of the interpretations made by the therapists were on the level of describing or validating the young people's feelings, as well as filling in implicit links. This kind of mirroring intervention sometimes extended to descriptions of the patients' behaviour, and to the thoughts that the behaviour suggested to the therapists. Often the therapists' descriptions were couched in terms of a shared atmosphere—"it feels sad", rather than "you are feeling sad". As treatment progressed, with the experience of holidays that brought the relationship between the young person and the therapist more into focus, transference interpretations became more frequent. However, these generally consisted of clarifications, descriptions, and validations of the patient's feelings towards the therapist, rather than suggestions that the patient's attitude towards some other figure in his or her life applied to the therapist as well. It may be that the oedipal connotations of this kind of link, which could have been felt to threaten the child's place, would have been particularly difficult for this client group to tolerate. As one of the therapists put it, "I feel that if I talk about myself, there's no room for her".[1]

This emphasis on mirroring, which the therapists largely arrived at intuitively, makes sense in view of the lack of a solidly established sense of self in most of these young people. As Alvarez (1992) has written, it is important to name and describe before attempting to link. Descriptions of shared atmospheres ("it feels sad") imply that acknowledging emotions need not mean being isolated; this approach makes it more likely that the young person will feel validated rather than accused, trapped, or condemned. This is particularly important for children who may feel that their position is at least partly a function of family patterns, as well as of their own individuality.

## *Working within a research project*

It is probably fair to say that initially the therapists and supervisors expected working within a research project to be a source of unwelcome constraints. All sessions and supervisions were taped—a matter of greater concern to child psychotherapists than to family therapists, who use video-recording as part of their everyday clinical practice. Additionally, in a number of instances, the research team had to approach families during a particularly delicate phase of treatment in order to administer research questionnaires, which aroused considerable anxiety in the clinical team about losing the case. Again, using a Manual did not sit easily with the emphasis in child psychotherapy on the importance of responding individually to each child. Most fundamentally, the idea that it would be possible in the time available to make a worthwhile difference to these severely troubled young people was not immediately convincing to professionals who were both accustomed to working with children who needed prolonged input and aware of studies (Fonagy & Target, 1996) that pointed to the greater long-term effect of intensive work.

In practice, these worries proved to be unfounded. Research requirements did not interfere with the quality of emotional engagement with each client that is fundamental to child psychotherapy. On the contrary: all the therapists felt that the structure of the Project, and the degree to which thought was given to each facet of each case, provided them with an additional layer of structure and containment, which was beyond that afforded by the close cooperation within a multidisciplinary clinical team and by the supervision that was built into the Project. Cassidy gives a particularly telling example in connection with Sam, who put substantial pressure on her to extend his sessions, just as his mother put pressure on the parent worker. This could be rectified through the intervention of the case supervisor, who in turn could refer to the structure of the Project, and the overall Project coordinator.

This incident was particularly instructive because it meant that the whole team—but particularly, of course, the therapist and parent worker—had to take on board the possibility of failure. At the time of finishing, Sam was not yet back at school. The implication was that therapist and parent worker were being deliberately and wilfully withholding, that they would be to blame for Sam's continuing problems. As Cassidy has illustrated, dealing with guilt was a long-standing problem for all members of Sam's family, and one that perpetuated their unhelpful enmeshment. The fact that therapist and parent worker could face the imputation of guilt, and stick to their joint decision rather than allow themselves to be turned against the conditions governing the Project as a whole, meant that they were able to provide the example of a professional "couple" who did not allow a wedge to be driven between them, even while they could empathize with their clients' point of view. Such an example provides a fundamental sense of security for all patients, but is particularly important for children of divorced parents, who naturally hold themselves responsible for their parents' separation, however unrealistic this may be. Britton (1983) has pointed out how frequently the particular structure of clients' problems can be seen to resonate within the relationships in the professional network, and attention to the model provided by these relationships is an important component of an intervention. As I have said, the fear that they had damaged their parents' marriage was a recurrent theme in the children's material, and one that held them back from developing and asserting themselves. The therapists addressed these oedipal anxieties, but the message would not have been convincing had it not been reinforced by what the families could observe about relationships within the Project. (Indeed, there are cases in which this kind of modelling seems to be the major agent of change: Rhode, 2003). In the event, the parent worker helped Sam's mother to support his father's attempts to get him back to school, which were ultimately successful. At the research follow-up interviews, all members of the family were fulfilling their own lives in a way that was appropriate to Sam's age and contributed greatly to the improved relationships between them.

However, finishing treatment after only 30 sessions was a struggle for all the workers; these were very troubled young people, and ending often felt both wrong and cruel. One of the Athenian therapists voiced this for us all at a Project meeting. "We have three sessions left", he said, "and this boy has just begun to talk about his sexual identity. What in the name of Heaven do we think we're doing?" What the therapists could do, with support from the supervisors, was to address the young people's feelings of disillusionment with a therapist who was stopping when work remained to be done. It was important to acknowledge that this should not be happening, and that the ending could arouse feelings of hatred that were completely justified. It was the therapist's acknowledgement and understanding of this hatred that helped the young people to feel it might not be overwhelming, and which ultimately supported their confidence in the power of their own love. We believe that this work is an important component of the so-called sleeper effect—that is, the considerable improvement seen between the end of treatment and later follow-up in the children who had individual psychotherapy. This improvement suggests that something from the therapy has been internalized and continues to exert an effect. Interestingly, Long and Trowell's (2001) analysis of a previous study of sexually abused girls showed that two factors distinguished those children who did well: the parents' willingness to become involved in the treatment process, and the ability of the therapists to address negative feelings surrounding the end of treatment. While psychotherapists would expect this to be the case on theoretical grounds, the fact that it had been demonstrated with regard to a highly vulnerable group of children who had also been offered only 30 sessions was reassuring to therapists and supervisors alike.

This process of the work on ending the treatment seemed to us so important that we took care not to interfere with it by dwelling on the possibility of more treatment after the follow-up research interviews, even when this seemed to us to be desirable. In fact, when some of the young people were offered further work, they said that they did not feel the need for it at that point. Equally, some felt at the time of finishing that they were ready to move into the next stage of their lives. Partly, no doubt, this was realistic; partly, for some, it was a way of conveying to the therapist the painful sense of being outgrown and left behind, just as parents are left in the course of the developmental phase of adolescence.

Transgenerational enmeshment was typical of these families. Because of this, the structural place of supervision within the Project—as distinct from its function as a source of understanding—was more important than it might have been with a different kind of case. Supervision is often thought of as providing the triangulation of an additional point of view, with the supervisor in the role of a supportive partner to the therapist in her task of addressing the child's problems. The central role of this oedipal constellation in supporting thought and reflection (Britton, 1989) is obviously crucial to the child's development (Rustin, 1998), and particularly so with these children of separated parents. In addition, however, the supervisor could be seen to be fulfilling the function of a supportive grandparent, and I suggest that this may have played a significant role for families in which transgenerational issues were so prominent.

As a supervisor within the Project, it is certainly the case that I experienced powerful feelings to a greater degree than is usual in that role. For instance, one therapist repeatedly said how inadequate she felt and how convinced she was that she was not doing her job properly. This feeling persisted, in spite of the fact that she was working conscientiously and well, that the patient was responding, and that I was able to show this to her. However, before long I began to feel acutely that my best efforts to help her were not succeeding, that my suggestions were incomprehensible—in fact, that I was not doing *my* job properly. These feelings were so immediate and distressing that it took some weeks before I could see them as a reflection of the patient's own overwhelming feeling of inadequacy, communicated to her therapist and, by her therapist, to me.

## *Concluding remarks*

As it turned out, this intervention proved to be surprisingly successful for "double depression", which is notoriously difficult to treat, as well as for major depression and dysthymia (Trowell, chapter 2, this volume). Although this must remain speculative until a comprehensive analysis of the transcripts can been carried out, I would offer the suggestion that part of the reason for this success may lie in the particular kind of depression for which the instruments appear to have selected. These young people showed all the preoccupation with the consequences of aggression that Freud (1917), Klein (1940), and others highlighted as the central factor in states of depression. In ordinary clinical practice, psychotherapists might expect such preoccupations to take a considerable time to modify. What seemed to distinguish the young people in this study was the degree and urgency of their existential anxiety: whether they existed as separate people, whether they had the right to exist, whether their own development occurred at the expense of their parents—all these were central issues. Perhaps a relatively brief intervention that focused on recognizing and describing their experience, and which in this way directly supported their sense of identity, could for this reason bring about more improvement in this particular group of depressed young people than might be expected in another group for whom existential anxiety was less important.

## *Notes*

Previous versions of this chapter have appeared as part of Trowell et al. (2003).

1. For a longer discussion of some of these technical questions, see Trowell, Rhode, & Hall (2010), as well as Hall, chapter 5, this volume.

# PART III

# FAMILY THERAPY

*The family therapy group used the opportunity of the Childhood Depression Project to give themselves permission to spend time meeting to review their work, viewing the tapes and discussing the sessions. Throughout the Project, the group met monthly, in addition to the supervision that was integral to the Project. Again, after the end of the Project the supervisors David Campbell, Emilia Dowling, Sara Barratt, and Renos Papadopoulos continued to meet to review the work. David Campbell also developed a study looking in detail at some of the sessions.*

*The chapters here arise from these discussion groups.*

*The therapists Sue McNab, David Pentecost, Vicki Bianco, and Henia Goldberg consider the issues of the Project for the family therapists. Emilia Dowling and Sara Barratt consider the issues for the supervisors of family work. Finally, David Campbell reports on his project, a detailed micro-analysis of some sessions.*

*All the family therapists found working within the Project challenging and, additionally, that the amount of external liaison involved was much greater than usual.*

*CHAPTER NINE*

# The family therapists' experience

*Sue McNab, David Pentecost, Vicky Bianco, & Henia Goldberg*

## *The research context*

We are four family therapists who worked in London on the BioMed/ERC outcome study on childhood depression, based in three European cities. This research study set out to compare (1) individual psychotherapy combined with parent work with (2) family therapy, as a treatment for children under the age of 15 who had been given a diagnosis of depression based on a self-report measure and a psychiatric interview using *DSM–IV* criteria (APA, 1994). Our task as family therapists was to offer up to 14 sessions of family therapy to these children and their families. Between 1999 and 2003 the four of us met twelve families comprising six boys and six girls: eight were white, three from a dual heritage background and one Asian. Three families were made up of two parents both living at home: three were families being raised by sole mothers with no contact with fathers, and the remaining six families were mothers with varying amounts of contact with fathers following family separation. We worked in pairs, using either a one-way screen or in-the-room consultation, coupled with a reflecting-team approach.

Being a small but nonetheless important part of a large research study was a new experience for us all. The research context has its own requirements and peculiarities which naturally impacted on our work. The first prerequisite was the time-limited nature of the work—a maximum of 14 meetings with each family. Initially, we felt rather anxious about this condition, particularly as our psychotherapy colleagues were given 30 sessions of individual work and 15 sessions of parent work. Although, they rightly considered this to be short-term work in their experience, the differential in therapeutic input between the modalities had the potential to set up a competitive dynamic between the professionals involved. However, as we got into the work, we began to appreciate the usefulness of this protocol. It meant that we and the families had to keep a clear focus to the work and to be very mindful about the process of change and about the pace at which it needed to occur. We found ourselves reminding families at each session of the number of sessions remaining. Over time, we noticed a pattern emerging. Changes in relationship, beliefs, and behaviour started to occur between Sessions 8 and 10, and the remaining meetings concentrated on consolidation, review, and endings. Interestingly, the majority of the families went "the full course" of 14 appointments even when changes had become embedded some months before. This may have demonstrated their own attachment to the research process.

A second stipulation involved working from a Research Manual devised by John Byng-Hall, David Campbell, and Renos Papadopolous (1996). Fortunately, this Manual was very wide ranging and gave us the freedom to work within our preferred models of therapy and systemic theory.

Throughout the Childhood Depression Project, we were very aware that our research colleagues were collecting data on a regular basis from the families. While we were not able to be party to the results, we naturally became very curious about the research process itself and its impact on our therapeutic work. It also raised our anxieties about therapist performance and the fear of failure in a public arena. As a group of family therapists, we were also involved in researching our therapeutic processes as well as searching for common themes in the work. This endeavour therefore operated at a number of levels and was a demanding enterprise, so we were grateful that the London family therapy team also comprised four very experienced supervisors. They occasionally offered live supervision to the therapy, but more usually they provided a monthly consultation space for tape review and discussion. Throughout the four-year project, we also had annual meetings with colleagues in Greece and Finland, which provided an invaluable opportunity to share the progress of our work and our differing styles and models, together with dialogues concerning the emerging themes unfolding in our work with childhood depression. Across the three countries, we discovered a great deal of common ground, not only in the issues we found ourselves tackling in the work itself, but also in the shared experiences of the effects on therapists of working with childhood depression.

This chapter aims to outline some of these ideas, to give a flavour of what we all learnt, both professionally and personally, about working with childhood depression as a result of being involved in this research project, and hopefully it will be of clinical value to our systemic colleagues in the field.

## *What is childhood depression?*

"In a clinical sense the term 'depression' denotes an illness characterized by a change of mood that is persistent and sufficiently severe for it to be labelled a disorder" (Kolvin, 1995). Misery and sadness can occur as symptoms in children of all ages, although it is only over the last twenty years that the concepts of depressive syndromes in childhood have evolved (Carlson & Cantwell, 1980). Symptoms include low mood, poor sleep, lack of concentration, poor appetite, social isolation, and low self-esteem. Different theoretical models posit diverse views about the causes of childhood depression—including trauma and adversity, loss, cognitive deficits, interpersonal difficulties, and dysfunctional family relationships—and will espouse a variety of interventions to relieve the symptoms (Harrington, Whittaker, & Shoebridge, 1998).

As systemic practitioners, we assume a multi-systems perspective in our work (Falicov, 2003; Pentecost & McNab, 2007). We take into account the bio-psychosocial approach to depression, considering the complex, circular interactions between biological makeup, psychological and relational issues, and sociocultural contexts. We are, of course, acutely aware of the "research bias" of this particular therapeutic endeavour and the fact that, to enter the study, the young people had to fit into very tight diagnostic criteria. At the same time, we are more attuned to questioning such labels and taking a social constructionist view, thinking of depression as arising in and being influenced by various contexts—sociocultural, familial, and relational. We therefore see sadness in children as an interactional phenomenon influenced by, and in turn influencing, the complex interactions that make up the daily life of children in their families and other contexts.

The children in our sample had all suffered a loss of some kind—mostly of a parent, either through death or marital separation. A number of them had serious difficulties in school, and two had not been in school at all during the past year. To varying degrees, they were isolated from their peer group. In our sample, the mother was the most centrally involved parent and in none of the twelve families did the two parents work together in clear, supportive roles. In some families, the children acted as supporters/confidants to their parents, many of whom were also suffering from depression. In fact, in almost every family we encountered, more than one family member was struggling with depressive symptoms, which must also beg the question of the genetic basis of depression and its transmission across the generations.

One of our first, powerfully over-riding impressions when meeting these children was that "depression" comes in many different guises. We did encounter young people who had turned their backs on the world and were isolated at home. However, the majority of the children were very similar to the ones we all meet daily in our clinical practice—angry, impulsive, aggressive, and defiant, as well as sad and lonely. It made us question how much "depression in children" we might be missing in the work we do in our agencies and how we might "treat" these children in the study differently from our home populations.

## *Working with hope and hopelessness*

Grappling with hope and despair is an over-arching theme in meeting people in the grip of a depressive episode, and we discovered that working between these polarities affected our positions as therapists and the way that we worked in a number of ways. We agree with Carmel Flaskas (2007) when she says that as therapists it can be our job to hold on to hope for clients in seemingly hopeless situations, and that hope is something we can do with others. We have also found it very useful to consider, in retrospect, Flaskas's (2007) ideas around the coexistence of hope and hopelessness. She describes how language promotes the oppositional polarity of these two states, whereas she feels that it is very rare that we experience unbounded hope—the two states exist side by side. This idea makes the hopeful/hopeless journey easier for all to navigate.

### *Connection*

Our first undertaking as therapists is to engage families in a collaborative therapeutic process. The diagnosis of depression and decision about inclusion in the study was being made by our psychiatric colleagues after a battery of psychological tests, and the delivery of therapy—either psychodynamic or systemic—was prescribed randomly with what appeared to us to be scant regard for the impact that these foregoing interventions might have on the delicate engagement task. We became curious about how this whole research procedure affected the mood of the families as we first encountered them. Some presented themselves in a resigned, exhausted fashion—others seemed wary and prickly around the edges, and, again, others saw us as a last hope, so much was invested in the process.

We found that engaging with "depressed systems" is a complex task, given that one of our stock-in-trade skills is in facilitating conversations. We rely on joining skills to engage emotionally with clients through the subtle nuances of body language, facial expressions, tone of voice, and humour. Depression, on the other hand, has the tendency to silence its sufferers and cuts down opportunities for the easy flow of communication. At times, we found it hard work to get things going—we had to dig deep into our professional tool bags in order not to feel deskilled, useless, and shamed by our initial failure to make a connection . We had to resist the temptation to retreat and disconnect from our clients. Therapeutic perseverance is a given in such circumstances, and with one family, where the young person barely spoke through the entire therapy, we had to work hard to decipher her shrugging shoulders and her head and facial movements as a guide to what she was trying to say. When she eventually found her voice, we all celebrated! We came to appreciate more fully that depression masks a myriad of other emotions—despair, anger, rage, shame, and blame, to name a few—and that reaching these different levels of affect was a crucial part of the work. (McNab & Kavner, 2005). Flaskas (2007) talks of the emotions of hope and hopelessness as internal feeling states and warns us that we ignore at our peril the individuals' emotional experience. To do so can also create a chasm in our empathic relationship with families. We would add the imperative of exploring our own emotional experience of depression in this work.

## *Action/reflection*

As our co-working developed, we became aware of the pull we felt towards active, first-order interventions for therapists who predominantly place themselves in a post-Milan/social constructionist frame. We began to consider how much the issue of risk and safety impacted on our abilities to remain curious practitioners, and how risk assessment had to be incorporated into our work on an ongoing basis. Lang, Little, and Cronen's (1990) domain theory provided a useful framework to guide our thinking. They talk of three different domains of production, explanation, and aesthetics that we, as therapists, move between in our daily work. For example, at times we found ourselves being catapulted into the domain of production when we took on the assessment of risk in child protection situations or high levels of risk of self-harm. At other moments, we could take more time to explore meanings and explanations, and throughout the whole we needed to pay close attention to our ethical or aesthetic stance. We talk later of the impact that depression can have on therapists' own affect and the care that is demanded to maintain a respectful stance.

> *Reena*, a 14-year-old Asian girl came to the first session with her parents, Sanjit and Meira. The problem as presented by the parents centred around Reena having been out of school for several months, isolated in a darkened bedroom because she was worried about the spots on her face. The family spoke of a number of tragedies that had befallen them over the past few years, including the death of their older son, Sanjit's own ill-health, and the long-standing marital difficulties between the couple. The themes were heavily overladen with emotion, and the therapists began to feel overwhelmed and uncertain about which of the many avenues presented to pursue. As the session continued, Reena put her hands up to her face to cover the very small spots present, and her hands remained over her face for the next 12 or so meetings. Her parents talked of their concerns about their daughter's safety following a recent incident in which she had taken a number of paracetamol tablets. This worry then became the highest context marker, and it took precedence in the conversation as the therapists entered the domain of production in undertaking a risk assessment and exploring the need for a psychiatric intervention and discussions around safety precautions.

Throughout the work with this family, we had to keep moving between reflections of meanings and action—at times, being very directive about the possible need for inpatient admission and the involvement of other child services. This last intervention prompted the parents to begin to find their own culturally congruent help for their relationship difficulties, which was the beginning of Reena's re-emergence into life. While they could allow us to work with their daughter, discussing their own marital difficulties with people from another culture was too shameful. Shame was a very potent emotion for the whole family. Reena had literally had to cover her face from the shame of her parents' marital battle and felt unable to show her face in public.

Being more active as a therapist can also be a way of keeping hope alive in seemingly hopeless situations. It becomes a way of counteracting our own sense of helplessness in the face of a depressed system. As already stated, in almost all the families we met, depression sat not only with the young person but with at least one other family member as well. Being active and authoritative may also act as a mask to hide the diffidence we feel about owning any knowledge base or skill in relation to families with a depressed member. The experience for families where hope has diminished and hopelessness has become a way of life may be debilitating and uncomfortable, but it may also feel safe—more of the same provides certainty, and there is no risk of being let down. As a therapist, it can feel like entering a no-man's-land: devoid of skills and ideas; sinking in with the family, never to be seen again. Holding on to a professional persona can be very difficult in such circumstances, and "doing something—anything" might feel like an imperative. Perhaps we also felt that, as other adults joining a defeated family, we should either take responsibility for risky situations or model a more active, problem-solving stance to kick-start parents into being more energetic. We describe elsewhere (Campbell et al., 2003) the theme of "reclaiming responsibilities". It was as if, for some parents, depression had sapped the life out of them and deprived them of their ability to think, organize, and help their young person regain his or her life. We were then invited to help parents focus on their parenting tasks, and our more directive position made a good fit for exhausted parents.

Conversely, we felt as therapists that depression might take away our ability to be helpful, and at times we felt the need to mount our own campaign against what psychologists have termed the cognitive transference of depressive feelings. We believe that we are now more finely in touch with the power of sadness to infiltrate the therapeutic relationship and can use our self-reflexive practices to try to understand and counteract its effects.

The opposite end of this dynamic continuum was the need to bear witness to the pain and suffering endured by families. We discovered that, at times, it was validatory both for families and for ourselves as clinicians to sit quietly with our powerlessness or impotence to "put it right". By sitting with the distress, it became possible to access a meta-position both for the families and for ourselves, thereby opening space for the entrance of new ideas or of re-storying the past as one of survival against the odds. We also had to reflect on our own survival in relation to what we are expected to manage in our work.

Elsa Jones and Eia Asen (2000) talk of the importance of having some control over the work environment in a research project, and for us this was not without its complications. We often worked late into the evening, in an institution that was not our primary workplace and where rooms had to be negotiated, files found, and new equipment struggled with. We would therefore recommend that more than "good-enough" opportunities for supervision and support are available for co-workers embarking on this work.

## *Team work and networking*

We were very fortunate in this project to be able to work with another co-therapist and to have an ongoing dialogue with very experienced colleagues. Over time, we began to appreciate that this so-called good fortune is actually an essential part of good systemic practice in work with childhood depression. Having sat with "depressed families" and felt hope fading and thoughts drying up, the ability to work with an (ideally similarly trained) colleague who can remain meta to the process in the room has been vital to us. While one of us might be on our knees and "out of" ideas, the other, from a different position, can maintain curiosity, highlight and connect strengths, and introduce and look for difference. By not becoming bogged down by the problem-saturated story and pursuing small openings in the fixed narrative, small shifts can be encouraged, which may then signal the promise of change both for the family and for the therapist. Working as a team, it is then possible to hear the story surrounding depression that needs to be heard without losing hope and becoming either paralysed into inactivity or fleeing into over-activity.

This "binocular" approach contributed towards our ability to notice and expand the small "sparkling moments" (White & Epston, 1990) for family member and for ourselves.

> With *Reena* and her family, a number of conversations took place about her return to school and suggestions made about leaving the house in spite of the shame of the spots on her face. Reena surprised us all by informing us that she had already done this on a number of occasions and had not found it as hard as we might have predicted.

Much has been written about the potential for systems to mirror each other; nowhere was this more apparent than in the supervisory process. We were fortunate indeed to be held in a warm, collaborative supervisory relationship with four very experienced colleagues. As time went by, we noticed how the supervisory level of context both influenced, but was also influenced by, the work in progress, in a reflexive loop. For example, in the live supervision, supervisors were invited to become more directive in their approach, particularly when they felt the therapist was being too exploratory in potentially risky situations.

> *David* was an only child living with his mother, Jean, and stepfather, Isaac. He was a very unhappy boy with a poor relationship with both his parents—his stepfather having only recently joined the family. David also had real difficulties at school, and there was a query about whether he should have a diagnosis of ADHD. During the third session, the therapists were exploring the family pattern of communication—one in which Jean cried at length and both David and Isaac ignored her. The therapists attempted to unpick the meaning of this pattern, but they were encouraged by the supervisor from behind the screen to take a much more directive approach and set the family a task of communicating together in a different style in the room.

With another family, the therapists and supervisor found themselves caught in a disagreement about the possibility of child protection issues, with the supervisor wishing to move more swiftly into the production domain. Of course, these situations called into question the issues of clinical accountability and with whom clinical responsibility lay within the team. The research context itself created something of a knife-edge in this respect, as we were aware that substantial changes in the child's position—for example, being prescribed medication—would result in them being withdrawn from the study.

At the other end of the scale, at times the therapists could feel overwhelmed by the amount of new ideas and hypotheses being raised by the supervisors—both trying to help unstick situations of impasse and, we also felt, as a way of throwing a lifebelt to drowning therapists.

Building safe networks around families and the young people in them became an important feature of our work of counteracting depression—particularly in relation to making good connections with schools and with other educational services for those young people out of school

> *William*, a bright youngster aged 14, had experienced very severe bullying in the early terms of secondary school and had subsequently dropped out of school, much to the dismay of his parents, who had high hopes of his academic achievement. His seclusion into the safer walls of home also coincided with his father's separation from the family. Close liaison with school staff was a requisite in repairing poor relationships between the family and the school and in paving a way back into full-time education for William. This work also involved visits to the school and the sixth-form common room—which was a very disarming experience for the therapist and gave her more understanding of the challenges for William!

On reflection, perhaps the overall theme of this section is that working with depression can be depressing but that there being more than one therapist makes it manageable. Again, this theme makes a very good fit with Flaskas's (2007) ideas around the relational and social context of hope and hopelessness and how important it is to tap the resources of the family, the community, society, and the therapeutic community in order to support hope and undermine hopelessness.

## *Shifting fixed narratives*

Families told us their stories around the entrance of depression into their lives. They shared their explanations for this with us, gave us vivid descriptions of the effect of depression on all of them, and related their sense of bafflement and despair at being up a blind alley in their search for freedom from its clutch. As you would expect, these were problem-saturated narratives, and the central characters included major losses such as death of a child or a parent, terminal illness, family separation, or struggles against oppression such as bullying, unhappy childhoods, racism, the impact of ADHD, and anorexia. These dominant stories had become very fixed over time in the life of each family and had invited the members to view themselves and their young people as "damaged" or "failures". Although there are obviously life circumstances such as these that may not change, they are not necessarily "the problem". It is the beliefs about them that may become constraining powers in a person's life, so that other identities or more liberating stories are kept from view.

> *Billy* is a 10-year-old boy living with his mother, stepfather, and younger sister from this new union. While his stepfather, Eddie, demonstrated real commitment to the therapy (and therefore to his stepson) attending every session, the parents were keen to impress on the therapist that the reason for Billy's sadness was the fact that he was growing up in a "single-parent" family. Billy's mother, Sarah, had very strong beliefs about what constitutes "family", and she believed that only growing up in a "complete" family (i.e., with two birth parents) could assure a child's happiness. Hence, she felt she had failed her son by leaving his biological father, John. Sarah made strenuous efforts to keep a connection between Billy and John, but she did not hear Billy's frustration and resentment for the effort he needed to make continuously to stay connected to a man he felt he hardly knew, a man he could not really call Dad, a man who made every effort to keep Billy at a distance. Eddie, on the other hand, worked and provided for Billy, played with him, and helped him in disciplinary

matters, all the while never receiving any overt or clear sanction to do so from Sarah.

In the process of therapy, we allowed enough stories of lived experiences in the family's daily life that counteracted the dominant beliefs to emerge before starting to challenge the adults' framing of these stories. Subsequent conversations brought forward the closeness between Billy and his stepfather, and Sarah began to shift her view that only a biological parent is a proper parent. This process happened alongside helping to create first-order changes regarding hierarchies between the two generations. Encouragement was given to the parents to work more closely together, to feel more confident in their parenting together, and to relieve Billy of some of his age-inappropriate responsibilities.

White and Epston (1990) say that frequently the problem is created for people by the gap between their own experience and the way they are having their experience storied by others, which does not represent their lived experience. Their lived experience contradicts some dominant narrative. We never felt that Billy felt "obliged" by the adults' narrative; however, the strength of the adults' belief in what constitutes a happy family meant that, before the therapy, Sarah could not hear her son's voice and could not accredit the right meaning to his experience and validate it.

Using ideas from narrative therapy can also be a powerful antidote to the disempowering effects of depression and can help to keep our souls alive (O'Hanlon, 1995). We think that working with childhood depression often positions therapists as repositories of hope, and listening acutely for small "unique outcomes" and bringing them into the spotlight assists us to find hope and possibilities in seemingly dire situations.

## *Self-reflexivity*

We are all operating in a social context that tells us that depression is at epidemic proportions and more practitioners need to be recruited to combat its effects on us all. It is therefore more than likely that we will be touched personally as well as professionally by this malaise and that we need to consider carefully how this may play itself out in our therapeutic relationships. For example, failure to keep hope alive in a personal story may encourage perseverance and stick-ability in a clinical context where the feeling is that failure is not an option. This may result in overworking, doubling ones' efforts, and perhaps taking too much responsibility for change. Conversely, it may promote a high sense of despondency and despair and freeze creative possibilities. It was not always easy to bring these personal stories into the team process—shame and failure are always difficult issues to tackle head on—perhaps even more so in an international research context, where competition inevitably rears its head.

As we have outlined, there are a number of emotions that we have come to see as companions in our work with depression. One such we did not anticipate, but which we now look out for, is "mania".

> *Paul* became sad and angry following his parents' separation and came to sessions with his parents and older sister. During an individual session with his mother, Jeanette, she told us about her shoplifting habit and narrated an elaborate story of more and more risky and audacious behaviour. At one level, we were in tune with the desperation leading to such activities—at another, we become fascinated by how she did it and, more than that, how she got away with it. We began to laugh and launch into our own more fantastic humorous storytelling and hypothetical bad endings.

This is only one example of many where we found ourselves literally getting carried away in almost uncontrollable laughter, and we began to recognize it as the consequence of "working on the edge" with life-threatening situations. Initially, we were very shocked by our responses, feeling that we were being very disrespectful to our clients; however, in dialogue with our colleagues in the different European centres, we learnt that we were not alone in this experience. We developed a strategy for managing such emotional episodes through the use of what we called the "third eye"—a device for keeping a close watch not only on the therapeutic process but also the team and supervisory processes.

## *Conclusion*

Being involved in this project has been an enriching and rewarding clinical experience. We have learnt the importance of taking a broad systemic view of "childhood depression", which sees it as lodged in the contextual relationships that surround children and their families. We have admired the courageous way that families have worked together to bring more hopeful ways of being into their lives and have been touched by their persistence and attachment to the Project. We have followed their stories through the follow-up research data and have been heartened that improvements have been maintained over time. The two young people who had been out of school for such a long period are both now at university.

Our ongoing work in our own agencies has, of course, been impacted by this research experience. We can make use of our own emotional barometers to alert us to the presence of depression and may use more focused questions to track its interactional path between family members and to uncover its impact through generations. For those of us working in adult mental health settings, there is an even greater imperative to bring children into the work, with the knowledge of the likelihood of depression being shared out between family members. We try to work with other colleagues where possible and make positive use of supportive and honest supervision in this work. We have felt positive about the efficacy of family therapy as a treatment for childhood depression. While overall there appears to be very little difference in the choice of modality between individual psychotherapy and family therapy in improving the effects of childhood depression, one of the research results indicated that levels of anxiety in children and families depreciated more quickly in the family therapy sample, which is a good marker of the benefits of working with several family members together.

CHAPTER TEN

# Systemic supervision in the context of a research project: the supervisors' perspective

*Sara Barratt & Emilia Dowling*

This chapter aims to describe the experience of the supervisory process in the context of a rigorously designed research project set up to compare the outcome of individual analytic child psychotherapy and systemic family therapy in the treatment of childhood depression. As systemic supervisors, we drew on social constructionist ideas about remaining curious, trying to ensure that we did not adhere rigidly to one view about the dynamics of the family and that we remained open to multiple perspectives. The structure that we developed was one in which it was possible to hear different versions of events and to challenge dominant discourses. Systemic psychotherapists are committed to the idea of working in teams as a safeguard against the dangers of becoming too wedded to the idea of one reality. The discussions and debates within the group meant that we gave up ideas that we felt certain of and listened to those of others in order to ensure that we were able to contribute to a richer narrative (Vetere & Dowling, 2005).

Within the family therapy arm of the Childhood Depression Project, the supervisory team were members of the systemic psychotherapy discipline in the department. The therapists were recruited through the alumni organization of the Clinic and were all experienced systemic psychotherapists. As a systemic team we decided to hold monthly group sessions where the different clinical sub-teams met for discussion and the development of ideas. These meetings were a crucial forum for sustaining the impetus of the work and for regaining hope.

## *What is systemic supervision?*

A key principle of systemic psychotherapy is the notion of "live" supervision in which the therapist working with a family is part of a team who actively participate in the therapeutic process, either in the room or from behind a one-way mirror. The therapist works with family members in a room equipped with toys and drawing materials so that children and parents can communicate their thoughts and feelings in different ways.

The team sits behind a screen to provide distance and the opportunity for ongoing reflections on the process of therapy. The team behind the screen usually meets the family early in the treatment, unless the family prefers not to meet them. The team's comments are offered in different ways: by phone, through an earpiece, or through a reflecting team. Common to all these variations is the idea of a collaborative way of working in which supervision is about offering thoughts for the family and therapist to work with (Anderson & Swim, 1995); it is, therefore, a transparent, respectful, and non-hierarchical process, although issues of clinical responsibility and client safety remain paramount. These are discussed further in this chapter. While "live" supervision is an essential component of family therapy training programmes, it is also widely practised in clinical teams working with families, as it gives therapists and families new ideas to use in the work (Brunetti, Dymond, M., Robins, & Vetere, 2005).

The supervisory input can take several forms:

» *In-room supervision*: The supervisor does not actively participate in the session but communicates her or his impressions to the therapist and family, who may then take up the ideas offered.

This method can be helpful to families who, as a result of their experiences, may feel intimidated by the use of a one-way screen.

» *Telephone*: The team behind the screen use the telephone to share their ideas with the therapist, who then conveys what seems appropriate to the family. The telephone can also provide a punctuation, which may enable a session to change direction, possibly to include more silent members or to disrupt repetitive and/or redundant patterns.
» *Earbug*: Although this was not used in the project, this method is commonly practised in training: the therapist has an earpiece, and the supervisor may actively guide the session through immediate input from behind the screen.

The structure of the sessions can include:

» *Break in session*: Family sessions are complex and intense, and families and therapist sometimes welcome and benefit from a pause in the process. The therapist may take a break and join colleagues behind the screen, bringing back the team's ideas for discussion with the family. The break gives the family the opportunity to be on their own without the team listening (the sound connection is interrupted). The therapist will listen to the ideas generated in the team discussion and decide which would be most useful to feed back to the family.
» *Reflecting teams*: The supervisory team joins the therapist and family in the room for a few minutes to reflect in their presence about the ideas that have emerged, while the therapist and family listen to the discussion. They may choose to discuss the comments further when the team has left the room (Andersen, 1991).

Live supervision gives therapists the opportunity for immediate feedback to their interventions. While the therapist talks with family members about their dilemmas, the team is able to think about the process of the session and the dynamics between family and therapist. The position of the "supervisor" is to attend to the process of the session and to contribute to the work by raising questions or by reflecting with the team members on their observations about the issues that may be arising for the family and the therapist.

### *The family therapy supervision context: using CMM as a conceptual framework for understanding the process*

Coordinated Management of Meaning (CMM) is a communication theory that provides a tool for exploring social processes and the relationship between lived experience and the stories told about these experiences (Bond, 2005). It is through the exploration of contradictions of meaning in different contexts that family therapists concern themselves and try to make sense of their relationships with their working environment and their clients.

As professionals, our thinking is organized by our beliefs and experiences, and we have to consider which context we are operating in. For example, a supervisor may be curious about a therapist's ideas following a clinical session but may also be a friend or a previous supervisor to the clinician. These relationships have an important effect on the way the therapist interprets the meaning of the question. The multiple relationships that we occupied provided opportunities for confusions in our work together, as we came to the task with different experiences and expectations of supervision which influenced and were influenced by the conversations we had about families.

Cronen and Lang's (1994) view that people listening to a conversation will all have a different understanding of that conversation was important in ensuring that there was the space to understand the different perspectives.

CMM provides a useful framework to examine the different layers of communication in the supervisory process and the relationship between them. Each level provides a context for every other level, reflexively. At times, the meanings at one level are in contradiction with those at another level. It is with these contradictions of meaning in context that systemic therapists must concern

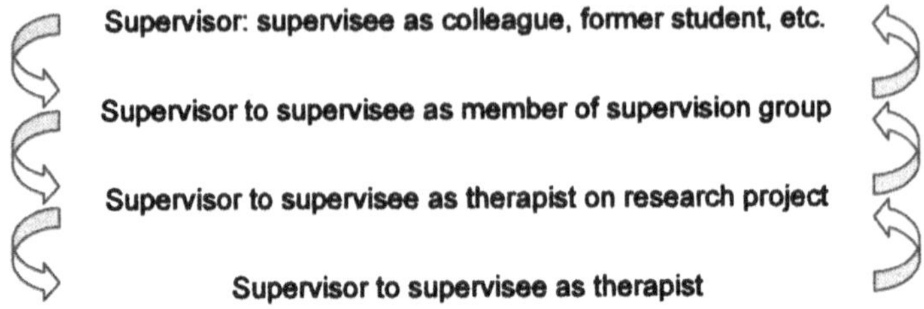


*Figure 10.1.* The influence of context on the supervisory relationship.

themselves. Figure 10.1 illustrates how the different contexts of the supervisory relationship influence one another—for example, the collegial relationship provided a context for the relationship as supervisor/supervisee on the research project and vice versa. As Figure 10.1 shows, the conversations between the therapist and the family were, at times, influenced by the supervisory team and sometimes provided a context for the work of the team/discussion groups.

## *Therapist to family*

In this relational system, the process of interaction between the different layers allowed different meanings and new conversations to emerge and helped us to take account of the different relationships that affected the way we talked to and listened to one another. Figure 10.2 illustrates the influence the conversations between therapist and supervision group, therapist and family, and therapist and clinical team had on the creation of new and more hopeful stories.

The idea of one truth was replaced by a co-evolving, richer story. Thus, the work between the therapist and the family generated ideas, which were expanded and commented on in the conversation between the therapist and the team. These ideas were further developed within the large team discussions. The therapists then decided how to use them in their work with the family.

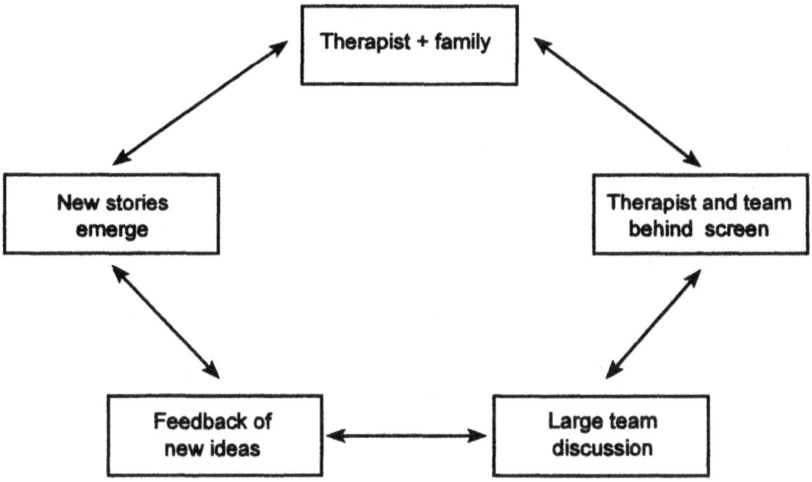


*Figure 10.2.* The process of creating new stories.

Fruggeri (2002) helpfully distinguishes two models of supervision as "supervision as teaching", as described above, and "supervision as reflection on one's practice". Our "supervisees" were experienced, qualified family therapists, like ourselves, and our model of supervision incorporated some supervision behind the screen but mostly consisted of whole group discussions and videotape review. Fruggeri says: "'Supervision as a practice of reflection' does not deal with ideas, attitudes, philosophical or ideological stances, feelings or emotions; rather it deals with the patterns and processes of interactions" (p. 14). Thus, our relationship was one of equals trying to work together to help the families.

In a social constructionist frame, the feedback from supervisor to supervisee is mutually influential, and ideas developed through the conversations between the professionals involved.

Cantwell and Holmes (1995) describe the task of the collaborative supervisor:

> The task of the therapist is to be a midwife for new meanings to arise, one who keeps the exchange going long enough for new meanings to be unwrapped and moves more easily towards a preferred future. A parallel process occurs in supervision. A

> therapist comes for supervision when looking for an expansion of options and new meanings. The supervisor cannot know what these new meanings and options will be but becomes a midwife, one who stays with the dilemmas long enough for new discoveries to emerge that fit for the one who is being supervised. [p. 36]

The guidelines we sought to use for supervision are described in Burnham (1993):

> Guidelines for organising the team discourse include: each contribution is treated as another option rather than right or wrong answers, promoting cooperation rather than competition, supervisors participating in conversations rather than pronouncing the right answer. [p. 365]

Burnham (2005) talks about the space between—relational reflexivity:

> I think of self-reflexivity as a process in which a therapist makes, takes, or grasps an opportunity to observe ... listen to ... question ... the effects of their practice, then use their responses to their observation/listening to decide "how to go on" in the particular episode or the work in general. Their responses might include: continuing with what they are doing ... recalibrating slightly ... or repositioning radically in how they act in relation to self and others. The practice of self-reflexivity tends to emphasize the "internal" activity of the therapist, as they search their own resources. [p. 3]

(The latter is similar to Tomm's, 1988, notion of "strategizing".)

The purpose of our supervision discussions was for the development of ideas through the clinical discussion and video review. An element of competition was inevitably a component of the conversations, as we were, in the back of our minds, aware of the evaluation of our work in comparison with that of our child psychotherapy colleagues. While we usually lost sight of this as we got caught up in our interest in the clinical discussions, we were aware of the danger for all therapists who feel under pressure to become more certain and less tentative, and Burnham's comment above that we were contributing ideas as an option rather than something that was right or wrong was an important message to us.

Davies and Harré (1990) helped us by distinguishing between role and position. They describe "role" as static, formal, and ritualistic, whereas "positioning" helps us to understand the fluidity of the way we change through language and over time. The positions that the different members of the team took in relation to the work at different times in the project led to divergence from some views and a coming together on others. The different ways in which we positioned ourselves in relation to the ideas and to one another was important in thinking about the way we worked together; the idea of "role" does, as Davies and Harre say, limit the way we can think about our work together, because we moved in and out of different roles in relation to one another. Thus, in making choices between contradictory demands, there is a complex weaving together of the positions (and the cultural/social/political meanings that are attached to those positions) that are available within any number of discourses: the emotional meaning attached to each of those positions that have developed as a result of personal experience; the stories through which those categories and emotions are being made sense of; and the moral system that links and legitimates the choices that are being made .

## *The supervisory process*

In this study, family therapists worked together in teams of two, with one supervising behind a one-way mirror. The supervisors joined the pairings from time to time, but much of the supervision was undertaken through monthly group meetings in which the four therapists and the four supervisors met to discuss the process of the work. Because the therapists were very competent and experienced, the project supervisors were able to take the role of consultants and were free to work with the therapists in developing ideas about the therapy rather than being concerned about the quality of the work. The therapists were undertaking complicated work with complex families, and the supervisors joined them in developing ideas and drawing out themes from the work. The families got to know the therapeutic teams well, and, for some families, it was decided that the supervising team member would stay in the therapy room, sharing thoughts and ideas with his or her colleague.

## *The nature of the work*

Family therapists working in child and adolescent mental health services usually focus on the interactions between family members and the repetitive patterns that have developed over time. We take account of the wider context of a family's life, bearing in mind constructs such as gender, culture, class, "race", sexual orientation, and disability. We are also mindful of different family forms, transgenerational patterns, and the different stages of development in the individual's and family's life cycle.

The research project started with the premise that childhood depression is a specific diagnosed illness. We were working with children who had been given a diagnosis of depression, together with their families. However, our work as family therapists is not usually organized by individual diagnoses, which are often derived from a deficit model. Traditionally, family therapists attempt to "de-pathologize" diagnoses that lie within a Western tradition: "The diagnosis of a psychiatric illness represents the analysis by a practitioner of the problems presented by a 'patient'—but one that conforms to a particular style and theoretical framework—the 'medical model'" (Fernando, 1991, p. 59).

As systemic psychotherapists, we usually start with an attempt to attend to the context of the problem, whereas in this study we started with an individual diagnosis. Our task was to work systemically with families who had signed up as participants in a project that came from a different premise. The context of the research Project and our need to find a way to work together within its confines meant that, as systemic psychotherapists, who were a minority within the dominant culture (both of the Clinic and of the Project) of psychoanalysis and the medical model, led us to operate as a minority group. We saw ourselves, a group of eight people, as "understanding one another" in the context of a range of different professional cultures.

In order to participate in the Project, the identified clients had met the criteria for certain levels of depression in the index patient as determined by quantitative measures. This meant that there was a certain amount of dissonance between the parameters of a scientific outcome study of childhood depression and the relational nature of systemic theory and practice.

When families first came for treatment, they would have already met several members of the research team for a variety of assessment measures, as described in chapter 1. This meant that therapists were forming a working relationship with the family within a framework of scrutiny and therapeutic allocation determined by research methodology, while trying to ease some of the desperation that both the children and the parents were feeling at different times. The dominant discourse of individual diagnosis had an impact on the therapists, who felt under pressure "to solve the problem". When professionals feel more anxious about their clients, they also tend to feel more responsible and take on the hopelessness of the different family members and thus may feel more responsible for creating change. During the process of therapy with the families, we felt at times hopeful and hopeless—both for the families and about our capacity to make a difference. Flaskas (2007) describes the juxtaposition of hope and hopelessness in the therapeutic relationship:

> To be attuned as therapists to the coexistence of strong hope and strong hopelessness, especially in experiences of abuse, trauma, loss and tragedy, allows us to stay open to witnessing more fully the realness of our clients' experiences. . . . To "know" that in some situations the experience of deep hopelessness cannot be cured or talked away allows us to stay more connected to our clients' experience. It also allows us to hold hope about the way in which hopelessness may come to be experienced as more tolerable across time, and the way in which the active nurturing of the feeling, thinking and doing of hope may change the quotient of hope and hopelessness. [p. 33]

As a working team, our supervisory meetings were important to contain some of the anxieties, particularly in connection with life-and-death issues.

In our meetings, we heard about the therapists' preoccupation with developing a therapeutic relationship and a sense of trust with the families. In a previous publication (Campbell et al., 2003), we have described the struggle to "keep hope alive" during the work. The group discussions distanced us from the distress that we often felt during the actual sessions. In these discussions, there was not the pressure and immediacy of "live" work, in which the therapist and team are organized by their reactions to the events of the session and the need to respond immediately. Watching a video clip that had been selected by the therapist for discussion enabled us to focus on the dilemmas for the therapist, which was the primary task of the supervision. As supervisors did not attend every family session, we felt that we came with a perspective that was sometimes too different for the therapeutic team. As therapy progressed, the relationship between therapist and family established a pattern and way of thinking about the difficulties that the child was experiencing. We felt that, at times, the therapist found it hard to develop his or her own ideas about the work with the family while taking account of the varied and different perspectives brought by the supervisors.

As supervisors, we were aware that, at times during those discussions, the ideas generated did not fit with the ongoing experiences of the therapists. It became a priority to make sure that we listened to the different voices and different perspectives of the therapists without marginalizing them with our supervisors' discourse. The group context enabled us to monitor this process, and, therefore, a richer and more complex narrative of the therapeutic process coevolved. Having the monthly discussions and review of videotapes enabled us to revisit family sessions and to talk about our different perspectives. This example illustrates this multi-layered process:

> The following comment came from one therapist in discussion about Family K:
>
> "The conversation is different; it's about trying to understand patterns of behaviour as something that family members have equal input as opposed to blaming one individual. To move away from blaming is a big move.
>
> "Looking at the family tree enabled them to see themselves as part of a heritage. That comes about through doing a genogram.

> The problem then becomes a trait they can be proud of, not ashamed of it. It's part of something big."

For this family, the genogram allowed a broader and more complex narrative to emerge, which enabled them to incorporate themes of culture, gender, and experiences contributing to new understandings of the difficulties. Genograms engage family members in developing a pictorial/diagrammatic story of their family together, focusing on the context of their relationship and perhaps helping parents and children to talk about more painful aspects of their family's story. The therapist felt that the completing of the genogram helped family members to make connections that could not have been achieved through language. She reported experiencing the mood as lighter. She could sit back, as an anthropologist, and be curious about it.

We all felt that we got to know the families very well through the group discussions and the live supervisions, and, therefore we experienced a real sense of teamwork. We were left with the question: "To what extent do we, as supervisors, have to pay attention to imposing our own ideas, which may not fit with where the therapists are at that particular time?"

There were questions around who "owned" the family, and we wondered how to position ourselves as supervisors when our attempts to be helpful could be construed as oppressive. We had to create a context in which it was possible to think independently and creatively without sabotaging the research framework.

As the work progressed, we became preoccupied with the constraints of the research design. As the seriousness and complexity of the cases became apparent, therapists worried that there were insufficient therapy sessions to properly attend to the clinical needs of the families they were working with. The research design allocated a maximum of 14 sessions to family therapy, as against up to 30 weekly child psychotherapy sessions with 15 parental support sessions. As supervisors we found ourselves at the interface of the therapists' clinical and ethical concerns and the dilemmas resulting from being part of a research project and feeling that some families allocated to family therapy were disadvantaged by the limited number of sessions in comparison with children and parents seen by our psychoanalytic colleagues.

## Conclusion

In this chapter, we have addressed the processes of systemic supervision and the constraints and possibilities for clinicians and supervisors when working together in the context of a research project.

The framework of the research project meant that the clinical/supervision team needed to attend to contextual dissonances in terms of structure and responsibility. Systemic psychotherapists are traditionally interested in relationships and patterns that contribute to symptoms and diagnoses. The centrality of childhood depression as a focus for the work led us to reach a better understanding of the meaning of childhood depression in interactional terms. It was important to us that the project was flexible enough to permit us to involve the wider systems such as schools and other networks central to the lives of the children, which is a central component of systemic practice. Working as a team was interesting and stimulating, as were the occasional meetings with colleagues working on other parts of the Project. The research framework helped us to understand and respect different approaches to the structure from our meetings with colleagues in Helsinki and Athens, and we were able to learn that, despite some clear constraints, interpretation is everything!

The clinical discussions helped us to broaden the narrative for the work with the families and develop new meanings for the depression in the context of family relationships. The complexity of the structures and of the work meant that both supervisors and clinicians could adopt a more collaborative relationship within the wider context of the Project. In spite of the initial anxiety about the level of scrutiny resulting from a comparative study, most of the children in the study got better, and families found that their work with us improved their relationships.

## Reflections

The role of the supervisor in family therapy literature stresses the importance of self-reflexivity. The supervisor of therapists in training works within a context in which there is permission to intervene and question in terms of personal resonances, life-cycle resonances, and so forth. Our position as systemic supervisors in this Project was less clear. We were supervising experienced and very competent therapists, and we may have felt that we did not have a mandate to address these issues.

A possible explanation as to why we got so caught up in the lives of the families and the content of the sessions could be that, because we were not properly attending to ourselves as supervisors and the relationship between ourselves and the therapists, generating ideas and hypothesizing about the families became all-absorbing.

Reflecting back on the experience, we can identify a number of dilemmas for supervisors:

- *Tensions between personal exploration and the task of the therapy:* How much do we reflect on our experiences from the personal domain? With hindsight, we think time would have been well spent attending to our own genograms and sharing our understanding of the beliefs we brought into the therapeutic task.
- *Negotiating differences:* As a team it would have been useful to explore our beliefs and experiences about gender, race, and religion as well as theoretical position. Making differences explicit and talking about them would have freed us to address some of these issues in our discussions about the families' dilemmas and would have enriched our understanding of the processes at work in the course of therapy.
- *Differences in approach and theoretical orientation in the wider context of the Project:* Talking openly about these might have generated vigorous debates that would have contributed to a better understanding of the processes involved in the treatment of childhood depression.

CHAPTER ELEVEN

# Co-morbidity: childhood depression and anxiety in family therapy

*David Campbell*

This chapter explores the family therapy process for children diagnosed with childhood depression who also showed a significant reduction of anxiety during therapy. It questions whether the concept of co-morbidity is helpful for systemic/family therapists, and proposes interventions that may help reduce anxiety in the context of family therapy.

The chapter is based on a qualitative research study that applied a discourse analysis of 17 transcripts from family therapy sessions with seven children and their families who were part of the larger outcome study that compared family therapy to individual child psychotherapy combined with parent work.

In the outcome study, approximately 25 instruments and questionnaires were used to measure the baseline, end of therapy, and follow-up levels of functioning for each of 72 children. One of the phenomena of childhood depression cited in the literature is the prevalence of anxiety along with the depression (Angold & Costello, 1993). This is referred to as co-morbidity, and the original study addressed this by including the Birmaher Anxiety Scales (Birmaher et al., 1996) among its 25 measures.

Analysis of the data from the twelve London-based family therapy cases showed that family therapy was effective in reducing reported levels of childhood depression, but a review of the Birmaher Anxiety Scales scores also indicated that four of twelve children had dramatic decreases in the levels of reported anxiety from the beginning to the end of therapy. There were also differences in anxiety reduction between the family therapy cases and the child psychotherapy cases in the study, suggesting that family therapy may offer a particular experience to children and families that directly reduces anxiety. We became interested in thinking further about this finding. Perhaps it would shed some light on questions such as:

1. What is the relationship between childhood depression and anxiety?
2. What can we learn about anxiety in a relational/family context?
2. Are there family therapy interventions that may be related to the reduction of anxiety?

With these questions in mind we transcribed 21 family therapy sessions (an early, middle, and late session for seven cases: the four children with significant decreases in anxiety and three others with non-significant changes in anxiety scores). Due to limited time and resources, 17 of the transcripts were subjected to a discourse analysis, which enabled us to study particularly the way family members, with the therapist, interacted to create their own realities about themselves, their family life, and the referring problem of depression.

## *Diagnosis and the systemic model*

Systemic therapists trained to see descriptions and labels as the product of a larger interactive, social process are often perplexed about what to make of traditional medical or psychological diagnoses, such as childhood depression. The strength of the medical/psychological model is that it allows us to cluster children together in one group, using one diagnostic label, and observe patterns or similarities among them, which lead to specific, targeted treatment. However, the risk is that therapists will lose sight of the specificity of each child and the wide range of resources that are apparent when diagnosis is seen as part of an ongoing process of building and maintaining relationships in a larger network.

We take the position in this chapter that the diagnosis is like a snapshot in time that reveals one important aspect of the child and the world he or she is part of. It is like one story about a child. But we also want to generate a curiosity about the process surrounding the diagnosis: what led up to it; what its meaning is for the child and the family; and how the diagnosis is maintained in the ongoing family beliefs and behaviours.

Therefore, in this study, we are using the children's own responses to an anxiety questionnaire to cluster them into a group to see if there are similar patterns in the way they interact in the therapy sessions.

## *Co-morbidity*

The presence of two or more diagnosable patterns of behaviour such as depression and anxiety is known as co-morbidity, and it is a helpful concept in that it widens the possibilities for understanding a child and his or her behaviour, and this leads inevitably to treatment interventions. For example, the literature shows that most children who are depressed are also anxious, but the converse is not true. Depression in children has typically been preceded by signs of anxiety; however, the majority of anxious children are not depressed, and this leads us to speculate about the nature of these behaviours and how to treat them. And in this small study, we may be able to say something about how depression and anxiety interact and how addressing one of these behaviours in therapy may be beneficial to the other.

### *Why co-morbidity is important*

Childhood depression has been identified in the literature as a phenomenon that is frequently present with other diagnosable behaviours such as anxiety and behaviour problems (Goodyer, 1995; Mitchell, McCauley, Bruke, & Moss, 1988). This means that clinicians and therapists may be responding to only part of what influences a child's behaviour, and underlying depression may be missed. In fact the concept of "masked depression" evolved to describe this pattern (Kovacs, 1996). Because there is a high rate of co-morbidity, we also run the risk of identifying causes of behaviour that may be related to the co-morbid condition rather than to the depression.

An appreciation of co-morbidity in childhood depression can affect the recognition of this syndrome, and, by recognizing it early, there may be increased chances of successful treatment. The literature suggests that childhood depression tends to be chronic and episodic (Angold & Costello, 1993), and in cases of co-morbid presentation it is generally signs of anxiety that have preceded depression and other behaviours such as conduct disorder.

When it comes to treatment, we may be able to treat children more effectively if we understand the full range of their experiences and the possible causes of their behaviours. For example, in a sample of 16 boys, Puig-Antich (1982), found that the onset of depression preceded that of conduct disorder, and the conduct disturbance resolved when the depressive episode responded to treatment in 11 of the 13 boys who had a full treatment response to the depression. In another study, Gittelman-Klein and Klein (1973) found that 81% of a sample of school-phobic children returned to school after treatment with an antidepressant, imipramine, whereas only 47% of children treated with a placebo returned to school.

The specific link between childhood depression and anxiety has been well documented. Mitchell and his colleagues (1988) found that depressed young people with coexisting anxiety disorders, particularly separation anxiety, appear to be more disturbed than their peers with depression alone. They show greater severity of symptoms and may be more difficult to treat. They conclude that clinicians should be aware that depressed children may present to the outside world these other problems and that the depression may only be uncovered through careful history-taking.

So, while we are making a case for the co-morbidity of depression and anxiety, we need to ask whether there are separate, distinguishing epidemiological or clinical features that allow clinicians to target their interventions for children's therapy. If, as the literature contends, anxiety precedes the presentation of depression in children, perhaps we should be alert to signs of anxiety in children and address this phenomenon directly. Or we may find that children who present with depression will respond more readily when we attend to their anxieties, and that depression diminishes as anxiety diminishes.

The measures used in this study have provided us with the opportunity to isolate those depressed children who also recorded a drop from high levels of anxiety to low levels of anxiety. We cannot answer the question here of whether a reduction in anxiety leads to a reduction in depression (or vice versa), but we do have a small sample of children for whom there is a correlation between the two measures. What we can address here is the question of whether there are particular things going on in the therapy of these children reporting a reduction in their anxiety. (It would be helpful to be able to compare this group with a group of similarly depressed children who did not report a reduction in anxiety, but our small sample dictates that this study will be limited to a qualitative analysis of the themes and discourses present in the sessions.)

## *What do we know about anxiety?*

Anxiety is a concept that represents a broad range of mental and emotional states, including anxiety states, panic, social anxiety, separation anxiety, post-traumatic stress, and so forth. Anxiety represents the most common mental disorder in the general population of children and adolescents—approximately 20%. It can be defined as a pervasive, persistent anticipation of a threatening but vague event. It is a negative affect closely related to fear and captured in the statement: "I constantly feel something bad is going to happen." The diversity of presentations has been reflected in the Birmaher Anxiety Scales, which include measures of school phobia, somatic, separation, and general anxiety. However, for this study we are going to consider it in its broadest manifestation and look to the literature for evidence of some relation between anxiety and family interactive processes.

Bowlby (1973) was the first to postulate a relationship between anxiety and disruption of the mother–child relationship, and subsequent attachment research has suggested a link between maternal overprotection and anxiety, particularly separation anxiety. Regarding parenting style, retrospective studies have demonstrated that anxious youths experience their parents as more restrictive and less warm than do control groups (Chavira & Stein, 2005), and observational studies of anxious children and their parents report an association between greater parental control and shyness. However, it is important to note that there is insufficient evidence for any causal connection.

There are many theories to explain the genesis of anxiety in children. from psychodynamic and attachment theory, to conditioning theory (Eysenck, 1980), cognitive theory (Beck, Emery, & Greenberg, 1985), and others. However, for this study we are going to base our thinking on the well-established link between anxiety and fear (Rachman, 1998) and assume that anxiety is more likely to develop in social groups, and families, where there are limited opportunities, for whatever reasons, for children to express their fears. This hypothesis leads us to consider how children express themselves in family therapy sessions—particularly how they express worries and fears to parents.

## *Methodology*

We analysed 17 transcripts from seven cases using discourse analysis (Edley, 2001; Gill, 1996; Wetherell, 1998) to examine the way constructs are altered "in relation to participants' orientation to their setting and conversational activities" (Wetherell, 1998) in therapy. In the *first phase* of the research, we immersed ourselves in the transcripts by reading through them with the therapists who had conducted the sessions. From these readings we identified four themes that seemed repetitive and integral to the way these families engaged in therapeutic conversations. The themes also allowed us to organize the text into areas that would be analysed using discourse analysis (Gill, 1996).

These four themes were:

1. *The child's voice:* This theme refers to the activities in the session that surrounded the child's own contribution to the therapeutic process. For example, what preceded the child's comments, and how did people respond to the child's comments?
2. *Negative affect*: This includes expressions of negative feelings such as sadness, disappointment, anxiety, or depression.
3. *Blame and responsibility:* This theme is reflected in discussions about blame, attribution, and locating cause and effect.
4. *Change:* This refers to the family's and therapists' talk about repetitive patterns and their attempts to change or see different perspectives.

These themes gave us a focus for the *second phase* of the research, in which we examined the way the family constructed their realities about these themes through their conversations among themselves and with the therapist. We wanted to learn how family members drew on certain discourses to build the constructs that supported these themes (Parker, 1992). We postulated that if we could look more closely at the way these discourses operated, we would learn more about the role of anxiety in therapy with depressed children and about the possibilities for therapeutic intervention.

Table 11.1 presents the decreasing anxiety scores for the seven children (A, B, C, . . . G) in this study. The changes in measures of childhood depression for the same children are presented in Table 11.2 (CDI: a self-administered questionnaire) and Table 11.3 (C-GAS: score results from psychiatric interviews).

**Table 11.1 Changes in Birmaher Anxiety Scale scores from baseline to end of treatment and follow-up**

| Anxiety-change group | Child | Birmaher Anxiety Scale score: Baseline | End of treatment | Follow-up | Difference: At end of treatment | At follow-up |
|---|---|---|---|---|---|---|
| High | A | 44 | 7 | 2 | –37 | –42 |
| | B | 49 | 20 | 20 | –29 | –29 |
| | C | 46 | 13 | 17 | –33 | –29 |
| | D | 28 | 2 | 9 | –26 | –19 |
| Low | E | 12 | 16 | 2 | +4 | –10 |
| | F | 15 | 10 | 10 | –5 | –5 |
| | G | 61 | 63 | 59 | +2 | –2 |

*Note:* Higher numbers indicate greater anxiety.

**Table 11.2 Children's scores on Childhood Depression Inventory (CDI) at baseline, end of therapy, and follow-up**

| Anxiety-change group | Child | CDI score: Baseline | End of treatment | Follow-up | Difference: At end of treatment | At follow-up |
|---|---|---|---|---|---|---|
| High | A | 31 | 3 | 7 | –28 | –24 |
| | B | 19 | 3 | 6 | –16 | –13 |
| | C | 22 | 18 | 16 | –4 | –6 |
| | D | 26 | 4 | 4 | –22 | –22 |
| Low | E | 22 | 3 | 3 | –19 | –19 |
| | F | 25 | 6 | 6 | –19 | –19 |
| | G | 38 | 39 | 38 | +1 | 0 |

*Note:* Higher numbers indicate higher levels of anxiety.

**Table 11.3 Children's scores on the Global Adjustment Scale (C-GAS) at baseline, end of therapy, and follow-up**

| *Anxiety-change group* | *Child* | *C-GAS score* | | | *Difference* | |
|---|---|---|---|---|---|---|
| | | *Baseline* | *End of treatment* | *Follow-up* | *At end of treatment* | *At follow-up* |
| High | A | 45 | 90 | 71 | +45 | +26 |
| | B | 35 | 75 | 68 | +40 | +33 |
| | C | 45 | 55 | 75 | +10 | +30 |
| | D | 48 | 75 | 84 | +27 | +36 |
| Low | E | 55 | 80 | 65 | +25 | +10 |
| | F | 55 | 62 | 85 | +7 | +30 |
| | G | 40 | 50 | 35 | –10 | –5 |

*Note:* Improvement is measured by higher score.

## *Findings*

The discourse analysis led us to speculate about what the family members were trying to do—what kind of realities were they trying to create through their interaction? We viewed their comments as positions they took within a range of discourses (which are emphasized in SMALL CAPS in the cases discussed below), and then we, as researchers, stepped back to identify a process we thought they were creating through this interaction.

We are therefore presenting in this section the eight interactive processes we have identified in the therapy transcripts:

» Tentative negotiation for parenting.
» Negotiating through blame and withdrawal.
» Shifting a mother–son relationship.
» Negotiating helpfulness.
» Mother and child sharing similar despair.
» Protecting the family from responsibility.
» Regulating a world view.
» Isolation from one's community.

Each one is accompanied by the text we used to identify the processes. Some full excerpts from the sessions have been included because we want to support our conclusions but also to invite the reader to generate her or his own alternative ideas.

### *Tentative negotiation for parenting*

In this process, children are exploring the nature of the parenting relationship with the help of the therapist. They seem to be trying to clarify what the parents' role is in the light of claims or concerns about their independence.

In the case of Child B, the parenting is explored through the theme of the mother's ability to cope with her own burdens and still promote B's independence. It seems that B needs to be reassured that her independence is something both she and her mother can adjust to. So she discusses the theme tentatively, and the therapist teases out the interactive aspects of B's independence. Here is an example from an early therapy session of B and the therapist discussing this theme.

Th: And last time we met you were going to stay over at someone's—how was that?

B (*quietly*): Yeah, it was great.

Th: Good you enjoyed it. Did mother miss you, do you think?

B (*nods, looks at mother*)

Th: How do you know she missed you?

B: Because she kept on phoning.

Th: To check that you were all right. Were you [B] worried about her [mother]?

B: Yeah.

Th: Can you tell when she is not happy?

B (*nods*)

Th: Can you tell straight away?

B: Yes

Th: How do you tell?

B: Well, she looks tired and doesn't smile, just frowns, sometimes stares into spaces.

Th: Is that something she has always done or something she does more now recently?

B: Well, she did it more when I got unhappy.

Th: Oh yes, right, because that's what you both talked about last time, how each other's moods affects the other one's.

The powerful family DISCOURSE ABOUT WORRY applies equally to mother and daughter in this case. It seems that B has to watch her mother for signs that she is ok, and the therapist points out that each person's moods will be affected by the other. Mother and daughter seem to share the belief that mother "missed out" as a child and therefore is limited in her parenting ability. This could be seen as a DISCOURSE ABOUT "DEFICIT", which is accepted by both. Understanding this will lead to the child being able to be more independent and to need less parenting.

In the next extract, parenting has been symbolized by hugs and physical proximity. It seems that B is seeking some certainty and reassurance that her mother will respond when she needs support. B puts her view into the discussion, and the therapist becomes active in providing an explanation: "having so much on their minds". Perhaps the therapist here is responding to B's request for certainty by offering something she believes the mother cannot offer.

B: I am a lot more used to eating now, but mother is still not sure about me.

Th: Would it be more helpful to you if she was more sure about you?

B: Yeah.

Th: Because I was wondering, if she was a bit brisker with you and didn't pussy-foot around you, would that be better for you?

B: Yeah. . . . Not to get upset so often because sometimes when my mother has been working hard, she ignores me when I talk to her and I get upset then. . . . As well, sometimes if I go away from my mother after an argument, she checks up on me a bit, and, um, I try and do what she does and say "can we be friends now" and she gives me a hug and a kiss, but when I try and do that she just walks away.

Th: So, what would you like her to do?

B: To listen to me a bit more when I'm upset.

Th: Yes, you talked a bit about her listening last time, and she said she would try to listen to you in a different way. I think grown-ups want to listen to children when they are upset but sometimes they have so much on their minds that they can't take it anymore, it all gets a bit too much, and I think that is what happens sometimes to your mother. But it's interesting that she says "can we be friends" and comes and gives you a hug. Do you ever say no, get lost?

B (*Shakes her head*)

There are many examples in our transcripts of parents and children arguing and "holding their ground", and we suggest that many of these incidents are attempts by the family to create a new construct of parenting based on DISCOURSES OF BLAME. It is as though the child is saying "you are wrong" and the parent is saying, "do not challenge my authority" or "do not criticize me". So the parent responds defensively, and neither parent nor child is able to negotiate any new understandings about parenting.

In the following example from the same case, B and her mother are discussing an argument and the therapist attempts to move the conversation to another level: the physical demonstration of parenting, the cuddle.

B: I say that when an argument comes we should deal with it and not try to make it go away, because if you just make it go away then it makes it worse.

Th *(to mother)*: Do you know what she means?

Mother: Yeah, but I feel that sometimes she pushes me on an irrelevant thing, it's something, nothing, like "mother, can I have a chocolate bar", "no", "why", I don't know. Not necessarily that, but it's a nothing thing. And then "why can't I have it", or "why don't you want it" and then I just answer it and then it's "why" again and this is just how I feel, that it's,. . . that I get pushed and pushed and it goes to a big thing for nothing. It's like the balance has been upset for nothing but as if she makes it go there.

Th: But I wonder, do you think she wants something else?

Mother: Yeah, that's what I wonder.

Th: It's not the chocolate bar, it's something else?

Mother: Yeah, it's attention, I presume, but that does get positive. . . . Yeah, how can one respond positively to that pushing, or is she pushing me to see how far I will go?

Th: Well, I expect it's a bit of both. (*to B*) Sometimes do you like to see how far you can push her?

B: Not in situations where I say "why". I say "why" once, and then I can see that my mother is getting upset so I say "why" again and then she tells me that she is getting upset, so I say "why are getting upset" and then she just snaps at me.

Th: So could she, for instance, if you said "can I have another chocolate bar", could she say "no, you have had two already, but you can have a cuddle instead"—what would that be like?

B: I think that would be quite nice, yeah.

### *Negotiating through blame and withdrawal*

The C case has been notable for the feelings of despair, and the belief that no one can change, that surrounds the definition of the relationships between C and his mother and the mother's recent live-in partner. C is a 13-year-old boy whose father lives in another country. He currently lives with his mother, who has a history of depression, and her partner. In an early session, mother had described her abusive childhood and her subsequent negative feelings about life.

C is asked about his mother's moods, which lead to his feeling of being isolated, too distant from his mother in the beginning and then overwhelmed by feelings as though he is too close. He is trying in the following sequence to clarify the emotional distance he wants in relation to his mother. The discourse for him is about BEING CLOSE WITHOUT BEING OVERWHELMED.

When C and the therapist are trying to build an explanation for his mother's moods, he draws on a DISCOURSE OF BLAME placed squarely on his shoulders. It then becomes apparent that his feeling responsible for his mother's moods leads him to give up.

C: Yeah. If she is not happy then she won't keep it to herself, she wants to spread it to everybody else. When my mother gets sad and sometimes she does and she cries and she drinks and when I go "oh not again" then she goes mad at me for days. Then she just wants to be left alone and if she has an argument with K (*the boyfriend*), then he will speak to me but she won't speak.

Th: And if mother is crying regularly, do you try and check out how she is?

C: No, I give up.

Th: You give up.

C: Yeah, I give up. I do feel sorry for her but sometimes she might cry because I have been bad at school, and it is like she gets upset about it and if something bad or nasty happens then I will comfort her, but something like that I don't know, if it is very serious, then she will say something like I'm a disappointment and I don't like that. It is very negative.

And then at a later stage of the therapy, C seems overwhelmed by his mother's emotion and once again backs away from the relationship.

Mother: He (C) asked why we were coming, and we said that the issue is depression and so it doesn't go on generation after generation. Yes, I think I touched on it, but it is a difficult topic. Anything that C asks me I will answer.

Th: (*to C*) Do you ask your mother about those things, about how she feels?

C: I used to, but I don't any more

Th: What stopped you?

C: Well, she cries every day and it is difficult. When she cries, I cry, and it is too often.

Th: There was a time when you would cry if you saw your mother cry?

C: Yeah, I would cry when she cries because it is not nice, but now it is uncontrollable.

Th: Right, are you saying that you have got used to it?

Mother: I think everybody has.

In a similar pattern to that observed in the B case, much of the continual bickering that went on in these sessions was an attempt to either solicit caretaking from the other, or to be acknowledged for caretaking that had not been appreciated. It seems as though they are saying "who will take responsibility for breaking this pattern and making me feel better?"

### *Shifting a mother–son relationship*

A puzzling feature of the C case is that, although C recorded a big drop in his own level of anxiety (accompanied by a drop on his CDI score), the family experienced a violent episode towards the end of therapy and felt relations in the family were as bad as they had ever been. K, who had not come to the session, was very upset by the verbal abuse of disrespect C was directing at his mother, and he hit C to punish and stop him. The mother is feeling demoralized and defeated by all of this, and she and C begin to construct an explanation for his behaviour based on a DISCOURSE ABOUT TRUST.

Mother: It must be like C says, he is always saying I'm a crap mother so it must be.

C: No, I'm only saying it because I'm angry.

Mother: Well, it must be, C, or else why the hell do you behave the way that you do? Why is it . . .?

C: It's because you do not trust me!

Mother: I trust you to go halfway across the world, what do you mean?

C: That is independence, trust is a different thing.

Mother: Trust comes into it.

C: If you can trust me with my friends, I told you I will swear on my life that I will behave properly, but no one listens.

In the context of what we have already said about C's family, his frequent, heart-felt appeals for trust can be interpreted as attempts to get support from a reference group, his peer group, for building new intimate relationships outside the family. They negotiate a new meaning of trust through this conversation, and it seems to rest squarely on support for C's ability to create more of his own world.

The intervention by K, the boyfriend, prompted a discussion of whose side he was on. He was clearly on the mother's side when he beat C, but at other times he and C had a good relationship and spent time together. C said the two adults ganged up on him, and he had to be more careful how he behaved in the boyfriend's presence. These sentiments are conveyed in the following discussion about strength and safety and C finding his voice:

Mother: My boyfriend went over the edge because C is so rude to his mother, because he would never do that and has never seen anyone do it.

C: I mean, I know that he will hit me if I'm rude to her. . . . That's the thing. . . my mother knows that I'm scared of him because he is big and it hurts when he punches me so she, . . . and what she does is, . . . because she knows that I can't express myself the same way as I can when he is there.

Mother: I get him to help me.

Th: It sounds like that.

C: When we are by ourselves, right, she, . . . I can express

> myself and say what I want but then when her boyfriend is there they gang up on me and they expect me not to hold any fingers up.

The feelings of blame and self-criticism became so intense they erupted into violence, and C now expresses his fear of the boyfriend, whereas the mother seems to feel supported by K's anger at seeing the mother disrespected. The frustration about not being able to shift their understandings of each other through words has led them to a physical, violent attempt to change C's behaviour, but, interestingly, his mother seems to make some meaning of this event by drawing on the DISCOURSE OF THE PROTECTIVENESS OF LOYAL PARTNERS.

But perhaps there are meanings at several levels here. C may also feel reassured that someone is prepared to fight for his mother's protection, and if he feels this is in place he may then be able to spend less time worrying about his mother and more time thinking about himself.

### *Negotiating helpfulness*

In many of the sessions we analysed, the referred child and parent disagreed, argued, and irritated each other. The children seemed to be drawing on DISCOURSES OF HELPFULNESS, but when they believed their efforts were not understood or useful, they became frustrated and the subsequent interactions showed this frustration, as well as a search for the frustration seems to come out in more awkward, fractious conversations with their parent.

For example, in another case, a 10-year-old boy, E, and his sister, F, are discussing how things have changed since their mother has been less depressed. E has been fidgeting for much of the session and finally something that seems to be a helpful discussion is suddenly interrupted.

> Th (*to children*): How have things changed for you as a result of mother coming out of her depression?
>
> F: The house is a lot cleaner.

Th: The house is a lot cleaner, great!

F: Things get done.

Th: How long have you noticed this, that things are really . . .

F: About four, no, about three months.

Th (*to E*): Would you agree with F that it's about three months?

E: Well, about.

Mother: Coming out of it and going to therapy, you know, it opens the wounds so I'm still shaky, but lately I have been a lot stronger.

Th: Right.

Mother: And now I can understand when I get depressed and think, "I know what that is" . . .

Th: Ummm, hmmmm.

E: The divorce leans on mother.

Mother: Oh, you're really irritating me E, why is it that you have to do attention-seeking the whole time?

Th: Well, how was this attention-seeking? You thought him talking about the divorce . . . ?

Mother: Have you not noticed that throughout the whole session he's been swinging, moving, jumping, that's what he's like all the time, all the time . . .

Th: Hmmmmm.

Mother: I find it hard work.

From the mother's perspective, the discussion about her depression touches on her efforts to get help and, in this case, resolve a painful, abusive divorce. We suggest this is irritating to the mother because the feelings are stirred up by her child, who is not in a position to offer the adult support she needs for this level of complex, painful feeling. He is 10 years old, lacking maturity, and because he is a boy, mother is not always able to "come to his level" in order to play or converse together.

Also, earlier in the session, mother has commented on the fact that E reminds her of her abusive husband (E's father), so it is more likely that feelings about the past will be stirred up in E's presence.

> Mother: Yeah, I do take it personally, so I suppose I relate it back, but I don't want E to turn out like his dad. That's not to say I don't want him not to love his dad and have a relationship with his dad, but there are very negative bad aspects there that I don't want passed on to E—is that fair?
>
> Th: Ummm, hmmmm.
>
> Mother: So maybe when he does these things, I take it personally in that way . . .
>
> Th: Maybe when he says things which he intends to, maybe, be different, you hear his dad's voice.
>
> Mother: Yeah, that's right, and then I notice myself slagging his dad off a lot and I notice that upsets him and I must, . . . I would like to try and do something about that because . . .
>
> E: I don't say anything to you, though . . .
>
> Mother: I know you don't . . .
>
> Th: You don't, but your mother notices that . . .
>
> Mother: And I can't stop myself and I think, "why am I doing it, it's not his fault", but I take it out on E, as if he's his dad.

This example illustrates that parents and children position each other in ways that make it difficult to clarify the possibilities for a parenting relationship. Here, mother has said she sees her ex-husband in her son, and this makes it very difficult to give him parenting he might desire or for her to see his behaviour as a message about what he needs and what he can offer, as a 10-year-old boy.

It is a common feature of many families referred for therapy that family members are trying to resolve traumatic experiences from the past. Here, we would say they are drawing upon a DISCOURSE ABOUT "RESOLVING THE PAST" and, in this case, the three family members participate in an exercise of resurrecting some of the experiences of the past and simultaneously separating the past from the present by seeing E as his own person, distinct from his father.

## *Mother and child sharing similar despair*

The G case consisted of a family of two parents and five children, one of whom was diagnosed with behaviour problems that led to continual, intrusive behaviour in the home. It seems clear from the transcripts that mother felt desperate and despairing about making any changes in family life while this son was spoiling the other children's chances of an ordinary life. For example, G, a girl aged 13, who was referred to the research study for depression and self-harm, could not invite friends to the house because they were harassed by her brother.

There is evidence in the sessions that G and her mother have a mutually protective, established relationship towards each other. Her mother gets some comfort from G, while also regretting that she doesn't have the time or peace of mind to give G the attention she deserves.

> Mother: It's like, I get sad,
>
> Th: I'm sure you do get sad because it is . . .
>
> Mother: Depressed, really, when I hear G say to the likes of you "oh I did this to myself but I didn't tell my mother because she has enough to deal with", and then you start judging yourself and think, oh my god, am I a terrible parent?

G and her mother recount a story of the father coming home drunk one night and the mother eventually retiring to bed. Father fell asleep on the sofa, but when he woke noisily in the middle of the night, it was G who went to the sitting-room and blocked the front door to prevent her father from going outside and disturbing the neighbourhood.

It is as though G and her mother find mutual support through what seems like interchangeable roles. In this excerpt, they jointly share their similar responses to similar feelings of despair. They are discussing the use of the bathroom as a retreat.

Mother: I use the bathroom, too.

Th: Do you?

Mother: Yeah.

G: It's the only room that has a lock.

Mother: I'm sure you will agree with me, because it is a toilet bathroom. You sit on the edge of the bath and then you get the knocks from the other kids, saying "what are you doing in there?" And you have to just say "I'm on the toilet", because that will cover it.

G: I'm the same.

Th: What is that like? Is it good to hear that mother does that same sort of thing, or is it worrying?

G: Yeah, it's not good, because even though we both think like that, it's not good because I know she's upset.

This case, compared to others, was striking for the level of helplessness conveyed by the mother. It seemed that the mother was periodically overwhelmed to the extent that she was no longer negotiating, or arguing, or challenging beliefs with others. And we see from the transcript that her daughter, G, has a strong identification with her mother and sees the world much as her mother does. It seems difficult in this interaction for the mother and daughter to conjure any idea of how they will lift themselves from this despair.

## *Protecting the family from responsibility*

The DISCOURSE ABOUT BLAME AND RESPONSIBILITY was utilized most powerfully in the case of the D family. Ten-year-old D was referred to the research project because of his depressive moods. The family was randomly allocated to family therapy, although they were not necessarily expecting to be seen all together.

Mother had lived as a lone parent with D for some years before she began living with her current partner. Now they also have a daughter together, aged 3, and all four of them attended the family sessions. After the first few sessions, D protested vigorously about coming to the sessions. He felt they were of no benefit, he didn't like them, and, besides, he was now feeling better in himself. His protests were countered by both parents, who found the sessions helpful in understanding more about their family dynamics. They discussed issues such as the stepfather's entry into the family and some of his frustrations about parenting D. D protested so consistently and with such strong feeling that it led us to speculate that he felt he was attending the sessions under false pretences—as though the "stated" reason was for D's depression and family relations, but that D's presence had another meaning, which was unacknowledged. Studying the transcripts for other discourses brought us repeatedly to the family stories about how they became a family: about the stepfather's role and mother being a depressed and stressed single parent; and the arrival of the new baby sister, signifying a new family unit.

These were powerful discourses filled with emotion and values. For example, mother believed that, as a depressed and unsupported single working mother, she was never able to look after D properly and she feels forever responsible for D's depression. She also felt ambivalent about the stepfather joining the family because she was aware that her own relationship with him would exclude D and that the arrival of the new baby would "cement" a new biological unit that excluded D further.

We have identified three important value-laden discourses that the family drew on to construct their narrative. The first is a DISCOURSE OF "FACING UP TO THINGS" which allows the family and D to take several positions. D takes the position that he can avoid certain issues or feelings by not taking part in the session, and this stimulates mother and stepfather to take the position that D should "face up to things". Each position influences the other, and the process generates continuous discussion about what D and his family should be talking about. The second is a DISCOURSE OF BIOLOGY, which offers positions that biological relations are important for parenting, and the other position that they are less so. Mother and stepfather may both hold to the former position, making it difficult to fully integrate D. At one point, the mother drew on this discourse, saying, "I feel grief for you, D, because you'll never have a biological father". The third is the DISCOURSE OF EXCLUSIVE RELATIONSHIPS. This suggests that belief in close, inclusive relationships such as that of the mother and D is supported by other positions in which someone is excluded from the relationship. This discourse may also generate positions that make it difficult to create a new, close-knit family.

If the family is only able to communicate their feelings within these discourses, it seems clear that D is placed in an impossible position. If he acknowledges being depressed prior to the therapy, he confirms that his mother is in some way responsible for his depression, so he tries to convince everyone he is fine and there is no need for the meetings. Yet he may also believe that being the centre of attention—"the problem"—is an opportunity for the family to come together in their attempt to help D feel better: a project that unites the family and eases some of mother's painful feelings. But this places D back in the position of having some responsibility for the family's future—a heavy burden, as though they would not have "faced up to" family issues if it had not been for D.

One important discussion in a later session drew on the discourse of who was responsible for the feelings and mood in the family. The therapist presents this idea, then asks mother to create a suitable exploration of responsibility with her son:

Th: Before you answer, let me share with you one of my observations. One of the main reasons you came here was centred around D, and that may be why D didn't want to come here—because he felt that everyone's problems were centred around him, and it is not necessarily so. We learnt today that a lot of it is about you (*mother*) worrying, which is not about D, so I wonder how you (*D*) will be able to make yourself say, "well, it is not me, it's not something I should take all the responsibility for". Do you understand what I am saying?

D: No, I don't.

Th (*to mother*): Do you understand?

Mother: Yes, I do.

Th: Would you be able to explain to D?

Mother: Um, that initially. . . . .

D: It doesn't matter, yes.

Mother: Initially D felt that we were here for him, then it turned into family therapy and, as the problem unwrapped, that maybe the problem wasn't to do with D but was about my worrying about the school.

D: Well, if it has taken us 14 sessions to work it out, then don't worry so much. Right, we have finished . . . let's go.

And a few minutes later the stepfather joins in to shift the focus to "us"—meaning the whole family—and mother has her own further reflection.

Stepfather: What I was trying to say is that initially when we first came here, you felt that it was about you, and now it is about us.

Th: So, actually, it has been a process of thinking "it is not about me".

D: If is has nothing to do with me, then why am I here?

Th: I am not saying it has nothing to do with you, I am saying that you are not the carrier of the thing that is difficult within the family.

Mother: So, you think that D takes on a lot of responsibility?

Th: I think it is something to take home with you and to think about. Maybe this is something that has changed, but maybe he was positioned in the family so that he was taking a lot of responsibility, or when things were not working, . . . well, it is easy to think, maybe it is because D is unhappy, or maybe because D is my son, but not his son. All kinds of things that may have had nothing to do with it.

Mother: And do you think he gets so upset about things that I don't see why he should get so upset is because he feels responsible?

This is another example of a depressed child and his family negotiating responsibility, but this excerpt clearly demonstrates a shift in the way the meaning of responsibility is negotiated. We see the parents openly acknowledging greater responsibility for what is happening in the family and thereby lifting some of the burden from D's shoulders.

## *Regulating a world view*

Several families in the study struggled to find the balance between their attention to difficulties and their appreciation of positives. We describe this as a DISCOURSE OF HOW WE SEE THE WORLD. We have observed family members taking different positions in the course of a session, as though holding one position for too long negates the other positions, perhaps associated with other emotions, and organizes relationships in a certain way.

A clear example of this comes from the later session of the previous family. The family are discussing the way the sessions seem, at some point, to just deteriorate and D seems to suggest it is not helpful to talk about positive things.

> Th: D said in the first half we didn't do anything, and what I understood from that is that D feels that when we are talking about positive things in the family, it is as if we are not doing anything.
>
> D: If we are talking about good things, then nothing is resolved.
>
> Th: And there is a feel that eventually we will really get into things, meaning it is always about getting to the painful things.

Then, a moment later, mother takes a similar position which is challenged by stepfather. This leads to a disagreement, and D quickly joins in to defuse any potential argument between the adults. When mother reports her own loss of energy, D draws attention to the end of the session by asking the time.

Mother: We haven't had a session yet where we haven't entered a grief moment, and in these sessions you don't expect to explore all the positive sides.

Th: So maybe that was the turning-point, expecting some grief moment.

Stepfather: You say that, but the positive, to say what is good about the dynamic, is so important rather than what is just bad about it.

Mother: I'm not saying that, you don't need to get angry about it

D: Hey, saying a thing like that is the point that things deteriorate, then you have an argument.

Mother: There is a slight expectation of something you know you, . . . I have a slight fear I suppose, and also on Friday evening at a certain point, I did feel my energy just die, didn't you? At a certain point?

D: What is the time?

Th: Also, you as a family need to think more with an emphasis on the positive things that are happening. Do we think that only if we get to the heavy nitty-gritty stuff that is of importance?

Mother: Oh, I definitely think I do when I think about it.

Th: So maybe it is something to think about.

Since the regulation of emotion is such an important feature of childhood depression (Kovacs, 1996), it is worth considering what we have observed in this study. This example typifies a process of social construction in which people may move from a positive outlook to a negative one in order to maintain a particular relationship. We believe that family members regulate emotion in the group, as a way of agreeing or disagreeing, supporting oneself or reaching out to stress, and so forth. In other words, we can see in this example with D that feeling positive or negative can be a strategy that, over time, becomes a pattern and a role within a family group. Our view is that therapists would be well advised to explore the way relationships are organized when positive and negative feelings are being proposed in cases with childhood depression.

### *Isolation from one's community*

The A case demonstrated to us a particular breakdown of communication between the 14-year-old referred client and her parents. A was the only child of two parents from an ethnic-minority background, who also had an older son who had died of a serious illness several years before the referral. The parents were mourning the death of their son and also had episodes of violence and discussions about separation. A seemed mightily to be pushing her parents away from her own life, yet she was closely involved in trying to intervene in her parents' violent relationship. Probably as a result of this bind, she remained silent for all of the therapy sessions, apart from the first fifteen minutes of Session 1. A did not want to speak in front of her parents nor be seen on a video camera, because she was deeply ashamed of spots on her face. The therapy team of two decided to split themselves, so that one therapist went to a separate room with A while the other remained to conduct a session with the parents. Usually, all rejoined at the end, and A's therapist made some comments to the parents which A wanted to pass on to her parents. For this reason, we could not do a discourse analysis to reflect the child's active participation in creating family meanings, but she was establishing her position by her absence.

At an early session, A gave a statement for the therapist to read out which said, "Stop making me have to worry about you"; at the next session, her longer message to her parents was:

> "I don't want my mother coming into my room all the time. I just want my spots to go away. I want to get better and then I'll go back to school and start going out. I don't want anyone to see me because it's embarrassing. And no more arguing and fighting. I want my dad to stop shouting at my mother for little things like food. I don't like everyone knowing about me not going to school and about my spots and I don't want my

> parents to tell any of my friends about my spots because they don't know that I'm not going to school because of the spots. I want my dermatology appointment to come quickly so I can get better quickly and I want schoolwork to do so I don't fall behind a lot."

So here are the therapists giving a powerful voice in an unorthodox way. And the anxieties A expressed are related to the parents' behaviour and to the shame she feels about not being a normal, attractive girl in her peer group. It seemed that A could not negotiate with her parents verbally, but she used the messages to negotiate a better relationship, a less shameful one, with her peers, and perhaps that was her solution to moving her parents closer to taking charge of their own relationship.

The opinion of the therapists in this case, and the researchers, was that family interactions and meanings were powerfully organized by the DISCOURSE OF SHAME. The shame the family felt in their own community was overwhelming, and the eventual reduction of anxiety reported by A was less about the content of what was discussed in the therapy sessions—such as seeing her parents change, discussing her parents deteriorating relationship, or seeing her father show some control over his violent behaviour, although these may have played a part—but more the result of a direct intervention by a member of her own community to reinstate A back into the normality of her school routine and neutralize the shame that seemed to be holding the family back.

## *Final discussion*

Our conclusions from this study are inevitably influenced by the setting in which we did our observation, and analysis and our bias led us to observe children in interaction with family members and to speculate about the impact of this interaction upon the experience of childhood depression and anxiety.

We have come to the view that family interaction provides the setting for two things to happen:

1. A child has an opportunity to negotiate for a different kind of parenting.
2. A parent has an opportunity to gain some confirmation or appreciation of him/herself as a parent, either by shifting a child's behaviour or by shifting the way the child sees the parent. It is like a living laboratory in which parents and children can use each other to gain some status, self-esteem, or pleasure, and the family has provided this opportunity from the beginning of the child's life.

Our view of childhood depression is that it results from some realization that this interaction will not lead to the desired outcome and then the participants withdraw from the interaction. Withdrawal can lead to hopelessness, which leaves children feeling helpless to change things and leads to depression as we can record it on our measures.

We have been struck by the way these families have struggled to use the DISCOURSES OF HOPEFULNESS AND CHANGE to sustain positive views of their lives only, to see their family interactions push them to positions of despair and inertia.

We observed many sessions in which children demonstrate protectiveness towards one or both parents, but this takes many forms, from angry rejection to argumentativeness, to abusive behaviour, to resignation, and to identification. In the family context, we have persisted in conceptualizing these behaviours as attempts to engage, or awaken, the parenting process. We have to assume that there is a scale for hopefulness within their available discourse, which allows us to hypothesize that some of our children have given up while some are still fighting.

Yet the families we have studied have all come forward into the large research project, so there must be some desire to seek something different. Why do they keep trying? Our suggestion is that as long as anxiety, depression, hopelessness can be embedded and expressed through interactions, such as those in these transcripts, the family members will keep trying to change the interaction, one way or another. If we believe that their individual identities are shaped by interaction, we must conclude that their chances for growth and development are also available in the interaction.

We have also learned about the importance of a wider network in addressing childhood depression, which is often conceptualized as an internalized experience. It will certainly be internalized, but we have seen examples from this sample of children being relieved of symptoms by talking in the presence of family members. This led us to re-evaluate the significance of the way children and the parents fitted into their wider family network or wider cultural community. Many of our cases consisted of relatively isolated families and individuals, and we speculate that when the adults feel less isolated, they can offer more as parents.

Another obstacle to "negotiated parenting" we have observed are the ghosts from the past. We had the impression here, and in a previous study (Campbell et al., 2003), that many adults are not free to parent, but are trying to resolve relationships from the past. We saw examples of a mother still negotiating with her own mother, and another mother trying to come to terms with an abusive ex-spouse, and we have seen how children can be drawn into the middle of this process and feel confused about why they are there and what they can reasonably do.

Because this was a small-sample qualitative study, we cannot make definitive statements about differences between the high- and low anxiety-change score groups; nevertheless, we can share clinical impressions gleaned from studying family therapy transcripts.

The most noticeable difference between the two groups in this study is that the high anxiety-change score group started therapy in a more anxious state (see Table 11.1) and, therefore, they may have been more concerned to address those feelings and reduce the anxiety—that is, they were feeling more fearful. They may have been more motivated to get into interactions that touched on this fearfulness directly and thereby reduced anxiety. Whereas one could argue that the depressed children with low anxiety-change scores had settled into depression with its low mood and feeling of helplessness—that is, being less aware of a fearfulness—they may also have been less motivated to address fears actively in the sessions.

It is interesting to note that the average CDI score at the start of treatment was 24.5 for the high anxiety-change group, whereas it was 28.3 for the low anxiety-change group (see Table 11.2).

One abiding impression from studying transcripts is that the high anxiety-change group seemed to demonstrate a greater ability to see different perspectives. In the course of the family therapy, members could be seen to alter their views. This was less obvious when we analysed the low anxiety-change group. They seemed to repeat their points of view more frequently, and they seemed less resourceful in getting out of their repetitive patterns.

None of the three cases in the low anxiety-change group had active, supportive fathers to add their perspective to the generation of meaning in the family. Our clinical impression was of mothers and their children fighting with depression with very little support (see Campbell et al., 2003).

Our final thoughts about the role of family therapy in reducing anxiety is based on the notion that anxieties arise when children do not have the opportunities early in life to have their fears—their basic fears—recognized by others. The family interactions we have studied, as fraught and stuck as many seemed to be, provided a forum for voices to be heard and for some anxieties to be recognized. The considerable amount of negotiating that went on to establish parenting relationships can be seen as the child's engagement in having their fears and needs attended to.

# PART IV

# RESEARCH

CHAPTER TWELVE

# Childhood depression: a place for psychotherapy

*Judith Trowell & Ilan Joffe*

Although considered clinically effective, there is little systematic research into the efficacy of individual psychodynamic psychotherapy or family therapy in the treatment of depression in children and young adolescents. Most available evidence concerning psychological treatments is for cognitive behavioural therapy (CBT) or inter-personal therapy (Elkin et al., 1989). While CBT is promising in the short term, previous studies (Birmaher et al., 2000; Brent et al., 1997; Wood, Harrington, & Moore, 1996) have found high rates of relapse, suggesting the need for continuation or booster treatment. Psychodynamic psychotherapy holds the promise of effecting more lasting changes in childhood depression by improving the capacity to resolve internal and external conflicts over time (Kolvin, Trowell, Tsiantis, & Almqvist, 1999).

With the serious nature of childhood/adolescent depression, it is crucial that treatments with efficacy and more than transitory effects, and with the potential for a reduction in the cumulative risks, be provided promptly and skilfully.

There is some evidence to support the use of antidepressant medication in the treatment of childhood depression. Previous placebo-controlled studies have reported response rates to fluoxetine monotherapy of 52% and 56% (Emslie et al., 1997, 2000) in cases of major depression. The Treatment for Adolescents with Depression Study (TADS; March et al., 2004) reported a response rate of 60.6% to fluoxetine monotherapy for major depressive disorder (MDD), and 71% when fluoxetine was combined with CBT. However, the use of selective serotonin re-uptake inhibitors (SSRIs) in the under-18 population is becoming more restricted because of the risk:benefit ratio (CSM, 2003). It is therefore important to identify alternative treatment modalities for depression in children and young adolescents.

While CBT has been found to be superior to comparison interventions in the treatment of MDD in children/adolescents in four out of six randomized trials (Harrington, Whittaker, & Shoebridge, 1998), some limitations have been identified: severe cases of depression have not been included, nor were cases with many co-morbid problems such as conduct disorder or repeated self-harm. A number of methodological limitations in the existing research to date were also identified in a review of the treatment research (Harrington, Whittaker, Shoebridge, & Campbell, 1998).

Muratori, Picchi, Bruni, Patarnello, and Romagnoli (2003) have shown that psychodynamic psychotherapy is effective in treating internalizing disorders in routine outpatient care; the benefits of such treatment were manifest both immediately and with delayed onset ("sleeper effect").

A number of factors suggest a place for family therapy in the treatment of depression in children. Parents can be important agents for behavioural change, as a positive parental attitude may be a powerful contributor to self-worth in childhood/adolescence (Harter, 1990; Kovacs & Bastiaens, 1995). There is now much evidence that the family environment can contribute to childhood depression (Diamond, Serrano, Dickey, & Sonis, 1996). Depressed children who live in a confrontational environment also have higher rates of recurrence (Asarnow, Thompson, Hamilton, Goldstein, & Guthrie, 1994).

There is strong evidence of an association between depression in children and problems in family members, including dysfunctional family relationships (Harrington & Dubicka, 2002). Factors such as high parental criticism, family discord, and poor communication between parent and child have been associated with the onset and course of juvenile depressive disorder. Goodyer, Herbert, Secher, and Pearson (1997) concluded that psychosocial interventions with first-degree relatives and current close friendships should be considered as part of a treatment strategy for first-episode MDD in children/adolescents.

The aim of this study was to conduct a trial of two established but as yet unvalidated forms of psychotherapy for major depression in childhood/adolescence: (1) focused individual psychodynamic psychotherapy (FIPP) ("individual therapy") with a focus on interpersonal relationships, life stresses, and dysfunctional attachments based on the model of Malan (Malan & Osimo, 1992) and Davenloo (1978) who provide guidelines about psychodynamics, training, and techniques in brief dynamic psychotherapy; and (2) systems integrative family therapy (SIFT) ("family therapy") with a focus on family dysfunction, but without specific attention to unresolved intra-psychic conflicts and early childhood. (Byng-Hall, 1995; Byng-Hall & Campbell, 1981; Will & Wrate, 1985). These treatments were compared in three culturally diverse settings, using a manualized approach.

It was hypothesized that individual therapy would be an effective treatment for depression and that improvement would be maintained and ongoing. Family therapy could also be effective in the treatment of depression. Based on the findings of Brent et al. (1997), which demonstrated a 37.9% response rate for depression with family therapy, it was hypothesized that family therapy might not be as effective as individual therapy in the treatment of depression.

Further hypotheses were made with regard to the sequence of response (internal change vs social interaction) and predictors of response between the two therapy groups using other measures as well as changes of psychosocial functioning based on the Social Adjustment Scale for Children and the Family Assessment Device. These will be reported in subsequent publications.

## *Methods*

A randomized control trial was conducted in London (Tavistock Clinic), Athens (Aghia Sophia Children's Hospital), and Helsinki (Children's Hospital), with 72 patients aged 9–15 years allocated to either individual therapy (FIPP) or family therapy (SIFT), based on standard randomization methods. Caseness was the only factor considered at randomization. Patients in each centre were randomly allocated to one of the two treatments (Tsiantis et al., 2005).

Ethical approval for the study was obtained locally in each of the three centres. The use of placebo controls was ruled out on ethical grounds (Kazdin, 1986; Parloff, 1986)

Based on previous studies of therapy with maladjusted children (Kolvin, MacMillan, Nicol, & Wrate, 1988; Kolvin et al., 1981), a power calculation was done to detect a difference in outcome of 30% between the two treatment groups. Accordingly, it was expected that 44 patients per group would be required to detect a 30% difference with 80% power, using a 5% test of significance. Following difficulties with recruitment, a further power calculation was carried out based on another review of the literature; using the sample size in the Brent et al. study (1997) as a guide, where there were 35–37 subjects in each treatment arm, the size of the treatment groups in this study was adjusted accordingly.

All participants were referred into the study from community child mental health services. The patients' progress within the study is illustrated in the CONSORT diagram (Begg et al., 1996) in Figure 12.1.

Entry to the trial followed screening using the Childhood Depression Inventory (Kovacs, 1981), a brief self-report measure. Children scoring >13 were included provided they subsequently met criteria for MDD and/or Dysthymia on the Kiddie-SADS (Chambers et al., 1985), a standardized semi-structured diagnostic interview.

Children had to be living with at least one biological parent, and any antidepressants or other psychotropic medication had to have been stopped at least four weeks prior to commencement of therapy, to ensure the exclusion of confounding variables.

Exclusion criteria included: depressive disorders meriting

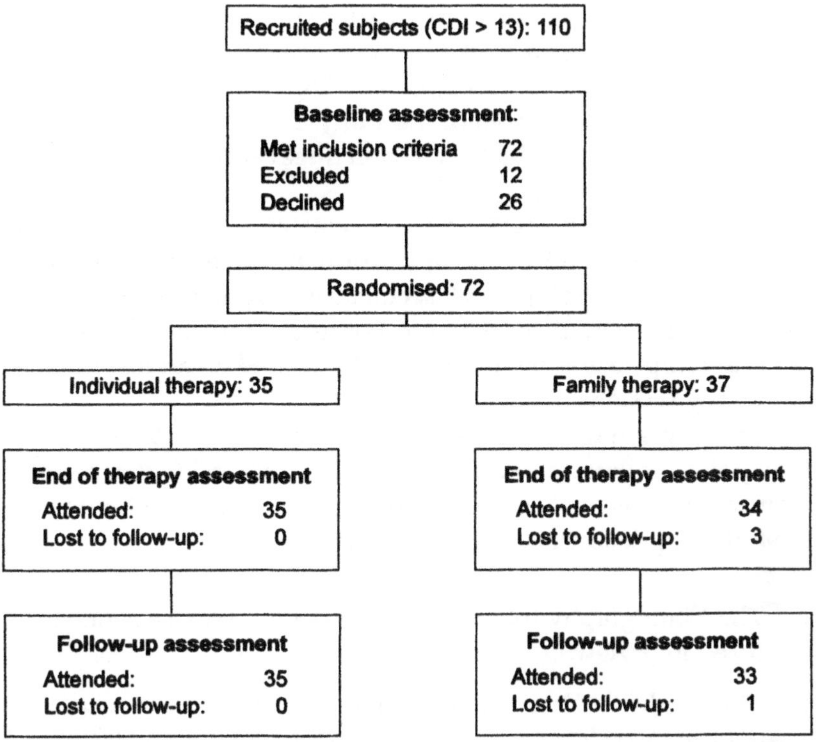


*Figure 12.1.* CONSORT diagram.

urgent hospitalization, bipolar and schizo-affective disorder, severe conduct disorder (considered likely to respond only moderately to psychotherapy), and parents with psychotic disorder or severe personality disorder.

Following screening, 24 cases entered into therapy in each country, divided equally between therapy types in London and Helsinki, with 11 in individual therapy and 13 in family therapy in Athens.

Treatment was conducted over a nine-month period and consisted of eight to fourteen 90-minute sessions of family therapy (mean = 11), or sixteen to thirty 50-minute sessions of individual therapy (mean = 24.7) plus individual parent sessions (one per 2 sessions of child's psychotherapy) by a separate case worker. There were between four and six individual therapists, and four and six family therapists in each of the three centres. The therapists in Athens and Helsinki had received training from the London team prior to the commencement of the study. Treatment Manuals were used to ensure comparability across all three centres, supplemented by cross-centre training.

Assessment took place prior to treatment ("baseline"), at the end of therapy ("end of therapy": primary endpoint) and again six months later ("follow-up": secondary endpoint). Patients "lost to follow-up" were those who did not return for "end of therapy" or "follow-up" assessment. They had attended a variable number of therapy sessions.

An extensive battery of instruments was administered at each time-point, collecting information about the child, the parents, their families, as well as relevant school measures. The findings of the following instruments are reported here:

1. The Demography Interview (Kolvin et al., 1991): a semi-structured interview.
2. The Kiddie-SADS (Chambers et al., 1985): this semi-structured clinical interview provides a measure of MDD and Dysthymia (based on *DSM–IV* criteria), and psychiatric co-morbidity. These included anxiety disorders (Generalized, Phobias, Separation Anxiety, and Panic Disorder), behavioural disorders (Oppositional Defiant Disorder, Conduct Disorder), Obsessive Compulsive Disorder, ADHD, and Anorexia Nervosa.
3. The Childhood Depression Inventory (CDI; Kovacs, 1981): this 27-item self-report questionnaire indicates the number of depressive symptoms and has a cut off indicating the presence of depression. A score of 13 was used as the threshold for entry into the study, based on research by Garvin, Leber, and Kalter (1991) for use of the CDI in clinical settings.
4. Moods and Feelings Questionnaire (MFQ: Angold, Costello, Messer, & Pickles, 1995; Angold, Costello, Pickles, Winder, & Silver, 1987): this 16-item self-report questionnaire provides a measure of depression. A threshold of 8 or more defines high scorers.

5. The Children's Global Assessment Scale (C-GAS: Shaffer, Gould, & Brasic, 1993): this clinician-rated scale provides a measure of overall impairment of child functioning (range of scores: 0 (lowest) to 100 (highest)).

## *Statistical analysis:*

A mixed-model repeated measures ANOVA was used to examine the extent of depression (as measured by the continuous instruments CDI, MFQ, and C-GAS) at each of the three time-points. Chi-square and exact tests were used for the comparison of the presence/absence of depression using cut-offs and the Kiddie-SADS.

Due to the small sample size in each country, most of the analysis was done for the three countries combined.

With regards to the Kiddie-SADS data, results have been calculated for separate disorders, but since they are known to occur together it was deemed appropriate to adjust the significance level to control for this association. A significance level of $p < .01$ was therefore used instead of $p < .05$. Also, the associations between these disorders are stated where applicable, and the significant results using these criteria are reported.

There were four "lost to follow-up" cases (one in Athens, three in London, all in the SIFT group). Intention-to-treat analysis principles were applied for these cases, with regard to the Kiddie-SADS scores, in order not to weaken the power of the sample size. Last-available scores were carried forward. With regard to the CDI and MFQ, we used a "mean substitution" method for dealing with missing data, where feasible and appropriate. Means were calculated for each instrument splitting by centre, time-point, and therapy type and imputed. Analysis carried out on the pre- and post-imputed data sets for each instrument confirmed that this did not change the statistical significance of any of the findings, other than to maintain the power of the sample.

A secondary analysis using multi-level modelling (ML-WIN) on the pre-imputed data was also carried out on the CDI, MFQ, and C-GAS data. The results of this (not presented here) confirmed the findings of the primary analysis. This also allowed us to examine factors related to improvement in each of the therapy groups.

## Results

### Characteristics of the sample

The mean age of participants was 12 years, almost two thirds (62%) were male, the majority were white and they represented all social class groups (see Table 12.1). Almost two thirds (62%) came from two-parent families (although not necessarily both biological parents). Just under half (44%) had a history of maternal psychiatric illness, while 15% had a history of depression in their extended family (siblings, grandparents, aunts, and uncles). Three quarters (76%) had been depressed for more than 6 months.

Overall, the sample characteristics were similar in each therapy type, except for a significantly higher percentage of males in the individual therapy group [$\chi^2(1) = 4.036$; $p < .05$] and a significant higher prevalence of paternal psychiatric history in the individual therapy group [$\chi^2(1) = 5.449$; $p < .05$]. A possible explanation for these findings is that demographic factors were not taken into consideration at randomization. These differences may have disappeared had the sample size been larger.

### Prevalence of depressive disorders

The prevalence of cases of MDD and/or Dysthymia, only MDD, only Dysthymia, and both MDD and Dysthymia ("double depression") have been examined. This was done to examine any differences in treatment effects in these clinically distinct groups of patients.

#### *Prevalence of depression (MDD and/or Dysthymia) before and after therapy based on the Kiddie-SADS*

At baseline assessment all the participants were diagnosed as depressed, with either MDD and/or Dysthymia, based on the

**Table 12.1 Characteristics of the sample[a]**

| | *Individual therapy N = 35 (%)* | *Family therapy N = 37 (%)* | *Combined N = 72 (%)* | *$\chi^2$/t-test* |
|---|---|---|---|---|
| Age | | | | |
| Mean (years) | 11.57 | 11.97 | 11.71 | NS |
| Standard deviation | 1.17 | 1.52 | 1.38 | |
| Range (years) | 9–14 | 10–15 | 9–15 | |
| Mode (years) | 11,12 | 10,12 | 12 | |
| Gender | | | | |
| Male | 26 (74) | 19 (51) | 45 (62) | $\chi^2(1) = 4.036$; $p < .05$ |
| Female | 9 (26) | 18 (49) | 27 (38) | |
| Ethnicity | | | | |
| White | 29 (82) | 34 (92) | 63 (87) | NS |
| Asian | 2 (6) | 2 (5) | 4 (6) | |
| Other | 3 (9) | 1 (3) | 4 (6) | |
| Missing | 1 (3) | 0 (0) | 1 (1) | |
| Socioeconomic status[b] | | | | |
| Class 1 | 1 (3) | 1 (3) | 2 (3) | NS |
| Class 2 | 7 (20) | 11 (30) | 18 (25) | |
| Class 3 | 12 (34) | 13 (35) | 25 (35) | |
| Class 4 | 5 (14) | 6 (16) | 11 (15) | |
| Class 5 | 4 (12) | 1 (3) | 5 (7) | |
| Missing | 6 (17) | 5 (13) | 11 (15) | |
| Parental marital status | | | | |
| Single/widowed/divorced | 11 (31) | 14 (38) | 25 (35) | NS |
| Married/living with partner | 24 (69) | 21 (57) | 45 (63) | |
| Missing | 0 (0) | 2 (5) | 2 (2) | |
| Maternal psychiatric history | | | | |
| Yes | 16 (46) | 16 (43) | 32 (44) | NS |
| No | 19 (54) | 21 (57) | 40 (56) | |
| Paternal psychiatric history | | | | |
| Yes | 7 (20) | 1 (3) | 8 (11) | $\chi^2(1) = 5.449$; $p < .05$ |
| No | 28 (80) | 36 (97) | 64 (89) | |
| Depression in extended family (excluding parents) | | | | |
| None | 29 (83) | 32 (86) | 61 (85) | NS |
| One family member | 5 (14) | 3 (8) | 8 (11) | |
| Two family members | 1 (3) | 2 (6) | 3 (4) | |
| Duration of depressive illness | | | | |
| 0–6 Months | 9 (26) | 8 (22) | 17 (24) | NS |
| >6 Months | 26 (74) | 29 (78) | 55 (76) | |

[a] Demography interview (Kolvin et al. 1991).
[b] UK Register General's Classification (Social Class 1 = highest; Social Class 5 = lowest).

Kiddie-SADS. By the end of therapy, of those receiving individual therapy, 74.3% were no longer diagnosed as depressed and none were diagnosed as depressed at follow-up (see Table 12.2). Of those receiving family therapy, 75.7% of cases of depression had improved by the end of therapy, and at follow-up only 18.9% were still diagnosed as depressed.

The change in prevalence of depression over the three time points in the individual therapy group was statistically significant [$\chi^2(2) = 77.537$; $p < .001$]. Further 2 × 2 chi-squares were performed to confirm between which time-points the significant changes had occurred. It was found that there was a statistically significant change in prevalence of depression from baseline to end of therapy [$\chi^2(1) = 41.364$; $p < .001$], from baseline to follow-up [$\chi^2(1) = 70.00$; $p < .001$] and also from end of therapy to follow-up [$\chi^2(1) = 10.328$; $p < .001$].

The change in prevalence of depression over the three time-points in the family therapy group, was also statistically significant [$\chi^2(2) = 60.953$; $p < .001$]. The 2 × 2 chi-squares performed as above found that there was a statistically significant change in prevalence of depression from baseline to end of therapy [$\chi^2(1) = 45.043$; $p < .001$], from baseline to follow-up [$\chi^2(1) = 50.455$; $p < .001$], but not from end of therapy to follow-up.

The prevalence of depression in the two groups was similar at the end of therapy. At follow-up there were significantly more cases with depression in the family therapy group [$\chi^2(1) = 7.335$; $p < .01$]. However, when the "lost to follow-up" cases were excluded, the prevalence of depression in the family therapy group at end of therapy was 13.4%, and at follow-up 8.1%. The comparison at follow-up between the therapy types was not statistically significant when the "lost to follow-up" cases were excluded.

### *Prevalence of MDD before and after therapy based on the Kiddie-SADS*

At the start of therapy more than 90% of the participants were diagnosed as having MDD (see Table 12.2). By the end of therapy only 6 (17.1%) still had this diagnosis in the individual therapy group and by follow-up none received this diagnosis. In the fam-

**Table 12.2 Presence of depression (MDD and/or Dysthymia), MDD, Dysthymia, and double depression (MDD and Dysthymia) at three time points by therapy type, based on the Kiddie-SADS**

| | *Individual therapy* *N* = 35 | | *Family therapy* *N* = 37 | | *Total* *N* = 72 | |
|---|---|---|---|---|---|---|
| | *Present* | *Absent* | *Present* | *Absent* | *Present* | *Absent* |
| Depression | | | | | | |
| Baseline | 35 (100.0) | 0 (0.0) | 37 (100.0) | 0 (0.0) | 72 (100.0) | 0 (0.0) |
| End of therapy | 9 (25.7) | 26 (74.3) | 9[a] (24.3) | 28 (75.7) | 18 (25.0) | 54 (75.0) |
| Follow-up | 0 (0.0) | 35 (100.0) | 7a (18.9) | 30 (81.1) | 7 (9.7) | 65 (90.3) |
| MDD | | | | | | |
| Baseline | 32 (91.4) | 3 (8.6) | 34 (91.9) | 3 (8.1) | 66 (91.7) | 6 (8.3) |
| End of therapy | 6 (17.1) | 29 (82.9) | 8[a] (21.6) | 29 (78.4) | 14 (19.4) | 58 (80.6) |
| Follow-up | 0 (0.0) | 35 (100.0) | 7[a] (18.9) | 30 (81.1) | 7 (9.7) | 65 (90.3) |
| Dysthymia | | | | | | |
| Baseline | 20 (57.1) | 15 (42.9) | 20 (54.1) | 17 (45.9) | 40 (55.6) | 0 (44.4) |
| End of therapy | 6 (17.1) | 29 (82.9) | 7[a] (18.9) | 30 (81.1) | 13 (18.1) | 54 (81.9) |
| Follow-up | 0 (0.0) | 35 (100.0) | 4[a] (10.8) | 33 (89.2) | 4 (5.6) | 65 (94.4) |
| Double depression | | | | | | |
| Baseline | 17 (48.6) | 18 (51.4) | 17 (45.9) | 20 (54.1) | 34 (47.2) | 38 (52.8) |
| End of therapy | 3 (8.6) | 32 (91.4) | 6[a] (16.2) | 31 (83.8) | 9 (12.5) | 63 (87.5) |
| Follow-up | 0 (0.0) | 35 (100.0) | 4[a] (10.8) | 33 (89.2) | 4 (5.6) | 68 (94.4) |

*Note:* Percentages in brackets.
[a] Including imputed data for 4 "lost to follow-up" cases

ily therapy group, the proportion with a diagnosis of MDD had dropped from 34 (91.9%) at baseline to 8 (21.6%) at the end of therapy and 7 (18.9%) at the follow-up contact.

The reduction in prevalence of MDD over the three time points in the individual therapy group was statistically significant [$\chi^2(2) = 71.595$, $p < .001$]. Further 2 × 2 chi-squares were performed to confirm between which time-points the significant changes had occurred. It was found that there was a statistically significant change in prevalence of MDD from baseline to end of therapy [$\chi^2(1) = 38.914$; $p < .001$], from baseline to follow-up [$\chi^2(1) = 58.947$; $p < .001$], but not from end of therapy to follow-up.

The change in prevalence of MDD over the three time points in the family therapy group was also statistically significant

[$\chi^2(2) = 51.371$; $p < .001$]. The 2 × 2 chi-squares performed as above found that there was a statistically significant change in prevalence of MDD from baseline to end of therapy [$\chi^2(1) = 37.220$; $p < .001$], from baseline to follow-up [$\chi^2(1) = 39.871$; $p < .001$], but not from end of therapy to follow-up.

The prevalence of MDD in the individual therapy group compared to the family therapy group at end of therapy was not statistically significant. The prevalence of MDD in the individual therapy group compared to the family therapy group at follow-up was statistically significant [$\chi^2(1) = 7.335$; $p < .01$]. However, this difference resulted from the inclusion of the 4 "lost to follow-up" cases in the family therapy group (there were no "lost to follow-up" cases in the individual therapy group). When the "lost to follow-up" cases were excluded, the prevalence of MDD in the individual therapy group compared to the family therapy group at follow-up was not statistically significant.

*Prevalence of Dysthymia before and after therapy based on the Kiddie-SADS*

At the start of therapy more than 50% of the participants were diagnosed as having Dysthymia (see Table 12.2). By the end of therapy only 6 (17.1%) still gained a diagnosis of Dysthymia in the individual therapy group and by follow-up none received this diagnosis. In the family therapy group, the proportion with a diagnosis of Dysthymia had dropped from 20 (54.1%) at baseline to 7 (18.9%) at the end of therapy and 4 (10.8%) at the follow-up contact.

As shown in Table 12.2, the change in prevalence of Dysthymia over the three time points in the individual therapy group was statistically significant [$\chi^2(2) = 32.308$; $p < .001$]. Further 2 × 2 chi-squares were performed to confirm between which time-points the significant changes had occurred. It was found that there was a statistically significant change in prevalence of Dysthymia from baseline to end of therapy [$\chi^2(1) = 11.993$; $p < .005$], from baseline to follow-up [$\chi^2(1) = 28.00$; $p < .001$], but not from end of therapy to follow-up .

The change in prevalence of Dysthymia over the three time

points in the family therapy group was also statistically significant [$\chi^2(2) = 19.425$; $p < .001$]. The 2 × 2 chi-squares performed as above found that there was a statistically significant change in prevalence of Dysthymia from baseline to end of therapy [$\chi^2(1) = 9.855$; $p < .005$], from baseline to follow-up [$\chi^2(1) = 15.787$; $p < .001$], but not from end of therapy to follow-up.

The prevalence of Dysthymia in the individual therapy group compared to the family therapy group at end of therapy was not statistically significant. This was also the case at follow-up.

*Prevalence of "double depression" (MDD and Dysthymia) before and after therapy based on the Kiddie-SADS*

At the start of therapy 48.6% in the individual therapy group and 45.9% in the family therapy group were diagnosed as having double depression (see Table 12.2). By the end of therapy only 3 (8.6%) still gained a diagnosis of double depression in the individual therapy group and by follow-up none received this diagnosis. In the family therapy group, the proportion with a diagnosis of double depression had dropped from 17 (45.9%) at baseline to 6 (16.2%) at the end of therapy and 4 (10.8%) at the follow-up contact.

As shown in Table 12.2, the change in prevalence of double depression over the three time points in the individual therapy group was statistically significant [$\chi^2(2) = 30.512$; $p < .001$]. Further 2 × 2 chi-squares were performed to confirm between which time-points the significant changes had occurred. It was found that there was a statistically significant change in prevalence of double depression from baseline to end of therapy [$\chi^2(1) = 13.720$; $p < .001$], from baseline to follow-up [$\chi^2(1) = 22.453$; $p < .001$], but not from end of therapy to follow-up .

The change in prevalence of double depression over the three time points in the family therapy group was also statistically significant [$\chi^2(2) = 14.389$; $p = .001$]. The 2 × 2 chi-squares performed as above found that there was a statistically significant change in prevalence of double depression from baseline to end of therapy [$\chi^2(1) = 7.633$; $p < .01$], from baseline to follow-up [$\chi^2(1) = 11.236$; $p < .005$], but not from end of therapy to follow-up .

The prevalence of double depression in the individual therapy group compared to the family therapy group at end of therapy was not statistically significant, and this remained the case at follow-up.

## *Additional measures of depression*

### *Childhood Depression Inventory (CDI)*

There was a significant difference in the mean CDI scores for both therapy groups at the different time-points, with the scores going down for both types of therapy (see Table 12.3; $p < .001$, power >99%). There was no significant difference between the individual therapy and family therapy groups by follow-up. There was a slightly significant difference between the two therapy groups over time ($p < .05$, power <80%).

In the individual therapy group, the mean drop in CDI score from baseline to end of therapy was 7.77, with a further drop of 5.49 from end of therapy to follow-up (total drop = 13.26). In the

**Table 12.3: Mean scores for depression based on the Childhood Depression Inventory (CDI) and the Moods and Feelings Questionnaire (MFQ), and Mean scores for the global functioning based on the C-GAS, at three time points by therapy type**

| | *Individual therapy* | | | *Family therapy* | | |
|---|---|---|---|---|---|---|
| | *Mean* | *SD* | *N* | *Mean* | *SD* | *N* |
| CDI | | | | | | |
| Baseline | 23.00 | 7.56 | 35 | 23.84 | 7.07 | 37 |
| End of therapy | 15.23 | 9.47 | 35 | 10.76 | 7.72 | 37 |
| Follow-up | cc | 6.15 | 35 | 9.08 | 7.82 | 37 |
| | 9.74 | | | | | |
| MFQ | | | | | | |
| Baseline | 14.09 | 6.27 | 35 | 16.06 | 6.20 | 37 |
| End of therapy | 7.88 | 6.87 | 35 | 6.11 | 5.05 | 37 |
| Follow-up | 5.54 | 4.74 | 35 | 4.92 | 4.70 | 37 |
| C-GAS | | | | | | |
| Baseline | 49.03 | 9.21 | 35 | 47.41 | 6.33 | 37 |
| End of therapy | 65.16 | 10.57 | 35 | 64.46 | 9.31 | 37 |
| Follow-up | 69.00 | 7.02 | 35 | 66.49 | 9.31 | 37 |

family therapy group, the mean drop in CDI score from baseline to end of therapy was 13.08, but with only a further mean drop of 1.18 from end of therapy to follow-up (total drop = 14.26).

Secondary analysis using ML-WIN confirmed the above findings.

### *Moods and Feelings Questionnaire*

There was a significant difference in the mean MFQ scores for both therapy groups at the different time-points, with the scores going down for both types of therapy (see Table 12.3; $p < .001$, power >99%). There was a slightly significant difference between the individual therapy and family therapy groups by follow-up ($p < .05$) but at low power (52%). There was also a slightly significant difference between the two therapy groups over time ($p < .05$).

In the individual therapy group, the mean drop in MFQ score from baseline to end of therapy was 6.21, with a further drop of 2.34 from end of therapy to follow-up (total drop = 8.55). In the family therapy group, the mean drop in MFQ score from baseline to end of therapy was 9.95, but with only a further mean drop of 1.19 from end of therapy to follow-up (total drop = 11.14).

## *Measure of impairment/level of functioning: Children's Global Assessment Scale*

There was a significant difference in the mean C-GAS scores for both therapy groups at the different time-points, with the scores increasing for both types of therapy (see Table 12.3; $p < .001$, power >99%). There was no significant difference between the individual therapy and family therapy groups by follow-up. There was also no significant difference between the two therapy groups over time, specifically at end of therapy.

In the individual therapy group, the mean rise in C-GAS score from baseline to end of therapy was 16.13, with a further rise of 3.84 from end of therapy to follow-up (total rise = 19.97). In the family therapy group, the mean rise in C-GAS score from baseline

**Table 12.4 Cases with one or more co-morbid conditions at three time points, by therapy type, based on the Kiddie-SADS**

| | *Individual therapy N = 35 (%)* | | *Family therapy N = 37 (%)* | | *Total N = 72 (%)* | |
|---|---|---|---|---|---|---|
| | *Double depression* | *No double depression* | *Double depression* | *No double depression* | *Double depression* | *No double depression* |
| Baseline | 29 (82.9) | 6 (17.1) | 29 (78.4) | 8 (21.6) | 58 (80.6) | 14 (19.4) |
| End of therapy | 16 (45.7) | 19 (54.3) | 19[a] (51.4) | 18 (48.6) | 35 (48.6) | 37 (51.4) |
| Follow up | 11 (31.4) | 24 (68.6) | 19[a] (51.4) | 18 (48.6) | 30 (41.7) | 42 (58.3) |

[a] Including imputed data for 4 "lost to follow-up" cases.

to end of therapy was 17.05, with a further rise of 2.03 from end of therapy to follow-up (total rise = 19.08).

Secondary analysis using ML-WIN confirmed the above findings.

### *Co-morbidity*

The presence of co-morbid conditions was assessed using the Kiddie-SADS (based on *DSM–IV* criteria).

The change in prevalence of cases with co-morbidity over the three time points in the individual therapy group, as depicted in Table 12.4, was statistically significant [$\chi^2(2)$ =19.821; $p < .001$]. The change in prevalence of cases with co-morbidity over the three time points in the family therapy group was not statistically significant, because of the absence of any decrease from end of therapy to follow-up. The prevalence of cases with co-morbidity in the individual therapy group compared to the family therapy group at each of the three time points, however, was not statistically significant.

## *Discussion*

In this study the following was found:

In the individual therapy group, 74.3% of cases were no longer clinically depressed following therapy, and 100% of cases were no longer clinically depressed six months later. Individual therapy appears to have been effective in cases of MDD, Dysthymia, and "double depression". This effectiveness appears to have been persistent, with no relapses six months following therapy. In addition, all remaining cases of depression (MDD, Dysthymia, and "double depression") had resolved at the follow-up point. This suggests an ongoing response to therapy following completion—the sleeper effect.

In the family therapy group, 75.7% of cases were no longer clinically depressed following therapy, and 81% of cases were no longer clinically depressed six months later. Family therapy also appears to have been effective in cases of MDD, Dysthymia, and "double depression". This effectiveness appears to have been persistent, with no relapses six months following therapy. In addition, further improvement in some of the remaining cases of depression (MDD, Dysthymia, and "double depression") was found at the follow-up point, particularly in cases of Dysthymia and "double depression".

Response rates for depression in the individual therapy and family therapy groups were not significantly different by end of therapy. While response rates appear to have been approximately 20% greater in the individual therapy group, compared to the family therapy group, at follow-up, this is very largely influenced by the inclusion of the 4 "lost to follow-up" cases in the family therapy group, who were considered as unsuccessfully treated cases following therapy. Without these 4 cases, the differences in response rates between the two groups are not statistically significant.

In addition to improvement as measured by cases no longer meeting diagnostic criteria for MDD or Dysthymia, similar improvement was found in both treatment groups in terms of level of impairment and level of functioning.

While the final outcome appears to have been similar in the two groups in many respects, the results from the CDI and MFQ suggest a different pattern of response or improvement. With regard to the MFQ, the family therapy group had a lower score at end of therapy, despite having had a higher score than the individual therapy group at baseline. While the power of this test was low (<80%), it does reflect the slightly different "path" for each of the therapy groups.

The family therapy group appears to have made greater improvement, in some respects, by end of therapy, compared to the individual therapy group. These differences, though, had disappeared by follow-up.

By follow-up, many of the family therapy trajectories appear to have plateaued, while the individual therapy group trajectories suggest the possibility of further, and possibly more rapid, improvement to follow.

The population groups in the three countries appear to have responded similarly to the treatment. Although not presented here, virtually no significant differences were found when similar analysis was done comparing the three treatment centres (London, Athens, Helsinki) in terms of response rates and patterns.

A significant number of cases in both therapy groups had co-morbid conditions. Almost a third of cases in the study had three or more co-morbid conditions. Following therapy, there was a decrease in co-morbid conditions, particularly anxiety disorders and conduct disorders, which are often associated with depressive disorders. This occurred in both therapy groups.

The results of this study suggest both individual therapy (response rate 74% by end of therapy) and family therapy (response rate 75% by end of therapy) may be more effective in the treatment of depression than are other forms of treatment. Previous studies have found a response rate in the region of 60% to CBT (Brent et al., 1997), 52–56% to fluoxetine (Emslie et al., 1997, 2000), and 71% to CBT and fluoxetine combined (March et al., 2004). An NNT[1] analysis was undertaken using the end of therapy results in this study. Using the placebo data in the TADS study as a comparator, the NNT for both individual therapy and family therapy is 3. This compares favourably with the NNTs reported in the TADS study, where the NNT for fluoxetine and CBT combined was 3, fluoxetine was 4 and CBT was 12. In the absence of a control group in our study, an NNT analysis was also conducted using the nondirective supportive therapy (NST) group from the Brent et al. (1997) study as an alternative comparator. The NNT for both individual therapy and family therapy was 6. It is important to note that in both the individual and the family therapy groups, further improvement was reported at follow-up. We would therefore expect to find lower NNTs at the follow-up point, were comparable data available.

The chronicity and severity of the depression in our study led us to believe that spontaneous remission was unlikely to have occurred in the vast majority of cases, particularly in light of the extent of co-existing dysthymia. Furthermore, the TADS study demonstrated a response rate of only 35% to placebo. The Brent/ Birmaher study (Birmaher et al., 2000; Brent et al., 1997) found that CBT did not confer any long-term advantage over family therapy or supportive therapy with regard to rates of remission, recovery, recurrence, or level of functioning. In that study, the median onset of recurrence was four months after recovery, whereas in this study, there had been no recurrences, with ongoing improvement six months post-psychotherapy. Further research will explore which components of the therapy were significant.

## *Conclusions*

Analysis has shown that both focused individual psychodynamic psychotherapy (with parent support work) and systems integrative family therapy were both effective in treating moderate to severe depression in children and young adolescents in three countries.

This includes cases of dysthymia and "double depression", which are generally considered to be more difficult to treat. There has also been an overall reduction in co-morbid conditions across the study.

### *Clinical implications*

1. This study provides evidence supporting the use of both individual psychodynamic therapy and family therapy in this age group.
2. It may be possible for trained therapists, with the help of the Manuals, to deliver effectively these focused forms of therapy.
3. Both treatments also appear to be exportable to wider settings in culturally diverse populations.

### *Limitations*

1. The study is limited by the sample size, which was influenced by recruitment difficulties. This becomes even more significant when comparing smaller sub-groups—e.g., countries and therapy groups within countries.
2. The effect of the 4 "lost to follow-up" cases is also significant, especially in relation to the total sample size, and more so because all of them were in the family therapy group. Intention to treat analysis principles were used in order not to lessen the power of the study or over-rate the effect of the treatments.
3. The absence of an "untreated" control group limits the study's ability to prove with certainty the efficacy of the therapies provided.

### *Further research*

Further analysis will be looking at whether differential predictors of response can be identified in the two therapy groups, and whether there are any significant differences across the three different cultural settings. Data from additional instruments about the child, his or her parents and family, and his or her environment will provide further insight into the current findings. It will also be important to establish whether any specific components of the respective forms of therapy were likely to have contributed to the patients' responses. Further studies should take measures to counteract the limitations as discussed above. Other factors to consider would include gender distribution and family mental health history, as well as user preference for therapy type.

## *Note*

1. NNT (Number Needed to Treat) is an epidemiological measure used in assessing the effectiveness of a health care intervention. It describes the difference between a treatment and a control in achieving a particular outcome.

CHAPTER THIRTEEN

# Psychodynamic and family psychotherapy for young people with major depression: preliminary findings on their psychosocial adjustment

*Gerasimos Kolaitis, Valeria Pomini, Vlasis Tomaras, Olga Maratos, Effie Layiou-Lignos, & John Tsiantis*

Child and adolescent depression is generally a common, recurrent, chronic, and debilitating disorder as it is associated with short-term and long-term functional impairment, morbidity, and mortality. Several case reports and open studies have suggested the efficacy of some psychosocial interventions in depressed young people, but very few controlled psychotherapeutic ones have been published (Michael & Crowley, 2002), while studies on the long-term treatment and management of young people with depression do not exist (Ryan, 2003).

In most of the studies, the main focus of outcome is depression, while other areas such as social impairment have been neglected, despite the existing evidence of a strong relation between depression and problems in these domains (Harrington, Whittaker, & Shoebridge, 1998). It is important, therefore, to examine systematically the psychosocial variables in studies of the etiology, course, and treatment of depressed young people (Puig-Antich et al., 1993). Hammen, Rudolph, Weisz, Rao, and Burge (1999) in their review of the empirical, methodological, and conceptual limitations of treatment for young people's depression have pointed out the relative neglect of assessment of youngsters' functional status compared to depressive symptomatology. They have concluded that all outcome studies should evaluate treatment effects for depressed children in areas such as academic, family, and social dysfunction that might contribute to future depression, as well as the impact of therapy on co-morbid conditions that contribute to poorer outcomes.

The association of depression in childhood with school and with peer difficulties had been described by Puig-Antich et al. (1985) and compared with normal controls. They have shown that depressed children and adolescents presented functional impairments in most aspects of their psychosocial behaviour.

Difficulties with peers were assessed both in depressed and non-depressed adolescents in the Newcastle Childhood Depression Project. However, the depressed group were more likely to absent themselves from school (Berney et al., 1991). Also, the findings of this study have underlined a more specific link between depression and school phobia. Furthermore, it was found that there is an association of a higher incidence of accidents with maladjustment that may reflect greater psychosocial stress in the depressed group as well as the relatively higher occurrence of conduct disorder (Berney et al., 1991; Kolvin et al., 1991).

Lewinsohn, Clarke, Seeley, and Rohde (1994) assessed the functional impairment in three social areas (with peer, with family, and in school) in a school population study in a randomly selected sample of 1,508 14- to 18-year-old adolescents with major depressive disorder (MDD). Of the adolescents with MDD, 13.3% presented no impairment, 30.7% presented impairment in one area of functioning, 37.0% in two areas of functioning, and 19.1% presented impairment in all of the three areas of functioning.

Cognitive behavioural therapies are the most frequently studied ones in treating depression, and they have been proved effective for depressed adolescents (Lewinsohn & Clarke, 1999). However, there are some studies showing that psychodynamic psychotherapy (PP) and interpersonal psychotherapy (IPT), having been modified for adolescents, have been promising for decreasing symptomatology as well as for increasing functionality in depressed young people (Mufson et al., 1994; Santor & Kusumakar, 2001; Trowell, Kolvin, et al., 2002).

Rossello and Bernal (1999) in their study found that IPT and CBT were efficacious treatments for depressed Puerto-Rican adolescents; IPT, in particular, was superior in the non-treatment group for increasing self-esteem and social adaptation. Muratori et al. (2003) have recently shown that PP is effective for treating internalizing disorders in routine outpatient care; the benefits of such treatment were manifested immediately and with delayed onset (sleeper effect).

Brent et al. (1997), even though they found CBT to have superior efficacy to systemic behaviour family therapy (SBFT) and nondirective supportive therapy (NST) for relief of depressive symptoms, found no treatment differences in the improvement of functional status, with all three treatments improving only to a modest degree on the C-GAS. This might be because relief of functional impairment lags behind relief of depressive symptoms, since psychosocial "scars" (evident characteristics after but not before the depressive episode, such as stressful major life events and excessive emotional reliance on others) of a depressive episode remain (Rohde et al., 1994). Alternatively, it might be because these adolescents have other problems, including nondepressive co-morbidity, that require additional or different interventions (Brent et al., 1997).

In the TADS study (Vitiello et al., 2006) the combination of fluoxetine with CBT was effective in improving functioning, global health, and quality of life in depressed adolescents. Fluoxetine monotherapy improved functioning. Kennard et al. (2008) compared antidepressant medication management (MM) and MM plus relapse-prevention CBT for six months in 11- to 18-year-old adolescents and found that the continuation-phase CBT reduces the risk for relapse by eightfold compared with MM. In addition, the two modes were equally effective in overall global functioning.

The main objective of this study was to examine the psychosocial outcome following the application of two psychotherapies—that is, individual psychodynamic and systemic family therapy—in a sample of children and adolescents with major depression. It was important to observe whether the decrease in depressive symptoms in the two samples following therapy (Trowell et al., 2007—see chapter 12, this volume; see also Tsiantis et al., 2005) was also accompanied by an increase in functional status in the areas of family, peers, leisure, and school. However, we report here only on the findings from the social functioning/adjustment evaluation.

## Methods

### The population

A randomized control trial was conducted in London (Tavistock Clinic), Athens (Aghia Sophia Children's Hospital), and Helsinki (Children's Hospital), with 72 patients aged 9–15 with depression who were allocated to either individual psychodynamic psychotherapy or family therapy. The detailed methodology of the trial has previously been described (Trowell et al, 2007—see chapter 12, this volume; see also Tsiantis et al., 2005). All patients' and parents' assessments were performed in both treatment conditions prior to treatment ("baseline"), at the end of therapy ("end of therapy"), and again six months later ("follow-up).

### The instrument

*The Social Adjustment Scale–Self-Report* (Weissman & Bothwell, 1976) includes a semi-structured interview, which measures social functioning, used to assess the social adjustment of children and adolescents. This is a reliable and widely used instrument that assesses six major areas of social functioning: work role (employment, housework, student work), social and leisure activities, relationships with extended family, role as a partner in primary relationship, parental role, and role within the family unit. There are 54 questions in total, each scored on a 5-point scale, with higher scores indicating poorer functioning.

### Statistical analysis

The paired comparisons Student's *t* test was used to evaluate any possible differences among baseline, end of therapy, and follow-up measurements for the scale variables. A repeated measures ANOVA was further used to evaluate the differences between the two groups (individual vs family therapy group) regarding the changes observed in the subscales during the follow-up period.

### *Results*

The mean scores reduction for all social adjustment subscales between baseline and end of therapy and between baseline and follow-up were statistically significant for individual and family therapy group ($p \leq .001$ in all comparisons). Also for the individual therapy group only, there was a significant score reduction on social leisure between end of therapy and follow-up ($p = .016$). The overall pattern for the social adjustment subscales during the three time periods was not different between the two therapy groups ($p > .05$).

## *Conclusion*

In Trowell et al. (2007; see also chapter 12, this volume), we presented the efficacy for two types of psychotherapy for decreasing depression while increasing the global functioning measured by the C-GAS . The results here demonstrate a significant improvement in social functioning at the end of treatment and at follow-up for both psychodynamic and family psychotherapy. The results of the global psychosocial outcome will be reported in an upcoming publication that will include findings on self-esteem, social functioning, parent and peer attachment, as well as the teachers' reports of children's school performance. Based on the experience of this trial, both types of psychotherapy seem to be effective and promising for depressed children and adolescents 10–14 years of age.

CHAPTER FOURTEEN

# Depressed children and young people: treatment outcome and changes in family functioning in individual and family therapy

*Finn Ferdinand Garoff, Kati Heinonen, Anu-Katriina Pesonen, & Fredrik Almqvist*

Emotional disorders cause young people and their families considerable distress. If left untreated, these disorders entail high social and personal costs that extend into adulthood (Lewinsohn, Rohde, Seeley, Klein, & Gotlib, 2003). Therefore, identifying efficient and effective treatments is a concern for scientists, practitioners, and policy-makers.

Fonagy, Target, Cottrell, and Phillips (2002) reported that 40–50% of depressed children and adolescents do not respond to medical or psychosocial treatments. Moreover, a recent meta-analysis of randomized controlled trials (RCT) reported only a moderate effect size of 0.34 for psychotherapy in child and adolescent depression (Weisz & McCarty, 2006). The treatment gains were maintained at 6-month follow-up, but not at 1-year follow-up. Therefore, pressure exists to develop more effective treatments and to better understand the mechanisms leading to positive treatment results.

As summarized by Carr (2007), research on the etiology of depression is converging in support of a diathesis-stress model. In this model, genetic factors render children and adolescents vulnerable to depression, and when this interacts with environmental factors, mood disorders can result. As pointed out by Lau, Rijsdijk,

Gregory, McGuffin, and Eley (2007), most life events and chronic stressors associated with childhood depression are embedded in the family context. Family environments with parental psychopathology, conflict, stressful divorce, domestic violence, and child maltreatment are significant sources of environmental stress, as are more subtle elements such as lack of parental attunement and expressions of affect and support (Shortt & Spence, 2006). These factors may also affect child development adversely, resulting in an inadequate capacity for emotional regulation, increased self-criticism, a lower sense of control over one's life, pessimistic cognitive style, insecure attachment representations, and insufficient social networks.

Hughes and Gullone (2008) defined family functioning as a family's ability to deal with everyday life and cope effectively with problems and changes. Families with a member who has major depression or other internalizing symptoms tend to experience more problems with family functioning. Asarnow, Jaycox, and Thompson (2001) have presented evidence of a bidirectional model in which parental depression and criticism, dysfunctional family interactional patterns, and family stress contribute to childhood depression, which in turn increases family stress and dysfunction.

Indeed, impaired family functioning in connection with a depressed family member is associated with a longer recovery time, a decreased treatment response, and an increased risk of relapse (Beavers & Hampson, 2000; Carr, 2000; Diamond, Reis, Diamond, Siqueland, & Isaacs, 2002; Hughes & Gullone, 2008). This lends support to the inclusion of families in the treatment process of youth depression. It has been suggested that family-based systemic interventions are likely to decrease family stress and promote social support within the context of the family (Carr, 2009). Family treatments may also decrease the risk of depressive episodes in other family members and improve family functioning as well as coping skills (Asarnow, Jaycox, & Thompson, 2001). Thus family therapy can be effective in treating and preventing depression among young people; it can also enhance family cohesion, adaptability, and resilience (Larner, 2009). However, given that the family environment plays an important role in childhood depression, relatively little is known about the role of family functioning in therapeutic interventions with depressed young people. This present study addresses this issue.

The research questions were as follows:

1. Does individual and family therapy affect family functioning differently?
2. Are the baseline levels of, or the improvement in, family functioning associated with decreases in depressive symptoms in individual and family therapy?

### *Time-limited systems integrative family therapy*

Time-limited systems integrative family therapy (SIFT) was developed within the systemic perspective of family therapy. The intervention was standardized by compiling a Manual that would allow for the differences between the schools of family therapy in use at the three clinical settings (Athens, Helsinki, London) participating in the Childhood Depression Project (Byng-Hall, Campbell, & Papadopoulos, 1996), the demographic characteristics of which are presented in Tables 14.1 and 14.2. Time-limited SIFT was conducted every two or three weeks by a pair of family therapists, for a maximum of 14 sessions. Each session was 90 minutes in length. After the first session, the parents were invited to participate. One out of three sessions was conducted with the parents only. Occasionally other family members participated in the sessions. In the work with the parents, the focus was co-parenting, rather than marital issues. The families participated in 8 to 14 sessions. The referral, screening, randomization, and assessment processes are presented in Figure 14.1

## *Family functioning*

The Family Assessment Device (FAD; Epstein, Baldwin, & Bishop, 1983) is a 60-item self-report questionnaire that has six subscales corresponding to the dimensions of the McMaster Model of Fam-

**Table 14.1 The demographic characteristics of the sample by clinical setting: the children**

| | *Athens* | *Helsinki* | *London* | *Total* | *Significant statistics* *F* | *p* |
|---|---|---|---|---|---|---|
| Age in years: mean (SD) | 12.2 (1.1) | 10.8 (1.2) | 12.1 (1.5) | 11.7 (1.5) | (2, 68) = 7.93 | .001 |
| Gender | | | | | | |
| Girls: *N* (%) | 10 (42) | 8 (33) | 9 (38) | 27 (38) | | |
| Boys: *N* (%) | 14 (58) | 16 (67) | 15 (62) | 45 (62) | | |

ily Functioning: problem solving, communication, roles, affective responsiveness, affective involvement, and behaviour control. In addition, the General Functioning scale assesses the overall level of family functioning. The FAD is scored by summing the responses (scored 1 to 4) for each subscale and dividing the sum by the number of items on each scale. The subscale scores thus range from 1 (best functioning) to 4 (worst functioning). The General

**Table 14.2 The demographic characteristics of the sample by clinical setting: the families**

| | *Athens* *N (%)* | *Helsinki* *N (%)* | *London* *N (%)* | *Total* *N (%)* | *Significant statistics* $\chi^2$ | *p* |
|---|---|---|---|---|---|---|
| Depressive ever: mother, biological | | | | | | |
| No | 17 (74) | 18 (82) | 21 (87) | 56 (81) | | |
| Yes | 6 (26) | 4 (18) | 3 (13) | 13 (19) | | |
| Family constellation | | | | | | |
| Single/widowed/ divorced | 8 (35) | 4 (17) | 13 (54) | 25 (36) | (2, *n* = 70) = 6.93 | .03 |
| Married/living with partner | 15 (65) | 19 (83) | 11 (46) | 45 (64) | | |
| Mother's educational attainment | | | | | | |
| School exams "lower" | 16 (70) | 13 (54) | 5 (22) | 34 (49) | (2, *n* = 70) = 11.0 | .004 |
| University studies or further qualification | 7 (30) | 11 (46) | 18 (78) | 36 (51) | | |

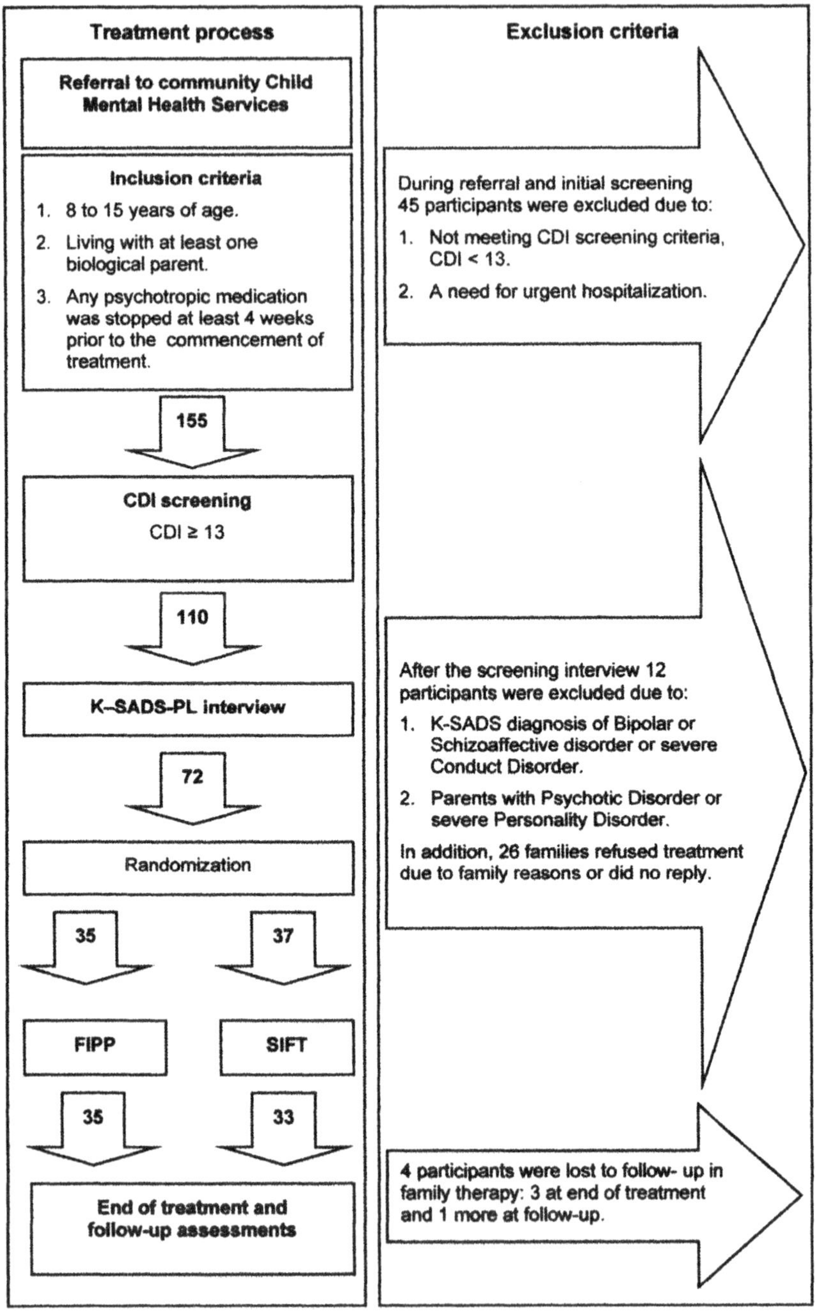


*Figure 14.1* The referral, screening, randomization, and assessment processes.

Functioning scale has been found to summarize family functioning well (Ridenour, Daley, & Reich, 2000) and has been designed to be multidimensional and to correlate to the other FAD scales (Miller, Ryan, Keitner, Bishop, & Epstein, 2000b). The FAD has shown reliability and predictive validity for several clinically relevant outcomes, and it can differentiate between clinical and non-clinical families (Kabacoff, Miller, Bishop, Epstein, & Keitner, 1990; Miller, Ryan, Keitner, Bishop, & Epstein, 2000a). In the present study, the FAD has been completed by participating mothers at baseline, end of treatment, and follow-up. The Cronbach alpha coefficient for the FAD was .76.

The Beavers Interactional Scales (BIS; Beavers, & Hampson, 1990) are based on the Beavers–Timberlawn family model. They consist of two observer-rated questionnaires for trained raters. The Beavers Interactional Competence Scale (BICS) is related to family structure and functioning, informational flows in the family, and the flexibility of the family system. It represents the overall level of health and competence of the family system. The subscales are summarized with scores ranging from 1 (optimal family functioning) to 10 (severely dysfunctional family functioning). The BICS has demonstrated high interrater reliability and high internal consistency across the subscales, as well as high discriminant and construct validity (Beavers & Hampson, 1990; Drumm, Carr, & Fitzgerald, 2000). The second scale, the Beavers Interactional Style Scale (BISS), indicates typical ways for the family to interact and relate that are not directly connected to the competence of the family system. The subscales are summarized with scores ranging from 1.0 (centripetal families, where family members strive to have their needs met exclusively within the family context) to 5.0 (centrifugal families, where members strive to have their needs met exclusively outside the family context). The BISS has shown high interrater reliability and internal consistency across the subscales (Beavers & Hampson, 1990), but in one study the scale showed only limited descriptive and discriminative power (Drumm, Carr, & Fitzgerald, 2000). In the present study, the BIS data is limited to the data collected from the 37 families in family therapy. The video recordings of the fourth (regarded as baseline assessment for the purposes of this study) and the last family therapy sessions (regarded as end-of-treatment assessment for the purposes of this study) were reviewed by the local team of family therapists who then rated the family interactions on the BIS scales. The Cronbach alpha coefficient for the BICS was .86 and for the BISS was .68.

## *The effects of treatment on family functioning, as assessed by the mothers*

The decrease in mean FAD General Functioning scores was relatively small: 2.2 ($SD$ = 0.5) at baseline to 2.0 ($SD$ = 0.4) at follow-up. A repeated measures ANOVA showed that the decrease on the FAD General Functioning scale across the different time-points was significant [$F(1.95, 130) = 3.53$, $p = .03$, partial $\eta^2 = .05$]. The changes in family functioning appeared during the treatment and were sustained, as indicated by within-subjects contrasts (from baseline to end of treatment $p = .02$; from end of treatment to follow-up $p = .14$). Significant interactions were found with gender [$F(1.95, 130) = 4.48$, $p = .01$, partial $\eta^2 = .06$] and clinical severity [$F(1.95, 130) = 4.51$, $p = .01$, partial $\eta^2 = .07$]. The FAD scores at baseline were lower for girls than for boys (girls: $M = 2.1$, $SD = .44$; boys: $M = 2.2$, $SD = .52$); by follow-up, FAD scores were lower for boys than for girls (boys: $M = 2.0$, $SD = .40$; girls: $M = 2.1$, $SD = .41$). The double-depression (DD) group had significantly higher FAD scores at baseline than did the no-DD group (DD: $M = 2.3$, $SD = .55$; no-DD: $M = 2.1$, $SD = .42$); by follow-up, the FAD scores of the DD group were on the same level as the scores of the no-DD group (DD: $M = 2.0$, $SD = .44$; no-DD: $M = 2.0$, $SD = .36$). The treatment group did not show significant within-subjects ($p = .98$) or between-subjects ($p$ =. 23) effects.

## *The effects of treatment on family functioning, as assessed by the family therapists*

The mean BICS scores decreased from 6.3 ($SD$ = 1.5) at first assessment to 5.3 ($SD$ = 1.5) at end of treatment. The repeated measures ANOVA showed that the improvement in BICS scores from first assessment to end of treatment was significant [$F(1, 31) = 7.56$, $p =$

.01, partial $\eta^2 = .20$]. Furthermore, participant age interacted significantly with time [$F(1, 31) = 4.94$, $p = .04$, partial $\eta^2 = .14$]; families with younger children experienced a significantly greater improvement in BICS during family therapy. No significant between-subjects effects for age ($p = .40$), gender ($p = .50$), or clinical severity ($p = .70$) were found. The mean BISS scores changed very little from 2.9 ($SD = .9$) at baseline to 2.8 ($SD = 1.0$) at end of treatment. This difference was not significant [$F(1, 31) = .605$, $p = .44$, partial $\eta^2 = .02$].

### *Family functioning as a predictor of change in youths' depressive symptoms: analyses with continuous scores of family functioning*

Linear regression analysis with baseline FAD General Functioning as independent variable and total CDI score change from baseline to follow-up as dependent variable showed that higher baseline family functioning influenced CDI score change positively ($\beta = .24$, $p = .04$, $R^2 = .06$). A similar analysis of BICS baseline scores showed a similar trend, although it was not statistically significant ($\beta = .27$, $p = .10$, $R^2 = .07$). Linear regression analysis with FAD General Functioning change from baseline to follow-up as independent variable and total CDI score change from baseline to follow-up as dependent variable was not significant ($\beta = .13$, $p = .30$, $R^2 = .02$), nor was the analysis using the change in BICS score as independent variable ($\beta = -.05$, $p = .8$, $R^2 = .003$).

### *Family functioning as a predictor of change in youths' depressive symptoms: analyses with binary family functioning improvement scores*

Table 14.3 summarizes the mean total CDI scores and standard deviations, at the different time points, in families that experienced improvement in family functioning during treatment and in those that did not, separately for the FAD and BICS improvement indexes.

**Table 14.3 Mean CDI total scores and SD, at different time points, for families with improved and not-improved family functioning during treatment.**

| | *CDI scores at:* | | |
|---|---|---|---|
| | *Baseline* *Mean (SD)* | *End of treatment* *Mean (SD)* | *Follow-up* *Mean (SD)* |
| FAD General Functioning improvement index (both treatment groups combined) | | | |
| No improvement (*n* = 30) | 24.3 (8.7) | 14.6 (10.3) | 12.0 (8.4) |
| Improvement (*n* = 42) | 22.8 (6.2) | 11.7 (7.6) | 7.57 (5.2) |
| BICS improvement index (only family therapy) | | | |
| No improvement (*n* = 13) | 24.5 (7.6) | 16.0 (9.7) | 13.8 (10.6) |
| Improvement (*n* = 24) | 23.5 (6.9) | 7.9 (4.5) | 6.5 (4.2) |

Repeated measures ANOVA analyses with the CDI score as within-subjects factor and the FAD improvement index as between-subjects factor showed no statistically significant effects. Within-subjects effects for the interaction between time and the BICS improvement index was significant [$F(1.85, 64) = 5.24$, $p = .01$, partial $\eta^2 = .14$]. Within-subjects contrasts indicated that this effect was related primarily to the changes in CDI scores from baseline to end of treatment [$F(1, 32) = 7.53$, $p = .01$, partial $\eta^2 = .19$ for the BICS index interaction effect]. The BICS improvement index was also a significant between-subjects factor [$F(1, 32) = 10.7$, $p = .003$, partial $\eta^2 = .25$]. Figure 14.2 illustrates the change in total CDI scores in family therapy for the two groups.

## *Discussion*

This study concludes that both forms of therapy—FIPP and time-limited SIFT—improved family functioning significantly, as indicated by maternal FAD General Functioning reports and family therapists' BICS assessments. There was no difference between the treatments in this regard. Families with depressed boys showed

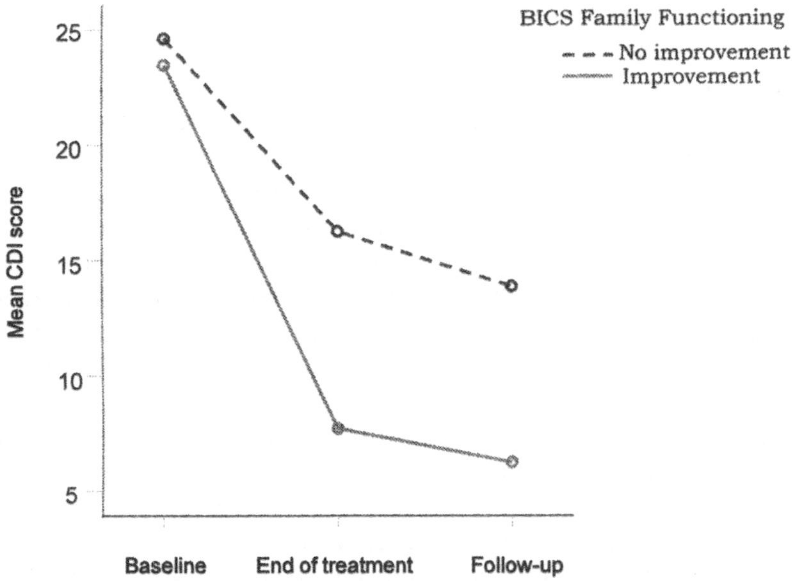


*Figure 14.2.* The estimated marginal mean CDI scores at different time points in family therapy, with separate lines for those with improved and not-improved family functioning according to family therapists' BICS assessments.

greater improvement in FAD scores, and families with younger children showed a greater improvement of family functioning on the BICS. However, the BISS of the family did not change during family therapy.

As has been reported previously (Trowell et al., 2007), both treatments were effective in decreasing self-reported symptoms of depression in children. However, the paths to improvement appeared to differ somewhat in the two treatment groups. Compared to the individual therapy group, the mean CDI scores were significantly lower in the family therapy group at end of treatment, but this difference disappeared by the follow-up. The faster treatment response in family therapy seems to be at odds with the study by Kolko, Brent, Baugher, Bridge, and Birmaher (2000) that suggested that family therapy may require a longer period of time to permit changes to take place in complex family interaction patterns and the treatment effect to be evident. In the present study, the faster treatment response in family therapy was related to the absence of double depression at baseline, since the CDI scores improved faster in family therapy than in individual therapy in the group without DD diagnosis. It is worth noting that a diagnosis of DD also predicted poorer outcome in the family therapy, but not in individual therapy.

Better baseline FAD scores predicted greater decrease in the CDI scores; a similar trend was not evident in relation to the BICS. In family therapy, classifying families according to improved family functioning on the BICS, or the lack thereof, yielded groups of families with different outcomes: families that had improved family functioning also showed significantly greater decreases in their children's CDI scores. These findings fit rather well the interactional model described by Asarnow, Jaycox, and Thompson (2001), where family factors influence the individual's depressive symptoms and vice versa. In addition, the results support previous evidence that family functioning influences treatment outcome in child depression (Beavers & Hampson, 2000; Carr, 2000; Diamond et al., 2002; Hughes & Gullone, 2008).

## *Clinical implications*

The results of this study support the use of the FIPP and the time-limited SIFT as effective treatments for depression in youths; the positive outcome of both therapy forms was maintained at the 6-month follow-up. However, the results also suggest that the time-limited SIFT may be more effective with younger children than with adolescents and in cases without a diagnosis of DD. This study supports the notion that treatment approaches with a focus on changing interactional patterns in the family that maintain symptomatic behaviour, such as systemic family therapy in general and the time-limited SIFT in particular (Byng-Hall, Campbell, & Papadopoulos, 1996), may contribute to the treatment of depression in young people (Larner, 2009). These treatments may be quite brief and yet effective, as in this study, but as Carr (2009) points out, depressive episodes have a tendency of recurring. Therefore, long-term re-referral arrangements should always be made. In addition, antidepressant medication and other interventions must be considered in cases less responsive to family therapy, as may be the case with severe cases of DD.

Our results indicated that family functioning is an important factor with regard to outcome when treating depressed youths in both family and individual therapy. Both FAD and BICS seem able to capture some aspects of family functioning relevant to treatment outcome. The changes in family functioning during treatment as measured on the FAD were significant, but were too small to be considered clinically significant. The changes in BICS scores were somewhat larger. It seems that the two instruments used to assess family functioning in this study differ somewhat in their sensitivities. The FAD General Functioning scale picked up baseline differences between the families that then influenced treatment outcome, whereas the BICS was more sensitive to clinically significant changes in family functioning during treatment. The clinical relevance of the BISS is not supported by this study.

## Note

*Grant support:* Medical Society of Finland, Finnish Foundation for Child Psychiatric Research, National Graduate School of Psychiatric Research of Finland.

# PART V

# CONCLUSIONS

CHAPTER FIFTEEN

# Reflections and thoughts: learning from the study

*Judith Trowell & Emilia Dowling*

Looking back, there is now time to consider what was learnt on the Project. It was a comparative outcome study, examining the outcome of two different therapeutic interventions. However, alongside the research criteria that established the initial diagnosis, we were also concerned to consider what we had learnt through the therapeutic interventions about the nature of childhood depression that might be of value to clinicians in the field. We have thought about the group of families recruited into the Childhood Depression Project, the family dynamics and patterns that emerged in the therapies, and the possible genetic inheritance, individual pathology, and internal dynamics of the children and young people. In this concluding chapter, we address the main ideas that have emerged: clinical issues; issues for professionals working with the families of depressed children; research issues; understanding childhood depression; and then some final thoughts arising from the Project.

## *Clinical issues*

A diagnosis of depression is a dramatic intervention for a young person, as well as for those around them: the family. It was also an issue for the clinicians within the Project. We were struck by the extent of the difficulties with which all the families were struggling. However, most of the children and young people did not initially present as seriously depressed, flat, low, or very sad. More often they were talkative, sometimes contemptuous and dismissive, giving a powerful impression of being cut off from their emotions. Often their sadness was masked by defiant behaviour or angry outbursts; sometimes it was manifested as emotional deadness. In many cases, the young people were in serious difficulties outside the family context, particularly in school, which made it essential for the therapists to connect with the professional network, to enlist support and understanding for the young person, and to assist the family in managing the problems.

### *Engagement*

As we have seen, the therapists did not find engagement with the young people and their parent(s) or families easy. In part, this was due to the extra demands of the research framework and the imposition of the initial research interviews, but there was something more: these families often felt in a desperate position and hopeless about the possibility of change. They wanted help but, at the same time, found it difficult to engage. The Project was perhaps the last hope, but alongside this was fear and suspicion, shame about the situation they found themselves in, and a disbelief that anything could change. Many of the young people and their families were wary of engagement: why risk themselves when the chance of change seemed unattainable? However, once established in the Project, the majority of the families attended most of their sessions, and the clinicians needed to hold on to this fact when they felt overwhelmed and full of doubt about what they had to offer.

### *Risk management*

Within such a group of very troubled children, risk management was an issue, and during the course of the Project serious concerns arose for a number of the young people. Where there were Child Protection concerns, the therapists liaised with the Local Authority in the usual way. Where there were concerns about deterioration in the young person's mental state, or the therapist was concerned about a possible psychotic episode, the Project Director, in role as consultant psychiatrist, was involved in a psychiatric review. In those cases where young people took an overdose of tablets, there was liaison in management with accident and emergency departments. The Project Director was involved in all such situations that aroused inevitable additional anxiety over the possibility of admission to hospital or the need for medication. In the event, with the work of experienced therapists, supported by senior professional supervisors, and with psychiatric support within the Project, it was possible to manage these situations and hold the treatment. However, the work involved was very stressful, and the therapists needed good backup, support, and containment of their inevitable anxiety.

### *Intergenerational issues*

Intergenerational issues were very real, with the extent of depression and mental health issues in the families ever present. On the one hand, as we have seen in many accounts in preceding chapters, parents were struggling with their own difficulties. Where parents were still together, in many cases they were locked into adversarial and acrimonious relationships that were destructive for the children. In these situations, the young people were either withdrawn and detached, or they were over-involved with one parent and hostile to the other and were often stuck at home and unable to get on with their own lives. Where there was a lone parent, the young person was often caught up with that parent in a merged relationship, finding it difficult to separate. Again, the young people were often the recipients of family projections and inappropriate expectations, sometimes related to the past. For example, one girl in individual therapy had a sister who was seen as the good, successful one, while she herself was struggling with depression and underachievement in school. This mirrored the experience of her mother, who had always seen herself as the underachieving one in her family of origin, with her own sister the bright, achieving, and successful person.

## *Liaison with other agencies*

Both for the co-workers in the work with the families, and with outside agencies, liaison proved to be essential. This was particularly important given the time-limited nature of the work, and the severity of the very real external problems presented by the young people. Professionals inside the Project needed to be constantly vigilant and mindful of the internal-/external-world boundary, to share issues as they emerged and to work closely together. At the same time, one member of the team needed to engage actively with the professional network. Since, initially, many of the young people were out of school, in these situations teachers, educational social workers, and educational psychologists all needed to be involved during the course of the therapy, either to facilitate the young person's re-entry into school or to ensure more regular attendance. For the most part, the young people did manage to get back into some form of education, but this was often with impressive input from outside professionals. Social Services and Mental Health Services were already involved with some families; here, too, liaison was important, as they had an important contribution to make, often extending far beyond the time of the Project.

## *Resilience*

The resilience of the young people was impressive. As is evident in the accounts of the work in previous chapters, they seemed able to free themselves from family projections and expectations through the therapeutic process and to grasp the opportunities available to them. Perhaps as the parents were able to use the support available for them, a space was made for the young people, giving them freedom to move out from the family and to get on with their own lives. Once back in a school setting and within their peer groups, they could begin to make important peer relationships and learn. In his chapter, David Campbell draws attention to the possible effects of co-morbidity (chapter 11): those young people who had been more anxious alongside their depression proved better able to grasp and maximize the available opportunities as their anxiety receded. On the other hand, some of those with behavioural problems were left still sabotaging themselves.

## *Professional issues*

Sue McNab and her family therapy colleagues have emphasized the emotional stress involved for the therapists in working with the families (chapter 9). All the therapists across the Project needed to tolerate the intense emotions of depression, despair, and hopelessness experienced by the families; to contain these feelings and continue to hope; to hold on to the capacity to think; and to maintain the courage to believe that they had something to offer. The Project provided a firm framework of supervision, case management, and support for the therapists from experienced colleagues, all committed to the research. There is no doubt that this firm holding structure made a very important contribution to the outcome of the clinical work.

There was a real issue for the therapists about the precise time-limited work required by the research, set in part by the limited funding available. At the outset, all the therapists considered that from their clinical experience, these children, young people, and their families would need long-term interventions. Such time-limited work was seen as a constraint, and throughout the Project the therapists struggled with their doubts and concerns about the efficacy of such an approach for such troubled families. However, despite these doubts, therapists of both orientations came to see that the work had led to positive outcomes for the families and young people. As Agathe Gretton writes (chapter 3), the very existence of the time limits led to a structuring of the work, which had positive elements for the young people, many of whom would have been unlikely to commit to long-term open-ended work. Commitment to time-limited work felt far safer. The clinical paper from Greece (chapter 6) highlights the usefulness of the structure for the professionals provided by the Manual.

All the therapists found the presence of the research team a mixed experience. The beginning research assessment was outside usual clinical practice, and the family therapists in particular felt intruded upon in their initial engagement with the families (Barratt & Dowling, chapter 10). Similarly, the ongoing monitoring meetings with the research psychologist at intervals throughout the therapy felt difficult, particularly at critical times in the therapy. The end-of-therapy and follow-up meetings with the research team had their difficulties for the therapists but were also reassuring for families and therapists alike, in that the Project research structure seemed to provide another layer of containment for this difficult work. The research also involved detailed notes and audio- and video-recordings, providing a wealth of clinical material to focus interventions and for subsequent clinical research (Campbell, chapter 11). While the family therapists were familiar with the use of video-recording in their day-to-day practice, the individual therapists were not accustomed to the presence of a tape recorder in the therapy room, and they have commented here on its impact, not always negative, on both the young people and the therapist (Cassidy, chapter 4).

Despite its demands, however, the Project provided a framework of supervision and support for the therapists without which the clinical work, with its intense emotional impact, could have foundered.

## *Research issues*

The nature of the research posed its own demands. It is always a problem obtaining an adequate number of participants (Trowell, Berelowitz, & Kolvin, 1995), and it was no different in this Project. Clinicians, otherwise willing to refer, were deterred by the research requirement of random allocation across the therapeutic approaches. Many of the young people in the London group were referred through the Tavistock Clinic Child and Family Department. It proved more difficult to recruit from further afield, where screening referrals for childhood depression might have yielded more cases. However, there were reservations both in the Clinic and in local clinics about routine screening of cases. Screening had occurred in secondary schools in a neighbouring borough, but those children found to be depressed through screening were seen in school, and not referred into the child and family mental health system. In retrospect, interventions in schools might have helped recruitment into the research. In his research project *Help Starts Here* (Kolvin et al., 1981), Kolvin offered a range of interventions in schools, and recruitment was more successful.

However, as we have said, random allocation proved to be a real difficulty for fellow clinicians reluctant to refer, not knowing which treatment would be allocated. Again, the random allocation took place following the first research interview, when it was clear that the young person met the criteria for the Project. Other factors later emerged as important: the mental health problems and incidence of depression in the family history, and the effects of co-morbidity, particularly where depression coexisted alongside anxiety or behaviour problems. While these factors proved important when looking at treatment outcome, they could not be taken into account at the point of random allocation. Had the numbers been greater, these additional factors would have lost their impact and become more evenly balanced across the treatment modalities. However, the small numbers have left unanswered research questions about these issues.

Another more fundamental issue was that of user choice. Those families who dropped out of the family therapy programme had been uncomfortable at the outset about being seen together as a family. One of these families had had previous experience of individual work, and another had issues that might have been better contained had the parent and child been seen individually. There were also other families who had strong preferences that happened to be met in the random allocation, but for whom there might have been a problem had this not been so. Where families have strong preferences, this may need to be considered in the allocation, and where numbers are greater, there might be a possibility of creating a small sub-sample that could take account of family preference.

The organization of an international research project takes considerable time and energy. The Project involved many planning meetings with senior staff from all three Centres: Athens, Helsinki, and London. Research instruments had to be agreed and translated, and time frames settled; Treatment Manuals for the individual therapists, parent workers, and family therapists also had to be written and translated. Total Project meetings for all the staff across the three Centres followed and were continued at intervals throughout the Project. These latter meetings were important occasions for discussion of clinical issues, while the research and management of the Project overall was held by the Project Management Group.

## *Understanding childhood depression*

The children and young people recruited to the Project formed an interesting group. Aged between 9 and 15 years, they were all on the verge of puberty and adolescence. This is a time of major transition for the young person and, in turn, for their families. The young person is coping with disturbing bodily changes, and the move to secondary education heralds interest in learning and thoughts about future-career pathways. Normal developmental processes are taking place, with participation in the peer group and with interest in relationships and sexual involvement, alongside group leisure activities and possible experimentation with alcohol and mind-altering substances.

In the main, the young people in this group had opted out of this phase. Physical changes were taking place, but emotionally they were still functioning as younger children. Many presented as individuals who were stuck, whose emotional development had been impaired, often with concrete thinking and a poor capacity to symbolize, and without the vocabulary or awareness of feeling states. In many ways, some resembled young people who have been severely traumatized or abused. Some lacked the sense of an internal life and space and seemed unable to have a dialogue within themselves to sustain themselves or to make sense of their thoughts and feelings. There was often a sense that they were children and young people struggling with the very basic question of whether they had a right to exist.

Many of the families were very fragile or troubled, which made it difficult for the children and young people. Without the family there to hold it all together, they did not feel that it was safe enough to leave and move on. On the one hand, this seemed linked to the lack of emotional resources in the family. However, adolescence is a difficult transitional stage for parents and children alike, and it felt as if the transition was too dangerous and the young people had retreated into the safety of childhood dependence. Children and young people need help and support to move on and to feel that the family can survive their going. Many of these families were struggling with very serious issues, and adults themselves were depressed. In addition, in some situations oedipal issues held parents and children in partner roles and locked them into their homes.

For a few young people, attempts to separate had led to strange "psychotic" bubbles of experience, episodes when events were described that were out of touch with reality. Voices and ghosts were presented, but these were later recognized as part of a struggle to explain sensations and thoughts that could not otherwise be named or understood. With these young people, much of the work seems to have been to give the young people a space and a language to explore their thoughts and feelings. They could then begin to understand themselves, their relationships and their conflicts.

*So how can one conceptualize childhood depression?* Since many of the families had long histories of depression and mental health problems, there was the possibility of genetic predisposition. However, the present complex family patterns and dynamics meant that these were emotional and social environments where depression seemed to be the norm. Many families seemed almost paralysed by a sense of isolation and of despair that nothing could change; many seemed overwhelmed by their situations and by emotional psychic pain that could not be processed. It is difficult to separate out the genetic from the psychosocial factors here. However, what became clear was that these young people were stuck, caught in a web of complex family dynamics; for some, it seemed that the world outside was a dangerous place. Most were at the hub of unconscious projections and projective identification that seemed to leave them lost and out of touch with their own thoughts and feelings, except, at times, of anger and despair.

What was striking was that once the families were engaged they felt relief and, for the most part, were able to use the treatment offered by the Project. The children and young people worked on their issues and, with help, were able to move out into their own world of school, peer relationships and friendships, and learning. The workers held on to hope, and the families themselves were enabled to have some hope that change was possible, knowing that the young people were in trouble and needed to move on. These time-limited interventions proved enough to free up apparently stuck and hopeless situations for the young people, though inevitably some parents were left needing further help.

## *Theoretical thoughts*

In the course of the Project, a number of ideas were particularly helpful in our thinking about childhood depression. In her book *Live Company*, Ann Alvarez (1992) talks of children who find it difficult to symbolize, seeing everything in a concrete way. This can also be the case with feelings that the child cannot recognize or name. She links this state with the existential anxiety felt by autistic children, saying that the work with them needs to be slow, giving them a language to name, explore, and own their feelings and so begin to feel aware of their own separate existence. In this work, the patient needs to sense that the therapist believes in the possibility of improvement and change and that things can change, that the situation can get better.

Herbert Rosenfeld, in *Impasse and Interpretation* (1987), describes the struggle for the therapist when confronted by objects in a patient's internal world that are determined to attack and destroy, to triumph over everything good (p, 110). He describes the situation where, when one destructive object is explored and ameliorated, others emerge to mock and triumph. It is all too easy for the therapist to give up and lose hope against the sustained attack of this negative state.

But perhaps the ideas that were most sustaining in thinking about the work are those of W. R. Bion. A number of Bion's papers in *Second Thoughts* (1967) were extremely helpful, in particular "A Theory of Thinking" (1962), distinguishing the psychotic from the non-psychotic part of the personality. Some of the young people had sensations, thoughts, feelings, and experiences that were extremely difficult to place. It was hard at times to be clear about whether these were psychotic symptoms, PTSD flashbacks, or pseudo-hallucinations. These states of mind seemed more than adolescent turmoil, and they needed to be recognized and carefully managed. It was helpful to see them as "bubbles of psychosis", with a partial loss of contact with reality, rather than a truly psychotic state, since they seemed to recede within the treatment.

McNab and colleagues (chapter 9) have referred to three major and interweaving themes that they found helpful in the family therapy work:

» Striking the balance between action and reflection
» Bearing witness to emotional pain
» Keeping hope alive

Both the family and individual work, in different ways, provided an opportunity to restructure relationships, often freeing the young person from the position of mediating between the parents or needing to take care of the parents. Both set out to enable parents to recognize issues that rightly belonged to adults and to create new opportunities for young people both within and outside the family.

## *Thoughts for clinicians*

We learnt many lessons from our work on the Project that could be helpful for those working with and identifying depression in young people:

- To be aware of behaviour and symptoms which may be masking depression. Reluctance to attend school, angry or despondent behaviour, and lack of interest and concentration at school could all be signs of an underlying depression.
- To involve the family in the treatment plan and promote communication between the family members; to listen to the voice of the child.
- To invest time and energy in connecting with relevant professional networks, which can further the lives of the child and his family. (In one of our families, finding and securing support for a marital couple within the culture and community of the particular family was an essential element of the overall work.)
- To enable the involvement of the school. Their understanding and support of the young people and their parents was often a key element in contributing to their improvement.
- To be aware of the emotional impact of the work and the difficulty at times of keeping hope alive. Where possible, to have good systems of supervision and professional support.

# GLOSSARY

## *Family therapy*

**Collaborative supervisor:** Fruggeri (2002, p. 12) makes a distinction between supervision as teaching and supervision as a reflection on one's practice. In the context of the BioMed/ERC study, the systemic supervisors worked with colleagues—the clinicians—to reflect on the clinical work and to collaborate to generate ideas about practice.

**Coordinated Management of Meaning (CMM):** This framework, developed by Pearce and Cronen (1980), theorizes communication as a process that allows us to create and manage social reality. Meaning can be seen to exist within a context. The context may not be hierarchically determined. They identify six levels of meaning, which may be defined differently according to the domain in which the relationship is taking place. The levels are: sociocultural norms, family myth, life script relationship, episode, and speech act (what is said) . Each of these contexts influences and is influenced by other contexts.

**Dissonance:** A tension between actions and beliefs—lack of agreement, consistency, or harmony.

**Genogram:** A therapeutic method whereby family members engage in developing a pictorial/diagrammatic story of their family together, focusing on the context of their relationships.

**Relational reflexivity:** "The intention, desire, processes and practices through which therapists and clients explicitly engage one another in coordinating their resources so as to create relationships with therapeutic potential. This would involve initiating, responding to, and developing opportunities to consider, explore, experiment with and elaborate the ways in which they relate" (Burnham, 2005, p. 4).

**Role:** The normal or customary activity of a person in a particular social setting: "what is your role on the team?" It is the prescribed or expected *behaviour associated* with a particular *position* or *status* in a *group* or *organization*. (www.businessdictionary.com)

**Social constructionism:** Social constructionist ideas fall within the framework of postmodernism. Social constructionism is an anti-essentialist ideology in which knowledge is constructed from social processes and between people. A central platform of social constructionism is that the function of language is not to represent reality but to enable us to engage in relations, and the meanings that we construe about the world result from these social interactions. (Campbell, 2000, pp. 12–13)

**Taking a position:** We choose to take positions within discourses, and we are also positioned by others on the basis of what we say and do. (Campbell & Groenbaek, 2006, p. 16)

## *Psychoanalysis*

**Acting in:** This is considered when therapists say or do things that come from their own unprocessed thoughts or feelings. This may arise from their own personal situation or from a response to their patient that is not contained and transformed.

**Acting out:** Freud described the subject as having powerful unconscious thoughts and feelings that may be acted out in the course of therapy, and can be understood in terms of the transference, but are not acknowledged as such by the patient. Acting out may take place within the session or in the outside world. (Freud, 1940 [1938], pp. 176–177)

**Alpha elements:** These were hypothesized by W. R. Bion (1962) as the means by which unconscious thoughts and feelings are transmitted from the baby to the mother, or from person to person. Alpha function is the capacity in the mind of the recipient to process and transform what was unthinkable and to manage the thoughts and feelings. This activity is containment.

**Containment:** The process by which the baby's emotions are received by the mother, who mentally "digests" them in her unconscious, so that the emotion can then be recognized and named as she is able to understand what is happening. (Bion, 1962; Rhode, 1997)

**Countertransference:** This term describes those feelings, conscious and unconscious, that are part of the therapist's response to the patient. It is made up in part by the therapist's own response to the patient, but also by the therapist's awareness of feelings communicated to him or her by the patient's unconscious. Thinking about and understanding the countertransference is a major part of a therapist's work. (Heimann, 1950; Rhode, 1997)

**Depressive position:** A state of mind characterized by the bringing together of splits, so that the baby recognizes that the idealized and hated mother are the same person. Relationships are with whole-objects for whom love and concern are felt (Klein, 1935). This leads to feelings of guilt for harm done in phantasy and to the wish to make reparation. In the working through of the depressive position, love mitigates hatred, and hope and security increase. If this fails, manic triumph may be resorted to, or paranoid-schizoid trends may be reinforced.

**Enmeshed:** Confused, unobjective, and preoccupied with or by past or present relationships or experiences.

**Internal objects:** Figures to whom the self relates and who have become internalized, so building up the "inner world" of object relationships. (Klein, 1940)

**Introjection:** The process by which the qualities of the self are built up through the phantasy of introjecting (taking in), and thus containing, objects with whose qualities the self can then identify.

**Mirroring:** The infant depends on its mother's facial responses when it looks into her face to establish a sense of self. (Winnicott, 1967)

**Object:** A technical psychoanalytic term for a person with whom the self (or subject) has an emotional relationship. An *external object* is such a person in external reality, while an *internal object* has been introjected and has thus become part of the inner world.

**Oedipal triangle:** In Freud's writings, the erotic desire for one of the parents and rivalry with the other make up the complex system of the developing child's oedipal constellation (Laplanche & Pontalis, 1973). Freud traced the importance of these triangular relationships for the individual's character and sexual life. More recent work has focused on the relationship between the negotiation of the oedipal triangle and the capacity for thought. (Bion, 1962; Britton, 1989)

**Paranoid-schizoid position:** A state of mind characterized by the splitting of objects into extremely good (ideal) and extremely bad ones (Klein, 1946). The self relates to *part-objects* rather than to whole, integrated ones; its prime concern is for its own survival, whereas in the depressive position the prime concern is for the good internal object.

**Projection:** Projection is an important developmental process—for example, the baby projects anger or fear into the mother, and the mother recognizes these feelings and soothes the baby, helping it to manage these emotions. Projection continues throughout life, usually as a way of getting rid of unpleasant or frightening feelings. The feelings are ascribed to another, and so awareness is avoided.

**Projective identification:** When an individual has unbearable thoughts and feelings, they can be evacuated into another person, and this other has to experience them. The originator may also exert control over the recipient as part of the response to these thoughts and feelings. It was thought to be a way of trying to avoid separateness. (Klein, 1946)

**Splitting:** Freud (1926) described a splitting of consciousness that permitted contradictory views to exist side by side. Klein (1946) viewed splitting as a means of dealing with anxiety when its excessive integration is interfered with. However, the split between good and bad is an important developmental step.

**Symbol formation:** The process by which one thing can be used to stand for another, without being pictorial, and which is the basis for creativity in the child and adult. In psychotic states, this capacity is interfered with, so that a symbol is equated with the thing symbolized, leading to what Segal (1957) has called *symbolic equations*. Thus, a child may feel that a drawing is the thing it depicts, rather than a representation of it.

**Transference:** First described by Freud (1895), it describes the process by which emotions from the past are re-experienced in the present in relation to the therapist.

**Unintegration:** Winnicott used this term to describe the internal state of the infant—that is, a state of not being integrated as a unit being who could have a sense of self and other, inside and outside, fantasy and reality.

## *Research measures*

**Beavers Interactional Scales:** Competence and Style Scales, as a system model of family functioning. Family interaction is observed over a 10-minute period, usually from videotaped material. Raters need training to reliability. (Beavers & Hampson, 2000)

**Birmaher Anxiety Scale:** This is a Screen for Anxiety Related Emotional Disoders (SCARED) consisting of 41 items, yielding five factors: panic/somatic, generalized anxiety, separation anxiety, social phobia, and school phobia. It has good internal consistency and discriminant validity. (Birmaher et al., 1999)

**Childhood Depression Inventory (CDI):** The CDI is a (27-item) self-report questionnaire, which indicates the number of depressive symptoms. (Kovacs, 1981)

**Children's Global Assessment Scale (C-GAS):** The C-GAS is a clinician rating of the overall impairment of a child's functioning. (Shaffer, Gould, & Brasic, 1993)

**Co-morbidity:** It is usual for a child with one diagnosis to have at least one other diagnosis, often several. This may be an artefact, the co-occurrence as a consequence of a single disorder having a complex pattern of symptoms which covers two disorders but is really one; or it may arise when two disorders share similar risk factors; or one disorder may lead to another; or a co-morbid constellation may be a distant syndrome in its own right. (Rutter, Taylor, & Hersov, 1994)

**Correlation:** A measure of relationships between variables describing the direction and degree of association between them. (Robson, 2002)

**Kiddie-SADS** A semi-structured clinical interview that provides a measure of MDD and dysthymia (based on *DSM–IV*) and psychiatric co-morbidity. (Chambers et al., 1985)

**Moods and Feelings Questionnaire:** A self-report questionnaire that rates depression. (Angold et al., 1987)

**Qualitative data:** Non-numerical data, usually in the form of written or spoken words, but also images etc.

**Quantitative data:** Data in the form of numbers.

# REFERENCES


Abbass, A. A. (2002). Short-term dynamic psychotherapies in the treatment of major depression. *Journal of Psychiatry, 47* (2): 193.

Abbass, A. A. (2006). Intensive short-term dynamic psychotherapy of treatment-resistant depression: A pilot study. *Depression and Anxiety, 23*: 449–452.

Abraham, K. (1911a). Giovanni Segantini: A psychoanalytic study. In: *Clinical Papers and Essays by Karl Abraham*, trans. H. C. Abraham & D. R. Ellison. London: Hogarth Press, 1955.

Abraham, K. (1911b). Notes on the psychoanalytic investigation and treatment of manic-depressive insanity and allied conditions. In: *Selected Papers on Psychoanalysis* (pp. 137–156). New York: Basic Books, 1953.

Alvarez, A. (1992). *Live Company*. London: Routledge.

Alvarez, A. (2000). Moral imperatives in work with borderline children: The grammar of wishes and the grammar of needs. In: J. Symington (Ed.), *Imprisoned Pain and Its Transformation: A Festschrift for H. Sydney Klein*. London: Karnac.

Andersen, T. (1991). *The Reflecting Team: Dialogues and Dialogues about the Dialogues*. New York: W. W. Norton.

Anderson, H., & Swim, S. (1995). Supervision as collaborative conversation: Connecting the voices of supervisor and supervisee. *Journal of Systemic Therapies, 14* (2): 1–13.

Angold, A., & Costello, E. J. (1993). Depressive co-morbidity in children and adolescents: Empirical, theoretical, and methodological issues. *American Journal of Psychiatry, 150*: 1779–1791.

Angold, A., & Costello, E. J. (2001). The epidemiology of depression in children and adolescents. In: I. M. Goodyer (Ed.), *The Depressed Child and Adolescent* (2nd edition). Cambridge: Cambridge University Press.

Angold, A., Costello, E., Messer, S., & Pickles, A. (1995). Development of a short questionnaire for use in epidemiological studies of depression in children and adolescents. *International Journal of Methods in Psychiatric Research, 5* (4): 237–249.

Angold, A., Costello, E. J., Pickles, A., Winder, F., & Silver, D. (1987). *Moods and Feelings Questionnaire: The Development of a Questionnaire for Use in Epidemiological Studies of Depression in Children and Adolescents*. London: Institute of Psychiatry.

Angold, A., Costello, E. J., & Worthman, C. M. (1998). Puberty and depression: The roles of age, pubertal status and pubertal timing. *Psychological Medicine, 28*: 51–61.

Angold, A., Costello, E. J., & Worthman, C. M. (1999). Pubertal changes in hormone levels and depression in girls. *Psychological Medicine, 29*: 1043–1053.

Angold, A., & Rutter, M. (1992). The effects of age and pubertal status on depression in a large clinical sample. *Development and Psychopathology, 4*: 5–28.

Antony, J., & Scott, P. D. (1960). Manic-depressive psychosis in childhood. *Journal of Child Psychology and Psychiatry, 1*: 53–70.

APA (1968). *Diagnostic and Statistical Manual of Mental Disorders* (2nd edition). Washington, DC: American Psychiatric Association.

APA (1994). *Diagnostic and Statistical Manual of Mental Disorders* (4th edition). Washington, DC: American Psychiatric Association.

Asarnow, J. R., Jaycox, L. H., & Thompson, M. C. (2001). Depression in youth: Psychosocial interventions. *Journal of Clinical Child Psychology, 30* (1): 33–47.

Asarnow, J. R., Thompson, M., Hamilton, E. B., Goldstein, M. J., & Guthrie, D. (1994). Family-expressed emotion, childhood-onset depression, and childhood-onset schizophrenia spectrum disorders: Is expressed emotion a non-specific correlate of child psychopathology or a specific risk factor for depression? *Journal of Abnormal Child Psychology, 22*: 129–146.

Barrows, K. (1990). Ghosts in the swamp: Some aspects of splitting and their relationship to parental losses. *International Journal of Psychoanalysis, 80*: 549–561.

Battle, J. (1981). *Self-esteem Interview*. Washington, DC: Special Child Publications.

Beavers, R., & Hampson, R. B. (1990). *Successful Families: Assessment and Intervention*. New York: W. W. Norton.

Beavers, R., & Hampson, R. B. (2000). The Beavers Systems Model of Family Functioning. *Journal of Family Therapy, 22*: 128–143.

Beck, A. T., Emery, G., & Greenberg, R. (1985). *Anxiety Disorders and Phobias: A Cognitive Perspective*. New York: Basic Books.

Begg, C., Cho, M., Eastwood, S., Horton, R., Moher, D., Olkin, I., et al. (1996). Improving the quality of reporting of Randomised Controlled Trials: The CONSORT statement. *Journal of the American Medical Association, 276*: 637–639.

Berney, T. P., Bhate, S. R., Kolvin, I., Famuyiwa, O. O., Barrett, M. L., Fundudis, T., et al. (1991). The context of childhood depression. *British Journal of Psychiatry, 159* (Suppl. 11): 28–35.

Bick, E. (1968). The experience of the skin in early object relations. *International Journal of Psychoanalysis, 49*: 484–486.

Bick, E. (1986). Further considerations on the function of the skin in early object relations. *British Journal of Psychotherapy, 2*.

Bifulco, A. T., Brown, G. W., & Harris, T. O. (1987). Childhood loss of parent, lack of adequate parental care and adult depression: A replication. *Journal of Affective Disorder, 12*: 115–128.

Bion, W. R. (1962). A theory of thinking. In: *Second Thoughts* (pp. 110–119). London: Karnac, 1984.

Bion, W. R. (1967). *Second Thoughts*. London: Karnac, 1984.

Birmaher, B., Brent, D., Chiappetta, L., Bridge, J., Monga, S., & Baugher, M. (1999). Psychometric properties of the Screen for Child Anxiety Related Emotional Disorders (SCARED): A replication study. *Journal of the American Academy of Child and Adolescent Psychiatry, 38* (10): 1230–1236.

Birmaher, B., Brent, D., Kolko, D., Baugher, M., Bridge, J., Holder, D., et al. (2000). Clinical outcome after short-term psychotherapy for adolescents with major depressive disorder. *Archives of General Psychiatry, 57* (1): 29–36.

Birmaher, B., Ryan, N. D., Williamson, D. E., Brent, D. A., Kaufman, J., Dahl, R. E., et al. (1996). Childhood and adolescent depression: A review of the past 10 years (Part 1). *Journal of the American Academy of Child and Adolescent Psychiatry, 35*: 1427–1439.

Bond, S. (2005). *An Exploration of a Relational Consultation Model for Use in the Exclusion Process with Primary School Aged Black Boys of African, African Caribbean and Mixed Race Parentage*. Doctoral thesis, University of East London/Tavistock Clinic, London.

Bowlby, J. (1960). Grief and mourning in infancy and early childhood. *Psychoanalytic Study of the Child, 15*: 9–52.

Bowlby, J. (1973). *Attachment and Loss, Vol. 2: Separation, Anxiety, and Anger.* New York: Basic Books.

Bowlby, J. (1980). *Attachment and Loss, Vol. 3: Loss, Sadness, and Depression.* New York: Basic Books.

Brenman Pick, I. (1985). Working through in the counter-transference. In: E. B. Spillius (Ed.), *Melanie Klein Today, Vol. 2: Mainly Practice.* The New Library of Psychoanalysis. London: Routledge, 1988.

Brent, D. A., Holder, D., Kolko, D. A., Birmaher, B., Baugher, M., & Bridge, J. (1997). A clinical psychotherapy trial for adolescent depression comparing cognitive, family, and supportive treatments. *Archives of General Psychiatry, 54*: 877–885.

Britton, R. (1983). Breakdown and reconstitution of the family circle. In: M. Boston & R. Szur (Eds.), *Psychotherapy with Severely Deprived Children.* London: Karnac.

Britton, R. (1989). The missing link. In: R. Britton, M. Feldman, & E. O'Shaughnessy, *The Oedipus Complex Today: Clinical Implications* (pp. 83–101), ed. J. Steiner. London: Karnac.

Brunetti, A., Dymond, M., Robins, D., & Vetere, A. (2005). When one became four: A systemic approach to supervision. *Clinical Psychology Forum, 152*: 24–27.

Burnham, J. (1993). Systemic supervision: The evolution of reflexivity in the context of the supervisory relationship. *Human Systems: The Journal of Systemic Consultation and Management, 4*: 349–381.

Burnham, J. (2005). Relational reflexivity: A tool for socially constructed therapeutic relationships. In: C. Flaskas, B. Mason, & A. Perlesz

(Eds.), *The Space Between: Experience, Context, and Process in the Therapeutic Relationship*. London: Karnac.

Byng-Hall, J. (1986). Family scripts: A concept which can bridge child psychotherapy and family therapy thinking. *Journal of Child Psychotherapy, 12*: 3–13.

Byng-Hall, J. (1995). *Re-writing Family Scripts: Improvisation and Systems Change*. New York: Guilford Press.

Byng-Hall, J., & Campbell, D. (1981). Resolving conflicts in distance regulation: An integrative approach. *Journal of Marital and Family Therapy, 7*: 321–330.

Byng-Hall, J., Campbell, D., & Papadopoulos, R. (1996). *Manual. Systems Integrative Therapy (SIFT): The Basis for an Integrative Approach*. London: Tavistock Clinic.

Campbell, D. (2000). *The Socially Constructed Organization*. London: Karnac.

Campbell, D., Bianco, V., Dowling, E., Goldberg, H., McNab, S., & Pentecost, D. (2003). Family therapy for childhood depression: Researching significant moments. *Journal of Family Therapy, 25* (4): 417–435.

Campbell, D., & Groenbaek, M. (2006). *Taking Positions in Organizations*. London: Karnac.

Cantwell, P., & Holmes, S. (1995). Cumulative process: A collaborative approach to systemic supervision. *Journal of Systemic Therapies, 14* (2): 35–46.

Carlson, G., & Cantwell, D. (1980). A survey of depressive symptoms and disorder in a child psychiatric population. *Journal of Child Psychology and Psychiatry, 21*: 19–25.

Carr, A. (2000). Editorial: Empirical approaches to family assessment. *Journal of Family Therapy, 22*: 121–127.

Carr, A. (2007). Depression in young people: Description, assessment and evidence-based treatment. *Developmental Neurorehabilitation, 11* (1): 3–15.

Carr, A. (2009). The effectiveness of family therapy and systemic interventions for child-focused problems. *Journal of Family Therapy, 31*: 3–45.

Chambers, W., Puig-Antich, J., Hirsch, M., Paez, P., Ambrosini, P. J., Tabrizi, M. A., et al. (1985). The assessment of affective disorders in children and adolescents by semi-structured interview: Test–retest reliability of the Schedule for Affective Disorders and Schizophrenia for school-age children, present episode version. *Archives of General Psychiatry, 42*: 696–702.

Chavira, D. A., & Stein, M. B. (2005). Childhood social anxiety disorders: From understanding to treatment. *Child and Adolescent Psychiatric Clinics of North America, 14* (4): 797–818.

Clouston, T. S. (1892). Developmental insanities and psychoses. In: D. H. Tuke (Ed.), *A Dictionary of Psychological Medicine, Vol. 1* (pp. 357–371). London: Churchill.

Cole, D. A., Peeke, L. G., Martin, J. M., Truglio, R., & Seroczynski, A. D. (1998). A longitudinal look at the relation between depression and anxiety in children and adolescents. *Journal of Consulting & Clinical Psychology, 66*: 451–460.

Cronen, V., & Lang, P. (1994). Language and action: Wittgenstein and Dewey in the practice of therapy and consultation. *Human Systems, 5*: 5–43.

CSM (2003). *Selective Serotonin Re-uptake Inhibitors (SSRIs): Overview of Regulatory Status and CSM Advice Relating to Major Depressive Disorder (MDD) in Children and Adolescents Including a Summary of Available Safety and Efficacy Data.* London: Committee on Safety of Medicines. Retrieved 14 May 2011 from www.mhra.gov.uk/Safetyinformation/Safetywarningsalertsandrecalls/Safetywarningsandmessagesformedicines/CON019494

Davenloo, H. (1978). *Basic Principles and Techniques in Short-Term Dynamic Psychotherapy*. New York: Spectrum.

Davies, B., & Harré, R. (1990). Positioning: The discursive production of selves. *Journal of the Theory of Social Behaviour, 20*: 43–65.

Diamond, G., Reis, B. F., Diamond, G. M., Siqueland, L., & Isaacs, L. (2002). Attachment-based family therapy for depressed adolescents: A treatment development study. *Journal of the American Academy of Child and Adolescent Psychiatry, 41* (10): 1190–1196.

Diamond, G., Serrano, A., Dickey, M., & Sonis, W. (1996). Current status of family-based outcome and process research. *Journal of the American Academy of Child and Adolescent Psychiatry, 35* (1): 6–16.

Dowling, E., & Gorrell-Barnes, G. (2000). *Working with Children and Parents: Through Divorce and Separation*. Basingstoke: Macmillan.

Drumm, M., Carr, A., & Fitzgerald, M. (2000). The Beavers, McMaster and Circumplex clinical rating scales: A study of their sensitivity, specificity and discriminant validity. *Journal of Family Therapy, 22*: 225–238.

Edley, N. (2001). Analysing masculinity: Interpretive repertoires, ideological dilemmas and subject positions. In: M. Wetherall, S. Taylor, & S. J. Yates (Eds.), *Discourse as Data: A Guide for Analysis*. London: Sage.

Edwards, J. (Ed.) (2001). *Being Alive: Building on the Work of Anne Alvarez*. Hove: Brunner-Routledge.

Elkin, I., Shea, M. T., Watkins, J. T., Imber, S. D., Sotsky, S. M., Collins, J. F., et al. (1989). National Institute of Mental Health treatment of depression collaborative research program: General effectiveness of treatment. *Archives of General Psychiatry, 46*: 971–983.

Emslie, G. J., Heiligenstein, J. H., Wagner, K. D., Beiderman, J., Carlson, G., et al. (2000). *Fluoxetine for Acute Treatment of Depression in Children and Adolescents: A Placebo Controlled, Randomised Clinical Trial*. Paper presented at the 39th Annual Meeting of the American College of Neuropsychopharmacology, San Juan, Puerto Rico, 10–14 December.

Emslie, G. J., Rush, A. J., Weinberg, W. A., Kowatch, R. A., Hughes, C. W., Carmody, T., et al. (1997). A double-blind, randomised placebo-controlled trial of fluoxetine in children and adolescents with depression. *Archives of General Psychiatry, 54*: 1031–1037.

Epstein, N. B., Baldwin, L. M., & Bishop, D. (1983). The McMaster Family Assessment Device. *Journal of Marital and Family Therapy, 9* (2): 171–180.

Eysenck, H. J. (1980). Psychological theories of anxiety. In: G. D. Burrows & B. Davies (Eds.), *Handbook of Studies on Anxiety*. New York: Elsevier/North-Holland Biomedical Press.

Falicov, C. (2003). Culture, society and gender in depression. *Journal of Family Therapy, 25* (4): 371–387.

Fernando, S. (1991). *Mental Health, Race and Culture*. Basingstoke: Macmillan.

Flaskas, C. (2007). The balance of hope and hopelessness. In: C. Flaskas, I. McCarthy, & J. Sheehan (Eds.), *Hope and Despair in Narrative and Family Therapy: Adversity, Forgiveness and Reconciliation* (pp. 24–35). Hove: Brunner-Routledge.

Fonagy, P., Gergely, G., Jurist, E. J., & Target, M. (2002). *Affect Regulation, Mentalization, and the Development of the Self*. New York: Other Press.

Fonagy, P., Steele, M., Moran, G., Steele, H., & Higgitt, A. (1993.) Measuring the ghost in the nursery: An empirical study of the relation between parents' mental representations of childhood experiences and their infants' security of attachment. *Journal of the American Psychoanalytic Association, 41*: 957–989.

Fonagy, P., & Target, M. (1996). Predictors of outcome in child psychoanalysis: A retrospective study of 793 children at the Anna Freud Centre. *Journal of the American Psychoanalytic Association, 44*: 2–73.

Fonagy, P., Target, M., Cottrell, D., & Phillips, J. (2002). *What Works for Whom? A Critical Review of Treatments for Children and Adolescents.* New York: Guilford Press.

Fournier, A. (1966). *Le Grand Meaulnes.* Harmondsworth: Penguin, 1990.

Fraiberg, S. H., Adelson, E., & Shapiro, V. (1975). Ghosts in the nursery: A psychoanalytic approach to the problems of impaired infant–mother relationships. *Journal of the American Academy of Child Psychology, 14*: 387–422. [Also in: *Clinical Studies in Infant Mental Health.* London: Tavistock, 1980. And in: L. Fraiberg (Ed.), *Selected Writings of Selma Fraiberg* (pp. 100–136). Columbus, OH: Ohio State University Press, 1987.]

Freud, A., & Burlingham, D. (1944). *Infants without Families.* New York: International Universities Press.

Freud, S. (1895) (with Breuer, J.). *Studies on Hysteria. Standard Edition,* 2.

Freud, S. (1917). Mourning and melancholia. *Standard Edition,* 16.

Freud, S. (1920). *Beyond the Pleasure Principle. Standard Edition,* 18.

Freud, S. (1940 [1938]). *An Outline of Psycho-Analysis. Standard Edition,* 23.

Fruggeri, L. (2002). Different levels of analysis in the supervisory process. In: D. Campbell & B. Mason (Eds.), *Perspectives on Supervision* (pp. 3–20). London: Karnac.

Garvin, V., Leber, D., & Kalter, N. (1991). Children of divorce: Predictors of change following preventive intervention. *American Journal of Orthopsychiatry, 61* (3): 438–447.

Gill, R. (1996). Discourse analysis. In: J. T. E. Richardson (Ed.), *Handbook of Qualitative Research Methods for Psychology and the Social Sciences.* Leicester: British Psychological Society.

Gittelman-Klein, R., & Klein, D. F. (1973). School phobia: Diagnostic considerations in the light of imipramine effects. *Journal of Nervous and Mental Disease, 156*: 199–215.

Glaser, K. (1968). Masked depression in children and adolescents. *Annual Progress in Child Psychiatry and Child Development, 1*: 345–355.

Golombek, H., & Kozenblum, M. (1995). Brief psychoanalytic psychotherapy with adolescents. In: R. C. Marohn & S. C. Feinstein (Eds.), *Adolescent Psychiatry: The Annals of the American Society for Adolescent Psychiatry, Vol. 20* (pp. 307–324). London: Analytic Press.

Goodyer, I. M. (Ed.) (1995). *The Depressed Child and Adolescent*. Cambridge: Cambridge University Press.

Goodyer, I. M., Germany, E., Gowrusankur, J., & Altham, P. (1991). Social influences in the course of anxious and depressive disorders in school age children. *British Journal of Psychiatry, 158*: 676–684.

Goodyer, I. M., Herbert, J., Secher, S. M., & Pearson, J. (1997). Short-term outcome of major depression: I. Co-morbidity and severity at presentation as predictors at persistent disorder. *Journal of the American Academy of Child and Adolescent Psychiatry, 36*: 179–187.

Goodyer, I. M., Herbert, J., Tamplin, A., & Altham, P. M. E. (2000a). First episode major depression in adolescents: Affective, cognitive and endocrine characteristics of risk status and predictors of onset. *British Journal of Psychiatry, 176*: 142–149.

Goodyer, I. M., Herbert, J., Tamplin, A., & Altham, P. M. E. (2000b). Recent life events, cortisol and DHEA in the onset of major depression amongst "high risk" adolescents. *British Journal of Psychiatry, 177*: 499–504.

Goodyer, I. M., Herbert, J., Tamplin, A. Secher, S. M., & Pearson, J. (1997). Short-term outcome of major depression: II. Life events, family dysfunction and friendship difficulty as predictors of persistent disorder. *Journal of the American Academy of Child and Adolescent Psychiatry, 36*: 474–480.

Goodyer, I. M., Kolvin, I., & Gatzanis, S. (1985). Recent undesirable life events and psychiatric disorder in childhood and adolescence. *British Journal of Psychiatry, 147*: 517–523.

Gorrell-Barnes, G. (1994). Family therapy. In: M. Rutter, E. Taylor, & L. Hersov (Eds.), *Child & Adolescent Psychiatry* (3rd edition, pp. 946–965). Oxford: Blackwell Scientific.

Gray, A. (1994). *An Introduction to the Therapeutic Frame*. London: Routledge.

Greene, V. (2000). Therapeutic space for recreating the child in the mind of the parents. In: J. Tsiantis, S. B. Boethious, B. Hallerfors, A. Horne, & L. Tischler (Eds.), *Work with Parents: Psychoanalytic Psychotherapy with Children and Adolescents*. London: Karnac.

Groves, J. E. (1996). Four essences of short-term therapy: Brevity, focus, activity, selectivity. In: J. E. Groves (Ed.), *Essential Papers on Short-Term Dynamic Therapy*. New York: New York University.

Gurman, A. S., & Budman, S. H. (1996). Theory and practice in brief therapy. In: J. E. Groves (Ed.), *Essential Papers on Short-Term Dynamic Therapy*. New York: New York University.

Guthrie, L. G. (1909). *Functional Nervous Disorders in Childhood*. London: H. Frowde/Hodder & Stoughton.

Haag, G. (1991). Nature de quelques identifications dans l'image du corps. *Journal de la Psychanalyse de l'Enfant, 9*: 73–92.

Hammen, C., Rudolph, K., Weisz, J., Rao, U., & Burge, D. (1999). The context of depression in clinic-referred youth: Neglected areas in treatment. *Journal of the American Academy of Child and Adolescent Psychiatry, 38* (1): 64–71.

Harrington, R., & Dubicka, B. (2002). Adolescent depression: An evidence-based approach to intervention. *Current Opinion in Psychiatry, 15*: 369–375.

Harrington, R., Rutter, M., Weissman, M., Fudge, H., Groothues, C., Bredenkamp, D., et al. (1997). Psychiatric disorders in the relatives of depressed probands. I. Comparison of pre-pubertal, adolescent and early adult onset cases. *Journal of Affective Disorders, 42*: 9–22.

Harrington, R., Whittaker, J., & Shoebridge, P. (1998). Psychological treatment of depression in children and adolescents. A review of treatment research. *British Journal of Psychiatry, 173* (10): 291–298.

Harrington, R., Whittaker, J., Shoebridge, P., & Campbell, F. (1998). Systematic review of efficacy of cognitive behaviour therapies in childhood and adolescent depressive disorder. *British Medical Journal, 316*: 1559–1563.

Harter, S. (1990). Causes, correlates and the functional role of global self-worth: A life-span perspective. In: R. J. Sternberg & J. Kolligian (Eds.), *Competence Considered* (pp. 67–97). New Haven, CT: Yale University Press.

Heimann, P. (1950). On countertransference. *International Journal of Psychoanalysis, 31*: 81–84.

Hinde, R. A. (1976). On describing relationships. *Journal of Child Psychology and Psychiatry, 17*: 1–19.

Hinshelwood, R. D. (1994). *Clinical Klein*. London: Free Association Books.

Horn, H., Geiser-Elze, A., Reck, C., Hartmann, M., Stefini, A., Victor, D., et al. (2005). Zur Wirksamheit psychodynamischer Kurzzeitpsychotherapie bei Kindern und Jugendlichen mit Depressionen. Prax. *Kinderpsycholoog Kinderpsychiater, 54*: 578–597.

Horne, A. (2000). Keeping the child in mind: Thoughts on work with parents of children in therapy. In: J. Tsiantis, S. B. Boethious, B. Hallerfors, A. Horne, & L. Tischler (Eds.), *Work with Parents: Psychoanalytic Psychotherapy with Children and Adolescents*. London: Karnac.

Houzel, D. (2002). *L'aube de la vie psychique*. Collection La vie de l'enfant. Paris: Editions ESF.

Hughes, E. K., & Gullone, E. (2008). Internalizing symptoms and disorders in families of adolescents: A review of family systems literature. *Clinical Psychology Review, 28*: 92–117.

Jones, E., & Asen, E. (2000). *Systemic Couple Therapy and Depression*. London: Karnac.

Joseph, B. (1987). Projective identification: Clinical aspects. In: J. Sandler (Ed.), *Projection, Identification, Projective Identification* (pp. 65–76). New York: International Universities Press. Reprinted London: Karnac, 1988.

Kabacoff, R. I., Miller, I. W., Bishop, D. S., Epstein, N. B., & Keitner, L. G. (1990). A psychometric study of the McMaster Family Assessment Device in psychiatric, medical, and nonclinical Samples. *Journal of Family Psychology, 3* (4): 431–439.

Kazdin, A. E. (1986). Comparative outcome studies of psychotherapy: Methodological issues and strategies. *Journal of Consulting Clinical Psychology, 54*: 95–105.

Keller, M., Beardslee, W., Dover, D., Lavori, P. W., Samuelson, H., & Klerman, G. L. (1986). Impact of severity and chronicity of parental affective illness on adoptive functioning and psychopathology in children. *Archives of General Psychiatry, 43*: 930–937.

Kennard, B. D., Emslie, G. J., Mayes, T. L., Nightingale-Teresi, J.,

Nakinezny, P. A., Hughes, J. L., et al. (2008). Cognitive-behavioural therapy to prevent relapse in paediatric responders to pharmacotherapy for major depressive disorder. *Journal of the American Academy of Child and Adolescent Psychiatry, 47* (12): 1395–1404.

Klein, M. (1935). A contribution to the psychogenesis of manic-depressive states. In: *The Writings of Melanie Klein, Vol. 1: Love, Guilt and Reparation and Other Works*. London: Hogarth Press, 1975.

Klein, M. (1937). Love, guilt and reparation. In: *The Writings of Melanie Klein, Vol. 1: Love, Guilt and Reparation and Other Works*. London: Hogarth Press, 1975.

Klein, M. (1940). Mourning and its relation to manic-depressive states. In: *The Writings of Melanie Klein, Vol. 3: Envy & Gratitude and Other Works*. London: Hogarth Press, 1975.

Klein, M. (1946). Notes on some schizoid mechanisms. *International Journal of Psychoanalysis, 27*: 99–110. [Also in: M. Klein, P. Heimann, S. Isaacs, & J. Riviere (Eds.), *Developments in Psycho-Analysis* (pp. 292–320). London: Hogarth Press, 1952. And in: *The Writings of Melanie Klein, Vol. 4*. London: Hogarth Press, 1975.]

Klein, M. (1955) The psycho-analytic play technique: its history and significance. In: *The Writings of Melanie Klein, Vol. 3: Envy & Gratitude and Other Works*. London: Hogarth Press, 1975.

Klein, M. (1957). Envy and gratitude. In: *The Writings of Melanie Klein, Vol. 3: Envy & Gratitude and Other Works*. London: Hogarth Press, 1975.

Kolko, D. J., Brent, D. A., Baugher, M., Bridge, J., & Birmaher, B. (2000). Cognitive and family therapies for adolescent depression: Treatment specificity, mediation, and moderation. *Journal of Consulting and Clinical Psychology, 68* (4): 603–614.

Kolvin, I. (1995). Childhood depression: Clinical phenomenology and classification. In: I. M. Goodyer (Ed.), *The Depressed Child and Adolescent: Developmental and Clinical Perspectives*. Cambridge: Cambridge University Press.

Kolvin, I., Barrett, L. M., Bhate S. R., Berney T. P., Famuyiwa O. O., Fundudis T., et al. (1991). The Newcastle Child Depression Project: Diagnosis and classification. *British Journal of Psychiatry, 150* (Suppl. 11): 9–21.

Kolvin, I., Garside R. F., Nicol, A. R., Macmillan, A., Wolstenholme, F., & Leitch, A. M. (1981). *Help Starts Here*. London: Tavistock Publications, 1987.

Kolvin, I., Macmillan, A., Nicol, A. R., & Wrate, R. M. (1988). Psychotherapy is effective. *Journal of the Royal Society of Medicine, 81* (5): 261–266.

Kolvin, I., & Sadowski, H. (2001). Childhood depression: Clinical phenomenology and classification. In: I. M. Goodyer (Ed.), *The Depressed Child and Adolescent* (2nd edition). Cambridge: Cambridge University Press.

Kolvin, I., Trowell, J., Tsiantis, J., & Almqvist, F. (1999). Psychotherapy for childhood depression. In: M. Maj & N. Sartorius (Eds.), *Depressive Disorders. WPA Series, Evidence and Experience in Psychiatry, Vol. 1*. Chichester: Wiley.

Kovacs, M. (1981). Rating scales to assess depression in school aged children. *Acta Paedopsychiatrica, 46*: 305–315.

Kovacs, M. (1986). A developmental perspective on methods and measures in the assessment of depressive disorders: The clinical interview. In: M. Rutter, C. Izad, & P. Read (Eds.), *Depression in Young People: Developmental and Clinical Perspectives* (pp. 435–465). New York: Guildford Press.

Kovacs, M. (1992). *Children's Depression Inventory (CDI) Manual*. New York: Multi Health Systems.

Kovacs, M. (1996). Presentation and course of major depressive disorder during childhood and later years of the life span. *Journal of the American Academy of Child and Adolescent Psychiatry, 35*: 705–715.

Kovacs, M., Akiskal, H. S., Gatsonis, C., & Parrone, P. L. (1994). Childhood onset dysthymia disorder. *Archives of General Psychiatry, 51*: 365–374.

Kovacs, M., & Bastiaens, L. J. (1995). The psychotherapeutic management of major depressive and dysthymic disorders in childhood and adolescence: Issues and prospects. In: I. M. Goodyer (Ed.), *The Depressed Child and Adolescent*. Cambridge: Cambridge University Press.

Kovacs, M., & Devlin, B. (1998). Internalising disorders in childhood. *Journal of Child Psychology & Psychiatry, 39*: 47–63.

Kovacs, M., Devlin, B., Pollack, M., Richards, C., & Mukerji, P. (1997). A controlled family history study of childhood onset depressive disorder. *Archives of General Psychiatry, 46*: 776–782.

Kovacs, M., Fenberg, T. L., Crouse-Novack, M. A., Paulauskas, S. L., & Finkelstean, R. (1984). Depressive disorders in childhood, I:

A longitudinal prospective study of characteristics and recovery. *Archives of General Psychiatry, 41*: 229–237.

Kovacs, M., Gatsonis, C., Paulauskas, S. L., & Richards, C. (1989). Depressive disorders in childhood, IV: A longitudinal study of comorbidity with and risk for conduct disorders. *Archives of General Psychiatry, 46*: 776–782.

Kovacs, M., Obrosky, D. S., Gatsonis, C., & Richards, C. (1997). First episode major depressive and dysthymic disorder in childhood: Clinical and socio-demographic factors in recovery. *Journal of the American Academy of Child and Adolescent Psychiatry, 36*: 777–784.

Kovacs, M., Paulauskas, S. L., Gatsonis, C., & Richards, C. (1988). Depressive disorders in childhood, III: A longitudinal study of comorbidity with and risk for conduct disorder. *Journal of Affective Disorders, 15*: 205–217.

Kovacs, M., & Sherill, J. T. (2001). The psychotherapeutic management of major depressive and dysthymic disorders in childhood and adolescence: Issues and prospects. In: I. M. Goodyer (Ed.), *The Depressed Child and Adolescent* (2nd edition). Cambridge: Cambridge University Press.

Lang, P., Little, M., & Cronen, V. (1990). The systemic professional domains of action and the question of neutrality. *Human Systems: The Journal of Systemic Consultation and Management, 1*: 39–55.

Laplanche, J., & Pontalis, J.-B. (1973). *The Language of Psychoanalysis*. London: Karnac, 1988.

Larner, G. (2009). Integrating family therapy in adolescent depression: An ethical stance. *Journal of Family Therapy, 31*: 213–232.

Lau, J. Y. F., Rijsdijk, F., Gregory, A. M., McGuffin, P., & Eley, T. C. (2007). Pathways to childhood depressive symptoms: The role of social, cognitive, and genetic risk factors. *Developmental Psychology, 43* (6): 1402–1414.

Laufer, M., & Laufer, E. (1975). *Adolescent Disturbance and Breakdown*. Harmondsworth: Penguin.

Leichenring, F. (2004). The efficacy of short-term psychodynamic psychotherapy in specific psychiatric disorders: A meta-analysis. *Archives of General Psychiatry, 61*: 1208–1216.

Leichenring, F. (2005). Are psychodynamic and psychoanalytic therapies effective? A review of empirical data. *International Journal of Psychoanalysis, 86*: 841–868.

Lewinsohn, P. M., & Clarke, G. N. (1999). Psychosocial treatments for adolescent depression. *Clinical Psychology Review, 19* (3): 320–342.

Lewinsohn, P. M., Clarke, G. N., Seeley, J. R., & Rohde, P. (1994). Major depression in community adolescents: Age at onset, episode duration, and time to recurrence. *Journal of the American Academy of Child and Adolescent Psychiatry, 33* (6): 809–818.

Lewinsohn, P. M., Gotlib, I., & Seeley, J. R. (1995). Adolescent psychopathology, IV: Specificity of psychosocial risk factors for depression and substance abuse in older adolescents. *Journal of the American Academy of Child and Adolescent Psychiatry, 334*: 1221–1229.

Lewinsohn, P. M., Rohde, P., Klein, D., & Seeley, J. R. (1999). Natural course of adolescent major depressive disorder, I: Continuity into young adulthood. *Journal of the American Academy of Child and Adolescent Psychiatry, 38*: 56–63.

Lewinsohn, P. M., Rohde, P., Seeley, J. R., Klein, D. N., & Gotlib I. H. (2003). Psychosocial functioning of young adults who have experienced and recovered from major depressive disorder during adolescence. *Journal of Abnormal Psychology, 112* (3): 353–363.

Long, J., & Trowell, J. (2001). Individual brief psychotherapy with sexually abused girls: What can we learn from the process notes? *Psychoanalytic Psychotherapy, 15*: 39–59.

Mahler, M. S. (1961). On sadness and grief in infancy and childhood. *Psychoanalytic Study of the Child, 16*: 332–354.

Malan, D. H. (1976). *The Frontier of Brief Psychotherapy*. New York: Plenum.

Malan, D. H., & Osimo, F. (1992). *Psychodynamics, Training and Outcome in Brief Psychotherapy*. London: Butterworth.

Mander, G. (2000). The therapist's tasks and roles in brief and focal therapy. In: *A Psychoanalytical Approach to Brief Therapy, Vol. 5* (pp. 81–99). Thousand Oaks, CA: Sage.

Mann, J. (1973). *Time Limited Psychotherapy*. Cambridge, MA: Harvard University Press.

March, J., Silva, S., Petrycki, S., Curry, J., Wells, K., Fairbank, J., et al. (2004). Fluoxetine, cognitive-behavioural therapy, and their combination for adolescents with depression: Treatment for Adolescents with Depression Study (TADS) randomised controlled trial. *Journal of the American Medical Association, 292* (7): 807–820.

Maudsley, H. (1867). *The Physiology and Pathology of the Mind*. London: Macmillan.

Maudsley, H. (1879). *The Pathology of Mind*. London: Macmillan.

Maudsley, H. (1895). *The Pathology of Mind* (2nd edition). London: Macmillan.

May, U. (2001). Abraham's discovery of the "bad mother": A contribution to the history of the theory of depression. *International Journal of Psychoanalysis, 82*: 283–306.

McNab, S., & Kavner, E. (2005). Shame and the therapeutic relationship. In: C. Flaskas, B. Mason, & A. Perlesz (Eds.), *The Space Between: Experience, Context and Process in the Therapeutic Relationship*. London: Karnac.

Meltzer, D. (1973). *Sexual States of Mind*. Strath Tay: Clunie Press.

Michael, K. D., & Crowley, S. L. (2002). How effective are treatments for child and adolescent depression? A meta-analytic review. *Clinical Psychological Review, 22*: 247–269.

Miller, I. W., Ryan, C. E., Keitner, G. I., Bishop, D. S., & Epstein, N. B. (2000a). The McMaster approach to families: Theory, assessment, treatment and research. *Journal of Family Therapy, 22*: 168–189.

Miller, I. W., Ryan, C. E., Keitner, G. I., Bishop, D. S., & Epstein, N. B. (2000b). Why fix what isn't broken? A rejoinder to Ridenour, Daley, & Reich. *Family Process, 39*: 381–384.

Mitchell, J., McCauley, E., Bruke, P. M., & Moss, S. J. (1988). Phenomenology of depression in children and adolescents. *Journal of the American Academy of Child and Adolescent Psychiatry, 27*: 12–20.

Mufson, L., Moreau, D., Weissman, M., Wickramaratne, P., Martin, J., & Samoilov, A. (1994). Modification of Interpersonal Psychotherapy with Depressed Adolescents (IPT-A): Phase I and II Studies. *Journal of the American Academy of Child and Adolescent Psychiatry, 33* (5): 695–705.

Muratori, F., Picchi, L., Bruni, G., Patarnello, M., & Romagnoli, G. (2003). A two-year follow-up of psychodynamic psychotherapy for internalising disorders in children. *Journal of the American Academy of Child and Adolescent Psychiatry, 42* (3): 331–339.

Muratori, F., Picchi, L., Casetta, C., Tancredi, R., Milone, A., & Patarnello, M. G. (2002). Efficacy of brief dynamic psychotherapy for children with emotional disorders. *Psychotherapy and Psychosomatics, 71*: 28–38.

O'Hanlon, B. (1995). *Problems and Possibilities*. Workshop, Tavistock Clinic, London, November.

Pankow, G. (1981). *L'être-la du schizophrene. Contribution a la methode de structuration dynamique dans les psychoses*. Paris: Aubier.

Parker, I. (1992). *Discourse Dynamics: Critical Analysis for Social and Critical Psychology*. London: Routledge.

Parloff, M. B. (1986). Placebo controls in psychotherapy research: A sine qua non or a placebo for research problems. *Journal of Consulting and Clinical Psychology, 54*: 79–87.

Parry-Jones, W. L. (1995). Historical aspects of mood and its disorders in young people. In: I. M. Goodyer (Ed.), *The Depressed Child and Adolescent* (2nd edition). Cambridge: Cambridge University Press.

Pearce, W. B., & Cronen, V. (1980). *Communication, Action and Meaning: The Creation of Social Realities*. New York: Praeger.

Pentecost, D., & McNab, S. (2007). Keeping company with hopes and despair: Family therapists reflections and experiences of working with childhood depression. *Journal of Family Therapy, 29* (4): 403–419

Puig-Antich, J. (1982). Major depression and conduct disorder in prepuberty. *Journal of the American Academy of Child and Adolescent Psychiatry, 21*: 118–128.

Puig-Antich, J., Kaufman, J., Ryan, N. D., Williamson, D. E., Dahl, R. E., Lukens, E., et al. (1993). The psychosocial functioning and family environment of depressed adolescents. *Journal of the American Academy of Child and Adolescent Psychiatry, 32* (2): 244–253.

Puig-Antich, J., Lukens, E., Davies, M., Goetz, D., Brennan-Quattrock, J., & Todak, G. (1985). Psychosocial functioning in prepubertal major depressive disorders, I: Interpersonal relationships during the depressive episode. *Archives of General Psychiatry, 42*: 500–507.

Rachman, S. (1998). *Anxiety* [Clinical Psychology, A Modular Course]. Hove: Psychology Press.

Ramani, R., & Paykel, E. S. (1992). Classification of affective disorders. *British Journal of Hospital Medicine, 47*: 831–835.

Rey, J. M., Sawyer, M. G., Clark, J. J., & Baghurs, P. A. (2001). Depression among Australian adolescents. *The Medical Journal of Australia, 175* (1): 19–23.

Rhode, M. (1997). Glossary. In: M. Rustin, M. Rhode, A. Dubinsky, & H. Dubinsky (Eds.), *Psychotic States in Children*. London: Duckworth.

Rhode, M. (2003) *Against the Odds: Points of Intervention in Complex Cases*. Plenary presentation on child psychotherapy, Fifth Three-

Section Conference of the European Federation for Psychoanalytic Psychotherapy: Psychoanalytic Psychotherapy in Our Time: When, Where and for Whom? Stockholm, 4–6 July.

Ridenour, T. A., Daley, J., & Reich, W. I. (2000). Factor analyses of the family assessment device. *Family Process, 38*: 497–510.

Robertson, J., & Robertson, J. (1971). Young children in brief separations. *Psychoanalytic Study of the Child, 26*: 264–315.

Robson, C. (2002). *Real World Research* (2nd edition). Oxford: Blackwell.

Rohde, P., Lewinsohn, P. M., & Seeley, J. R. (1994). Are adolescents changed by an episode of major depression? *Journal of the American Academy of Child and Adolescent Psychiatry, 33*: 1289–1298.

Rosenfeld, H. (1971). A clinical approach to the psychoanalytical theory of the life and death instincts: An investigation into the aggressive aspects of narcissism. *International Journal of Psychoanalysis, 52*: 169–178.

Rosenfeld, H. (1987). *Impasse and Interpretation*. London: Routledge.

Rossello, J., & Bernal, G. (1999). The efficacy of cognitive-behavioural and interpersonal treatments for depression in Puerto Rican adolescents. *Journal of Consulting and Clinical Psychology, 67*: 734–745.

Rushton, A., & Miles, G. (2000). A study of a support service for the current carers of sexually abused girls. *Clinical Child Psychology and Psychiatry, 5* (3): 411–426.

Rustin, M. (1998). Observation, understanding and interpretation: The story of a supervision. *Journal of Child Psychotherapy, 24*: 433–448.

Rustin, M. (2000). Dialogues with parents. In: J. Tsiantis, S. B. Boethious, B. Hallerfors, A. Horne, & L. Tischler (Eds.), *Work with Parents: Psychoanalytic Psychotherapy with Children and Adolescents*. London: Karnac.

Rutter, M., Taylor, E., & Hersov, L. (1994). *Child and Adolescent Psychiatry* (3rd edition). Oxford: Blackwell.

Ryan, N. D. (2003). Child and adolescent depression: Short-term treatment effectiveness and long-term opportunities. *International Journal of Methods in Psychiatric Research, 12* (1): 44–53.

Sandler, J., & Joffe, W. G. (1965). Notes on childhood depression. *International Journal of Psychoanalysis, 46*: 88–96.

Santor, D., & Kusumakar, V. (2001). Open trial of interpersonal therapy in adolescents with moderate to severe major depression: Effectiveness of novice IPT therapists. *Journal of the American Academy of Child and Adolescent Psychiatry, 40* (2): 236–240.

Schacht, T., Binder, J., & Strupp, H. (1984). The dynamic focus. In: H. Strupp & J. Binder (Eds.), *Psychotherapy in a New Key*. New York: Basic Books.

Segal, H. (1957). Notes on symbol formation. *International Journal of Psychoanalysis, 38*: 391–397.

Shaffer, D., Gould, M. S., & Brasic, J. (1993). A children's global assessment scale (C GAS). *Archives of General Psychiatry, 40*: 1228–1231.

Shortt, A., & Spence, S. (2006). Risk and protective factors for depression in youth. *Behaviour Change, 23*: 1–30.

Silberg, J., Pickles, A., Rutter, M., Hewitt, J., Simonoff, E., Maes, H., et al. (1999). The influence of genetic factors and life stress on depression among adolescent girls. *Archive of General Psychiatry, 56*: 225–232.

Spitz, R. A. (1946). Anaclitic depression. *Psychoanalytic Study of the Child, 2*: 313–342.

Steiner, J. (1993). *Psychic Retreats*. New Library of Psychoanalysis. London: Routledge.

Strober, M. (2001). Family-genetic aspect of juvenile affective disorder. In: I. M. Goodyer (Ed.), *The Depressed Child and Adolescent* (2nd edition). Cambridge: Cambridge University Press.

Sutton, A., & Hughes, L. (2005). The psychotherapy of parenthood: Towards a formulation and valuation of concurrent work with parents. *Journal of Child Psychotherapy, 31* (2): 169–188.

Todd, R. D., Reich, W., Petti, T. A., Joshi, P., DePaulo, J. R., Nurnberger, J., et al. (1996). Psychiatric diagnosis in the child and adolescent members of extended families identified through adult bipolar affective disorder probands. *Journal of the American Academy of Child and Adolescent Psychiatry, 35*: 665–671.

Tomm, K. (1988). Interventive interviewing, Part III: Intending to ask lineal, circular, strategic or reflexive questions? *Family Process, 27*: 1–15.

Trowell, J., Berelowitz, M., & Kolvin, I. (1995). Design and methodological issues in setting up a psychotherapy outcome study with girls who have been sexually abused. In: M. Aveline & D. A. Shapiro (Eds.), *Research Foundations for Psychotherapy Practice*. Chichester: Wiley.

Trowell, J., Joffe, I., Campbell, J., Clemente, C., Almqvist, F., Soininen, M., et al. (2007). Childhood depression: A place for psychotherapy.

An outcome study comparing individual psychodynamic psychotherapy and family therapy. *European Child & Adolescent Psychiatry, 16* (3): 157–167.

Trowell, J., Kolvin, I., Weeramanthri, T., Sasowski, H., Berelowitz, M., Glasser, D., et al. (2002). Psychotherapy for sexually abused girls: Psychopathological outcome findings and patterns of change. *British Journal of Psychiatry, 180*: 234–247.

Trowell, J., Rhode, M., & Hall, J. (2010). What does a manual contribute? In: J. Tsiantis & J. Trowell (Eds.), *Assessing Change in Psychoanalytic Psychotherapy of Children and Adolescents* (pp. 55–93). London: Karnac.

Trowell, J., Rhode, M., Miles, G., & Sherwood, L. (2003). Childhood depression: Work in progress, individual child therapy and parent work. *Journal of Child Psychotherapy, 29* (2), 147–169.

Tsiantis, J. (Ed.) (2000). *Work with Parents: Psychoanalytic Psychotherapy with Children and Adolescents*. London: Karnac.

Tsiantis, J., Kolvin, I., Anastasopopoulos, D., Trowell, J., Tomaras, V., Miles, G., et al. (2005). Psychotherapy for early adolescent depression (PEAD): A comparison of two psychotherapeutic interventions in three European countries. In: E. D. Hibbs & P. S. Jensen (Eds.), *Psychosocial Treatments for Child and Adolescent Disorders: Empirically Based Strategies for Clinical Practice* (2nd edition, pp. 267–293). Washington, DC: American Psychological Association.

Tsiantis, J., & Trowell, J. (2010). *Assessing Change in Psychoanalytic Psychotherapy of Children and Adolescents: Today's Challenge*. European Federation of Psychoanalytic Psychotherapy Series. London: Karnac.

Tustin, F. (1972a). Psychological birth and psychological catastrophe. In: *Autistic States in Children* (2nd revised edition). London: Routledge, 1992.

Tustin, F. (1972b). Psychotic depression. In: *Autism and Childhood Psychosis*. London: Hogarth Press, 1992.

Tustin, F. (1986). Falling. In: *Autistic Barriers in Neurotic Patients*. London: Karnac.

Vetere, A., & Dowling, E. (2005). *Narrative Therapy with Children and Their Families*. London: Routledge.

Vitiello, B., Rohde, P., Silva, S., Wells, K., Casat, C., Waslick, B., et al. (2006). Functioning and quality of life in the Treatment for Adolescents with Depression Study (TADS). *Journal of the American Academy of Child and Adolescent Psychiatry, 45* (12): 1419–1426.

Weissman, M. M., & Bothwell, S. (1976). Assessment of social adjustment by patient self-report. *Archives of General Psychiatry, 33*: 1111–1115.

Weisz, J. R., & McCarty, C. A. (2006). Effects of psychotherapy for depression in children and adolescents: A meta-analysis. *Psychological Bulletin, 132* (1): 132–149.

Wetherell, M. (1998). Positioning and interpretative repertoires: Conversation analysis and post-structuralism in dialogue. *Discourse and Society, 9*: 387–412.

White, M., & Epston, D. (1990). *Narrative Means to Therapeutic Ends*. New York: W. W. Norton.

WHO (1992). *The ICD-10 Classification of Mental and Behavioural Disorders*. Geneva: World Health Organization.

Will, D., & Wrate, R. M. (1985). *Integrated Family Therapy*. London: Tavistock Publications.

Winnicott, D. W. (1945). Primitive emotional development. *International Journal of Psychoanalysis, 26*: 137–143.

Winnicott, D. W. (1949). Birth memories, birth trauma and anxiety. In: *Through Paediatrics to Psychoanalysis*. London: Hogarth Press, 1975.

Winnicott, D. W. (1954). The depressive position in normal emotional development. In: *Through Paediatrics to Psychoanalysis*. London: Hogarth Press, 1975.

Winnicott, D. W. (1956). Primary maternal preoccupation. In: *Through Paediatrics to Psychoanalysis*. London: Hogarth Press, 1975.

Winnicott, D. W. (1965). *The Maturational Processes and the Facilitating Environment*. London: Hogarth Press.

Winnicott, D. W. (1967). Mirror-role of the mother and family in child development. In: *Playing and Reality*. London: Routledge, 1971.

Wood, A., Harrington, R., & Moore, A. (1996). Controlled trial of brief cognitive behavioural intervention in adolescent patients with depressive disorders. *Journal of Clinical Psychology and Psychiatry, 37*: 737–746.

# INDEX

For Product Safety Concerns and Information please contact our EU representative GPSR@taylorandfrancis.com Taylor & Francis Verlag GmbH, Kaufingerstraße 24, 80331 München, Germany

**Batch number: 10726009**

Printed by Printforce, the Netherlands